I0803701

EVERY MEMBER A SOUL WINNER

HELP FOR THE HARVEST

GLORIA J. BELL

REVIEW AND HERALD® PUBLISHING ASSOCIATION
Since 1861 | www.reviewandherald.com

Published by Review and Herald® Publishing Association, Hagerstown, MD 21741-1119

Review and Herald® titles may be purchased in bulk for educational, business, fund-raising, or sales promotional use. For information, e-mail SpecialMarkets@reviewandherald.com.

The Review and Herald® Publishing Association publishes biblically based materials for spiritual, physical, and mental growth and Christian discipleship.

This book was
Edited by Gerald Wheeler
Copyedited by Daun Redfield
Cover design by Ron J. Pride/Review and Herald® Design Center
Cover photo by © Thinkstock
Interior Design by Derek Knecht/Review and Herald® Design Center
Typeset: Minion Pro 11/13

PRINTED IN U.S.A.

18 17 16 15 14 5 4 3 2 1

Library of Congress Cataloging-in-Publication Data
Bell, Gloria, 1947-
Help for the harvest : every member a soul winner / Gloria Bell.
pages cm
ISBN 978-0-8280-2734-2
1. Witness bearing (Christianity)--Study and teaching. 2. Evangelistic work--Study and teaching. I. Title.
BV4520.B3575 2014
269'.2--dc23
2013015348

ISBN 978-0-8280-2734-2

HELP FOR THE HARVEST

To order additional copies of
Help for the Harvest, by Gloria Bell, call **1-800-765-6955**.

Visit us at **www.reviewandherald.com** for information on other Review and Herald® products.

Just before the return of our Lord, there will be a revival of interest in witnessing. Scores of laypeople will become actively involved in service. They will desire much more than the status quo. God's Spirit will move powerfully. Church members will discover their God-given gifts and use them in service for their Lord. Gloria Bell recognizes that God is calling a whole new generation of laypeople to become actively involved in soul winning. This practical volume on witnessing draws from Gloria's years of experience as a Bible instructor and lays out principles that really work. If you are an experienced soul winner or you are just beginning, you will be richly blessed as you read and put into practice the principles Gloria shares in this book. I hope you will be sure to place a copy in your library. I sure will want one in mine.

—Mark Finley

CONTENTS

INTRODUCTION

One of the most exhilarating aspects of being a follower of Christ is witnessing the conversion experience of someone who comes to know and accept Christ as their personal Savior. Rebirth takes third place in God's divine gifts to humanity—creation, procreation, and then re-creation, or rebirth. God created us in His own image and likeness. Next He gave us the command and ability to be fruitful and multiply and replenish the earth. Then, after the Fall, when all hope seemed lost and while we were yet sinners in need of a Savior, Jesus gave His life for us. He was treated as we deserve so that we could be treated as He deserves. The priceless gift of re-creation and restoration through Jesus Christ alone is the highest honor and opportunity ever made available to humanity. What an awesome privilege to be grafted into the family of God as sons and daughters once again for eternity.

As disciples of Christ, not only have we experienced rebirth and witnessed the spiritual rebirth of others, but in addition, God has chosen us for the high calling of laboring together as partners with Him in spreading the gospel of Jesus Christ. The charge goes out to all who have experienced rebirth, but unfortunately too few accept it. The harvest field is vast and ready and needs many more colaborers. Will you join together with God in the process of sowing the life-changing seeds of truth, nurturing the precious budding souls, and finally preparing nourished fruit for harvest? You will never be alone, "for we are labourers together with God" (1 Cor. 3:9).

Nothing could bring more joy than to have someone walk up to you years later and ask, "Do you remember me? I took Bible studies from you and was baptized. I am so excited to see you again to thank you and tell you how much my life has changed for the better. I appreciate you so much. I witnessed to my family, and they too have received Bible studies. What a blessing God has been to us since we joined the family of God." There can be no higher honor, no higher calling, no higher work than colaboring for the salvation of men and women.

The church of God is the established sanctuary for sinners, whether seeking salvation or saved by grace. It is God's divinely created means through which the light and love of the gospel of Jesus Christ is to reach out and reclaim the lost wherever they may be. As such, one of the purposes of the church is to create venues for evangelism and train its congregants to be light bearers from home to home and heart to heart.

From its inception, the Seventh-day Adventist Church has called upon all members to go door to door, home to home, giving Bible studies and leading both individuals and families to Jesus Christ. In more recent years, while the clarion call still rings out for all to be involved, "Bible instructor" has become distinguished as a title given to those who have responded to the divine summons to evangelistic ministry, whether for specific evangelistic endeavors, as a personal ministry, or as a full- or part-time vocation. Such colaborers are few in number compared to the enormous field to be worked. The church desperately needs many more.

> "After these things the Lord appointed other seventy also, and sent them two and two before his face into every city and place, whither he himself would come. Therefore said he unto them, The harvest truly is great, but the labourers are few: pray ye therefore the Lord of the harvest, that he would send forth labourers into his harvest" (Luke 10:1, 2).

As a part of its appeal to all members to become Bible instructors, the church offers, but does not require, collegiate training in one of many programs offered at Seventh-day Adventist universities for those seeking to enter the field of Bible instruction as a vocation. Because not all may be able to take advantage of such collegiate programs, the denomination encourages local congregations to provide training and supervised field apprenticeship to anyone desiring to become Bible instructors. *Help for the Harvest* is a comprehensive resource for supporting the local church's efforts to provide in-depth training for its Bible instructors in preparation for and during evangelistic meetings.

The evangelistic series encompasses and culminates a defined period of intentional outreach by all the departmental ministries of one or more local congregations through a major public campaign. Major evangelistic thrusts call forth from the Bible instructor the most heightened level of spiritual intensity and endurance. Every aspect of Bible instruction that would normally take months, if not years, to experience gets compressed into weeks during such series. For that reason, this Bible instructor's guide focuses in great detail on training people for public evangelism.

The Bible instructor has an essential role in the success of community and citywide evangelism. Unlike local church ministries, such meetings require Bible instructors to function at a multifaceted level of professionalism. Thus proper training of the Bible instructor to understand the complex interplay and organization of the evangelistic venue is crucial. *Help for the Harvest* is designed to supplement hands-on apprentice training.

This guide summarizes the insights I have gathered during more than 40 years as a Bible instructor as well as from actually working in dozens of evangelistic series of various lengths, types, and intensities. I had the honor of standing at my husband's side during his ordination to ministry in 1974 and serving as his Bible instructor until the day of his rest in 2011. In addition, I've had the privilege of working with numerous other Seventh-day Adventist pastors and evangelists. During those years I have witnessed hundreds give their hearts to Christ through baptism. I extend the deepest gratitude to all who unknowingly have contributed to what you will find in this training manual. This guide commemorates how God uses ordinary people who have dedicated themselves to Him.

It is my desire to share from my wonderful experiences as a Bible instructor those practices that I have learned from others through the years, methods I have been taught and/or examined, good counsel I have put into practice, as well as what I have in turn taught many others nationwide. The counsel in this guide I know from personal observation and experience will make for a more effective and efficient Bible instructor, especially in the evangelistic series setting. All names in this document have been intentionally changed and circumstances abbreviated to protect confidentiality.

This training manual is divided into five parts—Organizing for Evangelism, Preparing the Field, Let the Evangelistic Series Begin, Securing and Confirming Decisions, and finally, Follow-up Strategies. Each part contains several Chapters covering a specific practice for effective Bible instruction, particularly in preparation for, during, and following a major evangelistic thrust. Keep in mind that Bible instructing is a spiritual urgency woven into a person's lifestyle, not something merely done on the side or during an evangelistic series. It certainly doesn't mean that one cannot do Bible instructing part-time. But it does call for a continual desire for the salvation of others. It is passion that consumes the instructor's life, waking them in the early-morning hours to wrestle on their knees in spiritual battle for souls. The zeal for connecting with people they care about is what keeps Bible instructors in homes no matter what time of day and on the phone encouraging those struggling to know the joy of salvation. The Bible instructor can experience no greater thrill than seeing someone set free in Jesus. Only the joy in heaven over one sinner saved by grace can match it.

It is my hope that this in-depth study of Bible instruction as a vocation—or perhaps more accurately, a lifestyle—will encourage more individuals to join the worldwide team of Bible instructors. This manual is a comprehensive resource designed specifically for training Bible instructor teams in the local church. Be aware that if you are reading this training guide, God may be calling you to be His ambassador to humanity.

PART 1

ORGANIZING FOR EVANGELISM

CHAPTER 1

FIRE IN THE HOUSE

God established His church to be more than merely a sanctuary for worship and praise. "The church of Christ is organized for service. Its watchword is ministry. Its members are soldiers, to be trained for conflict under the Captain of their salvation. Christian ministers, physicians, teachers, have a broader work than many have recognized. They are not only to minister to the people, but to teach them to minister. They should not only give instruction in right principles, but educate their hearers to impart these principles."[1]

> "Every church should be a training school for Christian workers. Its members should be taught how to give Bible readings, how to conduct and teach Sabbath-school classes, how best to help the poor and to care for the sick, how to work for the unconverted. There should be schools of health, cooking schools, and classes in various lines of Christian help work. There should not only be teaching, but actual work under experienced instructors. Let the teachers lead the way in working among the people, and others, uniting with them, will learn from their example. One example is worth more than many precepts."[2]
>
> "More attention should be given to training and educating missionaries with a special reference to work in the cities. Each company of workers should be under the direction of a competent leader, and it should ever be kept before them that they are to be missionaries in the highest sense of the term. Such systematic labor, wisely conducted, would produce blessed results."[3]
>
> "Christian is to be united with Christian, church with church, the human instrumentality co-operating with the divine, every agency subordinate to the Holy Spirit, and all combined in giving to the world the good tidings of the grace of God."[4]

Once the membership gets into the spirit of evangelism, miraculous things begin to happen. They begin to think about their God-given calling to both in-reach and outreach ministry. The Holy Spirit fills their thoughts with names of friends, family, and coworkers, and they begin to see strangers differently. The Spirit of God awakens in them, and they become energized for the kingdom of God. Individuals associated with such church members will begin to listen. They are very often the first to respond.

The daily demonstration of the work of the Holy Spirit in the life of members constantly attracts others. The lyrics of the song carry much truth: "They'll know we are Christians by our love." Not only that, but many will want to know why you are a Christian and how they can become one. If you have been representing Christ day by day, their quick response will not be a surprise when you share with friends, family, and coworkers what you are doing and invite them to participate. Bible instruction starts in the heart and life.

> "Behold, the days come, saith the Lord God, that I will send a famine in the land, not a famine of bread, nor a thirst for water, but of hearing [and may I interject "seeing"] the words of the Lord" (Amos 8:11).
>
> "And I, if I be lifted up from the earth, will draw all men unto me" (John 12:32).

There is no limit to the ways in which we can witness to others the love of God toward us. Merely living the life of faith in action and sharing the goodness of God by word and action are powerful motivations to entering Bible work. On the one hand, the fields are ripe with those seeking to know and have a saving relationship with God. On the other, God is looking for many more who will dedicate their lives to sowing seeds of truth, watering the seed sown with Bible studies, and reaping the harvest of souls for Christ. The three aspects come together in the work of the Bible instructor.

Recruiting the Bible Instructor

Where we now find one Bible instructor active in a congregation, there should be teams of volunteers led by one designated Bible instructor coordinator, more often referred to as the head Bible instructor. Such individuals work interdependently with the in- and outreach ministries of every department of the church. The coordinator should represent the Bible instructor team in the planning process for evangelism and should be in ongoing collaboration with the personal ministries leader in every project. Well-trained and experienced, they should be willing and able to teach others the art and science of Bible instruction through training sessions combined with field apprenticeship. We will have more to say about the Bible instructor coordinator in chapter 4.

A congregation can recruit volunteer Bible instructor teams through a variety of means, including formal appeals by the pastor and/or the head Bible instructor, systematic training seminars offered once or twice per year, spiritual gift questionnaires, and personal invitations. Take care, however, not to urge people to become Bible instructors out of feelings of guilt or pressure, especially if someone has emphasized the high cost that Christ paid for our salvation. If that has undergirded your witnessing, go back to your prayer closet and meditate on the cross of Jesus Christ and recognize that there is no price you could pay that could even begin to repay our Lord for His enormous sacrifice.

Pray for the infilling of the Holy Spirit and His guidance in any appeal made for Bible instructors. In the words of Jesus to Nicodemus, "Ye must be born again" (John 3:7) "of water and of the Spirit" (verse 5). The baptism of the Holy Spirit fits us for witnessing, endowing us with the sensitivity for the salvation of others. It's amazing what we will do when motivated by the right spirit—the Spirit of God and a depth of love for our neighbors. It is crucial that people consider Bible work only for the right reason and motivation. Recruitment appeals for Bible instructors should reflect this.

The invitation to become a Bible instructor should be open to all willing to undergo a program of self-sacrificial training. It requires dedicated time in intense study, prayer, and sacrifice. Some will find that they feel the call of God for it, while others may conclude that that they can witness best in various other ways. In either case, employ no guilt-ridden pressure.

Do not turn anyone away before the training has taken place unless pastoral counsel advises otherwise. The training itself will provide the guidance needed to determine whether a person should join the Bible instructor team. On the other hand, do not choose anyone who has not gone through a training series or is unwilling to be an understudy in the field (just wants to do their own things). Misrepresentation in the home by poor methods and confused Bible knowledge can result in irreparable damage (resulting in a complete turn-off toward Seventh-day Adventists and/or a relationship with God). It is crucial that those who go into the communities representing God and the Seventh-day Adventist Church be thoroughly prepared with appropriate academic and field training and mentoring. More times than not I meet people who have erroneous notions about Adventists because of how someone presented the law of God and the Sabbath to them, who rebuked them with Ellen G. White quotes (often misquotes), were insulted because they spoke in tongues or believed their deceased loved ones were in heaven, etc. However sincere the intentions of those who did such things may have been, it was not proper Bible work!

In each home the Bible instructor should be a learner as well as a teacher. Bible work is as much an art as it is a science. I will say more about the art and science of Bible instruction later. But for now, in colaboring with the Holy Spirit, regard each individual as representing one chance, one opportunity that may never come in the same way again. Bible studies must be given appropriately and systematically, at the pace the recipient can handle. Dumping knowledge and backing the recipient into a corner with argument is not Bible instruction.

It is understandable that we all are eager to share our faith at times. Unfortunately, many embark upon Bible studies without the proper training and find themselves in embarrassing or argumentative situations that can destroy relationships and abruptly end what started out with genuinely good intentions. As a result, discouragement leads to a feeling of failure. But that need not be. Instead, we must provide good training and access to appropriate support.

Six months to one year prior to a major evangelistic program is a good time to offer the training. It should be a time when the focus is on evangelism. Utilize the first three months for training and the remaining months for sharpening field-work skills. The seminars in preparation for a major evangelism series should include, but not be limited to:

- comprehensive academic training sessions
- discussion groups on the various aspects of Bible instruction
- small and large group discussions on fundamental doctrines, difficult texts, etc.
- a study on and role play of each lesson presented in the homes
- role play of various situations, such as what to prepare beforehand, the initial home visit, supplies to have on hand, what to avoid in the contact's personal life, praying in the home, and calling for a decision.
- Student presentations on various topics, such as randomly chosen lessons, difficult passages and/or doctrines
- actual hours in the field developing interests

- partnering, preferably with an experienced Bible instructor who gives actual Bible studies
- small and large group discussion and role play on preparing for a baptism
- small and large group discussion on effective follow-up

Such training should be nonthreatening, creative yet practical, enthusiastic, encouraging, and effective. It should include demonstrations of various potential situations in the home and during the evangelistic meetings; be interactive; clarify understanding; involve if possible the pastor/evangelist and experienced Bible instructors from other areas of the country; provide access to a variety of study/research material; offer supervised field application; and be certifiable. Longer sessions of three to four hours each up to full-day intensives will offer a more comprehensive experience.

So often training gets rushed, because it happens in conjunction with a major evangelistic series that will begin shortly rather than being offered systematically at least once a year. As a result, too many people with great potential encounter challenges they are unprepared for. They, in turn, can discourage others who might have considered becoming a Bible instructor. But professional, comprehensive, and systematic preparation will produce a ready and ever growing pool of individuals who can shift their routine focus to a major evangelistic effort.

Using this approach, even though we didn't have all the resources now available, my husband and I built powerful teams from within every church we pastored, ranging from small towns such as Greenwood and Canton, Mississippi, and Decatur and Gadsden, Alabama, to larger cities such as Jackson, Mississippi, and one in southern California. Their memberships grew from fewer than 400 to more than 600, from around 40 to more than 300 (a new church spawned), a handful of members to more than 80 (new church spawned), fewer than 30 to more than 100 (new church spawned), and fewer than 100 to more than 350. Each of those explosive growth spurts occurred within a couple years. But they are merely examples of what could happen with well-trained local church Bible instructor teams. While some of them occurred under tents and in halls, most took place right in the local church. With ever-expanding teams of dedicated Bible instructors, there is no reason why God would not add to churches continuously through baptisms scheduled at least bimonthly (preferably monthly). In the early New Testament church, when the members were on fire for God, new believers joined daily. That same Holy Spirit power is available to God's fired-up pastors, Bible instructors, and churches today.

> "And they, continuing daily with one accord in the temple, and breaking bread from house to house, did eat their meat with gladness and singleness of heart, praising God, and having favour with all the people. And the Lord added to the church daily such as should be saved" (Acts 2:46, 47).

Chapter Activities

1. List some reasons Bible instructor training should be comprehensive for all, not presuming anything based on long-standing church membership or experience in other fields?
2. Discuss what it would take to begin a systematic program of Bible instructor preparation at your church.
3. Discuss and list the advantages of having a team of local church Bible instructors rather than depending on intermittently hired professionals.

Bible Instructor in an Evangelistic Series: The Benefits

Many hardworking, knowledgeable Bible instructors wonder why their daily efforts are so challenging and the results from their labors so few and far between. When they experience such feelings, it indicates that they should receive more on-the-job, supervised training. Sometimes the pastor can provide it when there are no experienced Bible instructors in the area, but nothing can kick new life into Bible work more than a major evangelistic series that provides daily, specific instruction and immediate application. Here are some reasons:

- Evangelistic series offer the opportunity to work with an experienced evangelist and head Bible instructor (usually from the outside) from whom one can gain a wealth of knowledge as well as ongoing training.
- The formal evangelistic series provides opportunity to engage in much more intense Bible work, forcing one to overcome inadequacies quickly.
- A major series lets those involved see within weeks the results of dedicated colaboring with God.

- It gives an opportunity to experience a different style of evangelism as compared to a pastor preaching weekly sermons and the usual ongoing church activities.
- Less experienced Bible instructors team up with more experienced ones and learn much as understudies.
- During an evangelistic series, the Bible instructor team can take notes each night and come to a better understanding of Bible doctrines and presentation style.
- A series affords the opportunity to experience the complete cycle of introducing someone to Bible studies, studying with them, clarifying Scripture, witnessing repentance and conversion and the challenges along the spiritual journey, and watching baptism and assimilation into the family of God during a compressed period of time.
- The evangelistic series provides an entirely different perspective in the role of Bible instructors because they will be coworkers on an evangelistic team directly under and in support of the evangelist.
- Formal evangelism becomes a time for personal spiritual renewal through special sessions of prayer and fasting for oneself and for those for whom the Bible instructor is laboring.
- Finally, it generates many new interests long after the series itself has ended. In fact, such follow-up should not only lead to continuous baptisms but also flow into the next major evangelistic campaign.

One's growth as a Bible instructor that could require years of laboring alone now can be compressed into weeks through working with an experienced Bible instructor team. Pastors are usually excited to have new Bible instructors who are willing to allow God to use them in such a capacity and, as a result, will eagerly support such interest. If you are serious about sharpening the gifts that God has given you for ministering to others, pray that He will open doors for you to work in an evangelistic series and that He will give you the faith and everything else needed to lead others to salvation.

> "But seek ye first the kingdom of God, and his righteousness; and all these things shall be added unto you" (Matt. 6:33).
>
> "But my God shall supply all your need according to his riches in glory by Christ Jesus" (Phil. 4:19).

Chapter Activities

1. Discuss how one's lifestyle can be a powerful witness for (or against) God's Word.
2. Discuss the benefits of training for Bible instructors.
3. How does an evangelistic series heighten the skills of the Bible instructor in a way that exceeds what is gained through local church activities?

---

[1] Ellen G. White, *The Ministry of Healing* (Mountain View, Calif.: Pacific Press Pub. Assn., 1905), pp. 148, 149.

[2] *Ibid.*, p. 149.

[3] Ellen G. White, *Medical Ministry* (Mountain View, Calif.: Pacific Press Pub. Assn., 1932), p. 301.

[4] Ellen G. White, *The Acts of the Apostles* (Mountain View, Calif.: Pacific Press Pub. Assn., 1911), p. 96.

CHAPTER 2

THE HIGH CALLING OF TORCH BEARING

"The conversion of souls to God is the greatest work, the highest work, in which human beings can have a part. By accepting this high calling, we become co-laborers with God, and partner with the Almighty in the salvation of precious souls He created to inherit eternal life. John 3:16 says, 'For God so loved the world, that he gave his only begotten Son, that whosoever believeth in him should not perish, but have everlasting life.'

"In the conversion of souls God's forbearance, His unbounded love, His holiness, His power, are revealed. Every true conversion glorifies Him, and causes the angels to break forth into singing."[1]

"Mercy and truth are met together; righteousness and peace have kissed each other" (Ps. 85:10).

"The highest of all sciences is the science of soul saving. The greatest work to which human beings can aspire is the work of winning men from sin to holiness."[2]

"We are not to feel that the work of the gospel depends principally upon the minister. To every man God has given a work to do in connection with His kingdom. Everyone who professes the name of Christ is to be an earnest, disinterested worker, ready to defend the principles of righteousness. Every soul should take an active part in advancing the cause of God. Whatever our calling, as Christians we have a work to do in making Christ known to the world. We are to be missionaries, having for our chief aim the winning of souls to Christ."[3]

"Are any tempted to make their circumstances an excuse for failing to witness for Christ? . . . Because of obstacles that seem insurmountable, the Christian may seek to excuse himself from obeying the truth as it is in Jesus; but he can offer no excuse that will bear investigation. Could he do this, he would prove God unjust, in that He had made for His children conditions of salvation, with which they could not comply.

"He whose heart is fixed to serve God will find opportunity to witness for Him. Difficulties will be powerless to hinder him who is determined to seek first the kingdom of God and His righteousness.... 'What time I am afraid, I will trust in Thee' (Ps. 56:3). To all who put their trust in Him, God will fulfil His promise."[4]

"Our work has been marked out for us by our heavenly Father. We are to take our Bibles and go forth to warn the world. We are to be God's helping hand in saving souls—channels through which His love is day by day to flow to the perishing. The realization of the great work in which he has the privilege of taking part ennobles and sanctifies the true worker. He is filled with the faith that works by love and purifies the soul. Nothing is drudgery to the one who submits to the will of God. 'Doing it unto the Lord' is the thought that throws a charm over the work that God gives him to do."[5]

"Let those who desire to work for God begin at home, in their own household, in their own neighborhood, among their own friends. Here they will find a favorable missionary field."[6]

"The formation of small companies as a basis of Christian effort is a plan that has been presented before me by One who cannot err. If there is a large number in the church, let the members be formed into small companies to work, not only for the church members but for unbelievers also."[7]

"Those who have had so great a sacrifice made for them that they might become partakers of His heavenly grace should in their turn sacrifice and deny self to aid in the great work of bringing others to the knowledge of the truth. Self-interest should be laid aside; selfish desires and self-comfort should not now stand in the way of God's work in saving souls."[8]

"Light, precious light, shines upon God's people; but it will not save them, unless they consent to be saved by it, fully live up to it, and transmit it to others in darkness."[9]

The torch-bearing relay became forever established in 1936 in Berlin, Germany, as the official announcement of the impending start of the Olympics. Since then, athletes have carried the Olympic flame around the globe and passed this iconic handoff down from generation to generation as an Olympic tradition.

We, the workers, stand today as the torch-bearers of the plan of salvation, one proclaimed since that fateful day that gave us Genesis 3:15. The plan announced a promise kept in John 3:16 and now proclaims the clarion call to remain faithful found in Revelation 22:7. The gospel torch represents a clear and distinct summons to prepare for the soon-coming Savior. We must keep the flames of Pentecost held high to every community so that we also may witness thousands baptized in a day. Our message must be unmistakable to generations to come until Jesus breaks through the clouds in all His royal glory and majesty.

No matter what your circumstances, you cannot use them as an excuse for failing to witness for Christ. You should see your witnessing power as directly linked to your spiritual fire. If you purpose in your heart to become a witness for the Lord because of your yearning to see others safe in the arms of Jesus, your own spiritual energy will become stronger and more resolute. And as you feel an inner urge to witness for God because He has saved you from eternal death and has given you the gift of salvation, you will find your spiritual powers strengthened.

You must believe that as you witness, it is actually the power of the Holy Spirit working through you to reach others. Therefore, the more you witness for Christ, the stronger and bolder will become your Christian walk and your testimony, regardless of your personal circumstances. Your witness for Christ should never be based on a response to guilt, or pressure for personal gain, or to impress others with your abilities. Such self-centeredness will not last very long before discouraging circumstances overwhelm you. The more you lend yourself to the Holy Spirit in faith, the more you will find your circumstances becoming your strength and motivation. This is God's work, and "no good thing will he withhold from them that walk uprightly" (Ps. 84:11).

I can think of at least three evangelistic campaigns, all Revelation seminars, in which the elders of the church joined arms with the Bible instructors in the lectures and Bible studies. During one of them I was among several elders asked to participate. Not only was it my first time to speak on any part of Revelation in public, but the subjects of Revelation 5-7 were an overwhelming challenge for me to understand, let alone present with passion. Expressing my feelings of discomfort with the subject matter and using any number of legitimate excuses to defer to someone more knowledgeable, I could have bowed out. But the Spirit of God rose up in my spirit and would not allow me. I labored on my knees and in the Word of God and other study resources until God gave me a word for His people. I praise Him that the battle is not mine but the Lord's. Others on the speaking team were no less challenged, but we believed that like Esther of old, God had chosen us for such a time as this. As a result, He kept His promise and drew 12 individuals to Himself in the first baptism. Others soon followed. Yes, I felt much pressure, but I had based my decision on Zechariah 4:6: "Not by might, nor by power, but by my spirit, saith the Lord of hosts."

> "Herein is my Father glorified, that ye bear much fruit; so shall ye be my disciples" (John 15:8).
>
> "Let us not be weary in well doing: for in due season we shall reap, if we faint not" (Gal. 6:9).

The attitude that motivates you as a Bible instructor to share the love of Jesus must come from the Spirit of God—from a relationship with Him and faith in His Word. It is the same unconditional level of agape love that motivates a husband who loves his wife or that drives parents to make extreme sacrifices for their children. Without question the same relationship that you have with God will reflect itself in how you share the plan of salvation. Whatever drives you to witness will be the same motivation that you will use to encourage others to know and serve God. That is why whatever compels you to witness must be for the right reason. If you serve God out of fear, guilt, pressure from others, spiritual indebtedness, etc., you will no doubt influence others to do the same.

Whatever shapes your relationship with God will become the filter through which you will present every Bible lesson. The prism through which you view your doctrinal beliefs will no doubt become the one through which you will share those beliefs with others. Calling on individuals to come to Christ and serve Him out of any type of fear or obligation, rather than urging them to embrace a relationship of love and appreciation, merely adds layers of burdens that will soon become too heavy for the new believer to bear. The length of time they hold to their new faith will tell the story. Unfortunately, too many are using misguided, faithless approaches to prey upon the desperate seeker of truth. You cannot effectively and passionately share with someone else something you do not have or have never known or experienced.

May you make a daily commitment to stay prayerfully in God's Word, enhancing a warm relationship with Him that does not cool under pressure but rather grows stronger with every challenge in life. Then not only shall you be more effective in leading others to Christ, but years later they will have remained because you have introduced them to the love of Jesus the right way.

Chapter Activities

1. Make a list of the stuff that is stifling the flames of the gospel torch held both by the church and by individuals.
2. How can you be a torchbearer in your own home? How can you pass along being on fire for Christ to the next generation?
3. Discuss what will keep your flame for spreading the gospel beaming, and what will cause it to eventually smolder.

Two Aspects of Bible Instructor Activity

As a local church Bible instructor, you can either give Bible studies alone or join with another member. You obtain names from following up various interests—such as Bible correspondence courses, church visitor lists, church events, mailers, surveys, community service, and personal ministries—and from interests developed through personal contact.

You will operate under the guidance and supervision of the local pastor and coordinate your efforts with the personal ministries leader. The associate pastor or the personal ministries leader may also perform this role of church ministry or share it with you. A vital part of the local church's outreach ministry is to have a designated person well trained to follow up on all interests, develop new ones, give personal Bible studies, provide training to those interested in joining the Bible instructor team, and prepare individuals for baptism. That person would be considered, or designated, the head or lead Bible instructor, or Bible instructor coordinator. We will discuss more about that important and specific role in chapter 4.

The Bible instructors in Seventh-day Adventist churches throughout a city or region may come together on a regular basis as a guild. The Pacific Union Bible Workers' Guild is a model for areas interested in forming such an organization. The focus of this Bible Workers' Guild is on the role of the Bible instructor in the local congregational setting, as well as during a defined evangelistic series conducted by an evangelist (or pastor-evangelist) and whose team of Bible instructors work under the direction of a lead/head Bible instructor, or Bible instructor coordinator. Expanding the guild across the nation would greatly benefit the mission and effectiveness of Bible instructors. It would provide a means for addressing responsibility and accountability among them, as well as being an invaluable resource for developing well-trained individuals.

Keep in mind that during an evangelistic series the evangelist is the center point. Your job as a Bible instructor is to make every effort to direct the attention of the attendee to the evangelist (and his or her designated associate) as the key person presenting the lessons, answering the questions, and directing how the series will go. Bible instructors are never in opposition or competition with the evangelist. On the contrary, your role is supportive and complementary. You repeat what the evangelist says, direct appropriate questions and concerns to the evangelist, and urge the importance of not missing any presentation of the evangelist.

Chapter Activities

1. Explore some of the differences between congregational Bible instruction activity and that involved in an evangelistic series.
2. Discuss how much of the work of God depends on the members and how much on the pastor.
3. Discuss why the Bible instructor is always under the supervision of a pastor/evangelist or the head Bible instructor.

---

[1] Ellen G. White, *Evangelism* (Washington, D.C.: Review and Herald Pub. Assn., 1946), p. 292.

[2] E. G. White, *The Ministry of Healing*, p. 398.

[3] Ellen G. White, *Testimonies for the Church* (Mountain View, Calif.: Pacific Press Pub. Assn., 1948), vol. 6, p. 427.

[4] E. G. White, *The Acts of the Apostles*, pp. 466, 467.

[5] E. G. White, *Testimonies*, vol. 9, p. 150.

[6] *Ibid.*, vol. 6, p. 428.

[7] E. G. White, *Evangelism*, p. 115.

[8] E. G. White, *Testimonies*, vol. 1, p. 431.

[9] *Ibid.*, vol. 2, p. 123.

CHAPTER 3

ROAD-TESTED PROFESSIONALS

> "Every Christian is bound to be a Bible worker, to do something in imparting to others the great present truth for this time. Communicate what you do know. Tell it, sing it, pray it. Work while it is day; for the night cometh, in which no man can work. God help you, is my most earnest prayer."[1]

Whether engaged in ongoing Bible studies for the local congregation or under the direction of an evangelist, your qualities and responsibilities as a Bible instructor are vital to successfully leading someone to Christ. Yet they are actually simple in nature. If you are excited about what God has done for you, you are ready to witness, and should do so everywhere you go and with whomever you meet. Your smile in public, intentional helpfulness, unsolicited acts of kindness, encouraging words, and good deeds will go a long way to draw people to you and to Christ. You won't have to wave a flag that you are a witness for Jesus—people will approach you because of your genuineness and consistency. They will ask you questions and seek your spiritual counsel, prayers, and Bible studies. If you love God with all your heart and feel empathy for those loaded down with the cares of life, you are already qualified to tell the world about Jesus and His love.

The Bible has many examples of new believers immediately sent to witness to all whom they knew. The woman at the well lived a shunned life, having had five husbands and now living an adulterous life when Jesus met her. Her encounter with Jesus truly converted her, and she went to tell others about the salvation she had received (John 4:1-30). After Jesus cast out the demons from the possessed man who lived secluded in the countryside of the Gadarenes, he denied the healed individual the opportunity to join Him in ministry but rather sent him back to his home to witness to others what he had experienced (Luke 8:27-39). Even though Jesus warned the leper that He had just healed not to say anything before the high priest had pronounced him clean, the man, so grateful to be free of his leprosy, could not hold back from telling everyone everywhere he went what Jesus had done for him (Mark 1:40-45).

These are a few of the many accounts in Scripture telling of those so thankful for salvation and healing that they immediately began witnessing of God's love and power. Although they did not understand all the doctrines of the church, they knew Jesus. While not formally trained, they had experienced the power of Christ's example and felt empowered with a testimony that was theirs to share. Through the personal testimony of their experience with the Son of God, many came to know and accept Christ as their Savior. Even though they did not give formal Bible studies, they led all those they encountered to the master Teacher. Unfortunately, many of those young in the faith, after giving their testimony, feel that they must defend it to the point of being obnoxious or combative. That is not witnessing. On the contrary, it indicates that they need proper training for witnessing while their enthusiasm is still strong.

The Seventh-day Adventist Church established the Bible instruction program as the teaching and training arm of evangelism. It is a vocation done by those who have experienced the love of Christ and have responded to God's call to devote their life, time, and focus as a colaborer with Him under the direct supervision of a pastor/evangelist. They may be either experienced in giving Bible studies in the home and have a track record of leading others to Christ, or they may be in training under a "road tested" professional. It is the only difference between the work of the Bible instructor and the daily witnessing done by all those who have accepted Christ. The Bible instructor team is the professional arm of outreach trained to present the gospel in the home. The general membership of the church will have already witnessed to many of the Bible study interests.

Chapter Activities

1. Describe the differences in witnessing for Christ and being a Bible instructor for the church.
2. How could those mentioned in the Bible be such effective witnesses after merely one encounter with Jesus?
3. Discuss what a new believer should do to refrain from getting into arguments over doctrinal differences.

Qualities and Responsibilities of the Bible Instructor

Following is a general outline of the qualities and responsibilities you should possess as a Bible instructor. The list does not seek to disqualify anyone. On the contrary, you should embrace it as more of a charge than a prerequisite. If you do not feel comfortable with, or know that you lack, anything on the list, work it out with God. The purpose of the list is to help you to recognize and understand better the traits and duties of a Bible instructor. You might find yourself struggling with some of the tenets below once you enter the work. Sincerely determine by the grace and power of God to be an overcomer. God must be first, last, and best in the life of the Bible instructor. It's never about "me." On the contrary, it's always about God and Him alone. "Not I, but Christ" in every word and action, every thought and deed.

We all struggle from time to time with feelings of discouragement and inadequacy, but that does not disqualify you for continuing as a Bible instructor. On the contrary, it is a time to pray, recommit, be restored by the power of God's Holy Spirit, and move forward in faith. A prayerful talk with the pastor or evangelist about any struggles with any of the tenets below should help you determine whether you should step aside until the struggle has been won.

If you are considering joining the worldwide team of Bible instructors in the Seventh-day Adventist Church, here are qualities and responsibilities for you to contemplate. As a Bible instructor, you should:

- **Have love for God and an appreciation for His love for you.** You will demonstrate not only love for God but also for those whom God is inviting you to love to Him.
- **Feel the call of God to evangelistic ministry**. It is a summons to devote your life to frontline soul winning, training for evangelism, and being actively involved in evangelism under the supervision of a pastor/evangelist.
- **Be a Seventh-day Adventist of firm principle and uncompromising character.**
- **Believe in the mission of the church to spread the three angels' messages.** Promote the fact that we are indeed living in the last days and that God's remnant church is the recipient and conduit of the last solemn message of warning and of salvation to the world.
- **Be willing to work the communities** door to door and participate in various evangelistic efforts.

- **Have a sincere love and burden for souls** and a desire to take part in the great commission of Matthew 28:19, 20: "Go ye therefore, and teach all nations, baptizing them in the name of the Father, and of the Son, and of the Holy Ghost: Teaching them to observe all things whatsoever I have commanded you: and, lo, I am with you alway, even unto the end of the world." As a Bible instructor you must truly value those for whom you labor while respecting their privacy and their choices, and keeping confidentiality.
- **Have a humble, teachable spirit** willing to follow the guidance and instructions of the pastor or evangelist and those appointed to lead the Bible instructor team, and to work just as cooperatively and harmoniously with all those on the evangelism team. If God has called you to be a teacher in any branch of the work of God, you should also expect to be a learner in the school of Christ. "One who works in harmony with the counsel of God, and in unity with the brethren, will be more efficient to do good than ten will be who do not realize the necessity of depending upon God and of acting in harmony with the general plan of the work."[2]
- **Understand the importance of Bible instruction.** You should feel that you have accepted the highest honor given by God to humanity—spreading the rays of light that heaven has shed upon you. Recognize that Bible study is essential to every type of evangelistic endeavor. Let nothing discourage you from this work.
- **Honor God in every aspect of your labor for Him.** It may require long hours and many self-sacrificing inconveniences, but it's not about you once you have made the commitment to an evangelistic effort; it's about being faithful to God and to those in your spiritual care each and every day.
- **Refuse to be diverted from your calling.** Instead, commit yourself to attend every nightly evangelistic lecture and Bible instructor meeting as far as possible, and faithfully dedicate yourself to home visits and the best possible practices.
- **Feel a sense of responsibility for the success of each nightly meeting and the evangelistic series as a whole.** Be willing to remain focused from the time you receive an assignment until you have completed it, and from the time you accept the care of a name until you have accomplished your part in being a colaborer with God.

- **Demonstrate in your life that you consider all the commandments sacred.** God has placed His sanctity upon His law and bids us to implement every principle in our life. As you "walk the talk," it will draw others as you follow in the footsteps of Jesus Christ.
- **Preserve personal integrity** at any cost to yourself, for you represent God and the Seventh-day Adventist Church. You may be the only image of Jesus that someone will ever know. This includes appropriate dress and speech, positive attitude, and professional, godly conduct. You understand that how you conduct yourself models the way for those for whom the team is laboring.
- **Spend dedicated time in the study of and meditation on God's Word, as well as in the development of the art and science of effective Bible instruction.** Be a continuous learner in the school of Christ and pursue various types of study and training for an ever-evolving and expanding ministry. Your prayer should be "Lord, I trust You to teach me, improve me, and use me to lead others to know Your love and love You in return." You must be open to and receive wisdom, knowledge, and understanding from God and the ability to apply them consistently each day. "The entrance of thy words giveth light; it giveth understanding to the simple" (Ps. 119:130).
- **Demonstrate leadership skills** in correct and appropriate verbal and written communication. Become capable of strategic planning, organizing and directing for successful in- and outreach, and be willing to train and guide others in the art and science of Bible study. Strong leadership is a goal toward which all Bible instructors should strive. Second Timothy 2:2 states, "And the things that thou hast heard of me among many witnesses, the same commit thou to faithful men, who shall be able to teach others also." Continuing to expand the Bible instructor force with well-trained individuals is an important part of this ministry.
- **Be respectful and respectable.** As a Bible instructor, you must be willing to respect people, space, and time and be able to work harmoniously, cooperatively, and supportively with pastors, evangelists, and others involved in evangelism. Utilize time efficiently and effectively. Be supportive, trustworthy, and truthful. Keep confidences and avoid wasting resources. Not only receive

correction, but be timely in giving it. Always respect peoples' homes, furniture, families, guests, and circumstances, and by all means, their opinions and beliefs.

- **Be a person of prayer, fasting, and faith.** Be one willing to let the Holy Spirit lead regardless of perceived obstacles and setbacks. Always remember that the battle is not ours but the Lord's (1 Sam. 17:47; 2 Chron. 20:15).

"Bible readings [studies] should be held in the homes of the people, and our literature should be circulated. Truth, precious truth from the Word of God, is to be presented, both in public and in house-to-house visitation. We have a message that is to prepare a people to stand amid the perils of the last days, and in proclaiming this message we need many men and women filled with the Holy Spirit and with a knowledge of God's Word."[3]

"You need not go to the ends of the earth for wisdom, for God is near. It is not the capabilities you now possess or ever will have that will give you success. It is that which the Lord can do for you. We need to have far less confidence in what man can do and far more confidence in what God can do for every believing soul. He longs to have you reach after Him by faith. He longs to have you expect great things from Him. He longs to give you understanding in temporal as well as in spiritual matters. He can sharpen the intellect. He can give tact and skill. Put your talents into the work, ask God for wisdom and it will be given you."[4]

"Let God's workers teach the truth in families, drawing close to those for whom they labor. If they thus co-operate with God, He will clothe them with spiritual power. Christ will guide them in their work, entering the houses of the people with them, and giving them words to speak that will sink deep into the hearts of the listeners. The Holy Spirit will open hearts and minds to receive the rays coming from the source of all light."[5]

"God will not permit this precious work for Him to go unrewarded. He will crown with success every humble effort made in His name."[6]

Chapter Activities

1. Discuss the importance of the local church when it comes to spreading the gospel of Jesus Christ.

2. Discuss your opinion about the qualities and responsibilities of the Bible instructor.
3. Discuss the question Is everyone who has accepted Christ a Bible instructor?

---

[1] Ellen G. White, "Words of Gratitude," *General Conference Bullentin*, April-June 1899.

[2] Ellen G. White, "Be of One Mind," *Review and Herald*, May 29, 1888.

[3] Ellen G. White, "Closing Days at the Oakland (Cal.) Camp Meeting," *Review and Herald*, Oct. 4, 1906.

[4] Ellen G. White, *Christ's Object Lessons* (Washington, D.C.: Review and Herald Pub. Assn., 1900), p. 146.

[5] E. G. White, *Evangelism*, p. 436.

[6] Ellen G. White, *Gospel Workers* (Washington, D.C.: Review and Herald Pub. Assn., 1915), p. 192.

CHAPTER 4

THE BIBLE INSTRUCTOR COORDINATOR

The size of the evangelistic team and how it assigns its various tasks will determine the extent of the Bible instructor coordinator's responsibilities. They may range from directly supervising the Bible instructor team to arranging the entire evangelistic series.

Essentially Bible instructor coordinators, or head Bible instructors, have the dual focus of conducting personal Bible studies and of administrating them and other evangelistic endeavors. On the one hand, they have the awesome responsibility of supporting the needs and functions of the Bible instructor team and supervising all their activity in preparation for, during, and following an evangelistic program. On the other hand, they are responsible for ensuring the full support of the evangelist by the Bible instructors and other evangelistic team members. They have had more experience in evangelism and are aware of what will work best for the success of the evangelist and his or her program. First of all, they are accountable to God and then to the evangelist for fulfilling responsibilities such as:

Study the Word of God with individuals, families, and groups, leading them from where they are to a full surrender of their lives to Christ.

Assist the pastor/evangelist and personal ministries leader with the development of plans and procedures for a major evangelistic program.

Coordinate and/or conduct training seminar series and field work coaching.

Develop interest in volunteer Bible instruction through rallies, presentations and appeals, special events, personal invitations, etc.

Support the pastor/evangelist in assisting, or conducting, regular review meetings with the Bible instructor team for the purpose of devotion and prayer emphasis, in which you distribute Bible-student interest assignments, hear and give input on reports of the Bible instructors about their progress with study interests, provide ongoing training and presentations, secure special speakers for Bible instructor enrichment, resolve issues and concerns, develop strategic planning, make announcements, give directives, and provide relationship-building activities.

Team up with individual Bible instructors for field work for the purpose of meeting and encouraging Bible study interests and modeling hands-on training.

Play an ad-hoc, advisory role on the pastoral/evangelist's team with regard to strategic planning for future evangelism and providing reports on the progress of the Bible study students, field work, and follow-up care of new members.

Be flexible and attentive during the nightly meetings to the activities of each Bible instructor.

Support the evangelist's procedures for decision and altar calls, preparation for baptism, baptismal arrangements, and events following the baptism.

Be available to assist Bible instructors in gaining decisions for baptism.

Be an ever-growing student of the Word of God in knowledge and personal life application, in presentation, and in teaching/training others.

Represent themselves as professionals of the highest calling and standards, and model a Christ-centered character at all times. The head coordinator should display an obvious love for God and those for whom He gave His life.

Other responsibilities that Bible instructor coordinators have had a role in are:

Work in collaboration with the platform chairperson and pastor/evangelist to ensure every aspect of the nightly meetings runs smoothly, especially as it pertains to the multifaceted role of the Bible instructor.

Assist the associate evangelist, if necessary, or assigned persons, to ensure that everything is functioning appropriately and supplied with the needed personnel, supplies, and equipment.

Work with various pastors in the targeted evangelistic area to develop and implement preseries strategies and provide training campaigns for recruiting and training volunteer Bible instructors as well as create interest in the upcoming meetings.

Assist the associate evangelist or point person in addressing special needs, concerns, and issues that arise before and/or during the evangelistic series.

Support the pastor and/or evangelist to ensure the care and follow-up Bible studies and/or reviews occur in a salvific manner and that special needs for support get referred to the appropriate resources.

To summarize: A Bible instructor coordinator should have strong experience in the various aspects of Bible work, have an administrative and supervisory background in the evangelistic setting, have a track record of soul winning, have the ability to develop and conduct Bible instructor training campaigns and presentations, and be flexible to work collaboratively with a diversity of evangelists, pastors, and other Bible instructors.

All congregations are not fortunate enough to have an experienced Bible instructor coordinator. But they should not hastily bestow the position even on those who may truly desire it if they have not yet been "road tested." The head Bible instructor role is highly visible and multifaceted, and it can get drawn in many directions by other departmental leaders, thus challenging inexperienced individuals in ways that they may not be able to handle appropriately.

I've known head Bible instructors who have never given a Bible study; never driven a car; never been responsible for a baptism; have lined their living room walls with certificates of training but never trained anyone else; do not know their way around the communities of their own city; will not go out after dark; seldom attend prayer meeting; do not get along with others on the Bible instructor team or with the pastor. More harm than good results for the Bible instructor team if such individuals receive the title without the qualifications. Head Bible instructors do not get made overnight. On the contrary, by being faithful over time, they develop each of the qualities listed above. It would be far better to begin developing *road-tested* Bible instructors and allow them to gain the necessary experience and character. Their readiness to take on such a position will become evident in time. The wait will have been worth it. Then the church will have a professional that can build a well-trained Bible instructor team.

I know of individuals who give as many as 10 actual Bible studies per day (that's a consistent 50 Bible studies per week), have trained hundreds, and have led hundreds to baptism. Some run their own home meetings and even full-scale evangelistic series. Powerful lay preachers, they bring many to Christ yearly. They are the road-tested professionals that we should call upon to expand the Bible instructor force of our church. Some have a college education, while others were trained in the field through the years by the Holy Spirit.

Chapter Activities

1. List challenges that an inexperienced Bible instructor may not be prepared to handle as head Bible instructor.
2. List things that you can learn from an experienced head Bible instructor that an inexperienced one could not yet teach.
3. In your opinion, what would be evidences that a Bible instructor is ready to take on the much larger role of head Bible instructor?

CHAPTER 5

SEEKING FRIENDS FOR ETERNITY

As a Bible instructor, you may find yourself teaming up with others in some capacity to generate potential interests and Bible studies, such as (but not limited to):

- community surveys
- community service, filling requests for special needs
- community outreach, participating in events designed to attract and interest the community in Bible studies
- door-to-door ministry to deliver introductory lessons and develop home Bible studies by leaving literature, door hanger announcements, flyers, etc., in the vicinity of the church
- interest follow-up, developed from the visitors' log, television and Internet media, and the other outreach ministries of the various departments of the church
- prayer ministry, as a participant in small-group intercessory prayers

While most people can learn to be outgoing, it is not a requirement to witness for Christ—being willing, available, and obedient is. Living a consistent life in Christ is an imperative. "If ye be willing and obedient, ye shall eat the good of the land" (Isa. 1:19). What you will say when you meet a stranger and are impressed to witness to them will come easier with experience. Keep in mind that God is touching hearts all the time, preparing them to be impressed by the love of God reflected through many avenues of witnessing, or seed sowing (including the Christ-centered life). You must believe that your ministry to people is one of those avenues that God has ordained and appointed for a specific moment of contact. That is why you should keep small tracts, sermon CD/DVDs, and Bible study enrollment cards in your car and purse. When words seem to fail you, immediately trust God and receive His promise in your spirit, by faith:

"For the Holy Ghost shall teach you in the same hour what ye ought to say" (Luke 12:12).

Diane was walking past the church one Sabbath morning when a Bible instructor warmly greeted her. It turned into a lengthy conversation about Diane's family and spiritual struggles and ended with an accepted invitation to suspend her business for the morning and attend church. Member after member received her with open arms. Later she accepted Bible studies, and the rest is history. A kind word at the proper moment nurtured a seed of yearning for the love of Christ that day and changed a life forever.

A conversation may start with something as simple as a catch phrase that you are accustomed to saying, such as "God is good," "With God all things are possible," or "It's a beautiful day." Even a pleasant smile on a peace-filled face can generate conversation. One of the mistakes many Christians make is to feel as though they must work at witnessing for Christ. Such an attitude puts the person in charge instead of the Spirit of God. The Word of God says, "Let your light so shine before men, that they may see your good works, and glorify your father which is in heaven" (Matt. 5:16). If your daily prayer is, "Lord, help me let my light shine for You today in every way so that someone is touched by Your love," God will be glorified through you even though you may never know how, where, or when. Rest assured that living a life filled with the fruit of the Spirit is a constant witness for Christ. Read about the fruit in Galatians 5:22, 23: "But the fruit of the Spirit is love, joy, peace, longsuffering, gentleness, goodness, faith, meekness, temperance: against such there is no law."

Every morning and throughout the day, pray that the love of God permeates your heart and keeps it from evil. Remember, it's "not by might, nor by power, but by my spirit, saith the Lord of hosts" (Zech. 4:6). Combining your prayer with the prayer of Jabez in 1 Chronicles 4:10 would also give strength, faith, and hope for the day: "And Jabez called on the God of Israel, saying, Oh that thou wouldest bless me indeed, and enlarge my coast, and that thine hand might be with me, and that thou wouldest keep *me* from evil, that it may not grieve me! And God granted him that which he requested."

Remember, it is not merely your personal testimony that witnesses to the goodness of God—it is your walk with Him each and every day. It is about being available to God for meeting human needs. New Testament writers refer to how Christians speak and carry themselves in what the King James Version of the Bible translates as their "conversation": "Having your conversation honest among the Gentiles: that, whereas they speak against you as evildoers, they may by your good works, which they shall behold, glorify God in the day of visitation" (1 Peter 2:12).

My partner and I finally found the address for Johnny. It was a mobile unit at the end of a country road. Johnny greeted us cordially but tried in the kindest of ways to inform us that he was not interested in the Bible study guides. Still he humbly accepted the first one, despite his attempts to beg off. When we returned, we saw him head away from us into the woods surrounding the dwelling but noticed another man in the mobile unit. It was his father. Invited into the roach-infested dwelling, we began what would be weeks of visits to comfort the elderly, bedridden Johnny senior. We had no idea that sometimes one of his daughters was in a back room listening to us sing and read scriptures and pray, until one day she sneezed. Oh yes, Johnny enjoyed praying in the old Southern style, and he loved to hear us pray.

On one visit another daughter called on the phone while we were there and cursed us for being in her father's house. To make a long story short, that daughter came to the house while we were still there and heard us singing and testifying and reading scriptures. She joined in and extended our stay with her own testimony. Other family members happened by during our later visits and appreciated our ministry to Johnny senior. This is what ministry is all about. Great-grandchildren often ran over when they saw us drive up. They loved the songs and scriptures and listened attentively to the Bible lessons we briefly presented. Johnny had 12 children and many grandchildren. Most lived out of town. Although we were not able to get Bible studies started within that family other than the abbreviated versions we shared with the older man, we can only hope and pray that we made an impression for Christ and that seeds were sown that will one day be watered and cultivated. They knew we were Seventh-day Adventists and had no problem with that. Although we never saw Johnny, junior, again, I have to believe that God sent us to minister to Johnny senior, and other members of his family during his final days.

Let the old cliché remind you of what witnessing is truly all about, "I'd rather see a sermon than hear one any day." Pray that those whom God brings into your life today see a sermon of God's love. Just as every sermon doesn't result in immediate responses to an altar call, you should not expect every sharing of God's love to lead to a Bible study. Don't be hard on yourself when a Bible study interest doesn't result from intentional sharing. Pray for a consistent life and faithful witness, and the Bible studies will come. Then pray for all those the Lord directs to take note of the sermon they saw in your life and that what they saw was acceptable to God. Pray that they will have an open and sincere heart to hear the Holy Spirit's leading. And pray that they will have a longing for personal change that only God through the Holy Spirit can fill. Never lose faith that God heard your prayer and your desire to be a witness. Only in heaven will you know how effective your often silent testimony was to the salvation of others.

Chapter Activities

1. Discuss the strengths and weaknesses of your congregation as it relates to witnessing to the community.
2. Role-play starting up a conversation with a stranger that leads to the topic of the love of God for them.
3. Discuss ways a person can get started in witnessing to others about spiritual matters.

Proven Outreach Ministries

Bible instruction touches the ministries of every department of the local church. Normally the outreach ministry leader will give detailed instructions and often role-play how to conduct the outreach project, especially those involving the entire church family. When challenged and rallied for the cause of Christ, the membership will embark upon outreach activity in small groups. The following often-used outreach avenues for church groups or corporate witnessing have had great success in initiating Bible studies.

- **Friend-to-friend ministry.** List the names of friends, coworkers, family, and anyone else you know by name who might be open to the gospel. Fast and pray for God to soften hearts and prepare them for the evangelistic series. Join with others to pray together for such individuals. Some you will be able to enroll in Bible studies. For others, it may be best that someone else contact them. And for still others, different types of invitations may be more appropriate—an invitation such as to attend church or a church event, to watch *It is Written* or *Breath of Life,* or to enroll in a Bible correspondence course.
- **House-to-house labor.** "This house-to-house labor, searching for souls, hunting for the lost sheep, is the most essential work that

can be done."* Teams of two going out on mapped assignments enrolling people for Bible studies from door to door will never become obsolete. It is a powerful witness for God and the local church and a way to meet (and get to know) those living in the community nearest the church.

- **SWAT.** The designation "SWAT" stands for Soul Winning Action Teams. An outreach auxiliary of a church, the team contacts those who visit the congregation. After the visitors receive a letter of welcome from the pastoral team, a SWAT team goes to their homes. SWAT's objective is to enroll the individuals in a Bible lesson course and then begin studies with them. Ultimately, the goal is to lead the visitors to a decision to accept Christ and join the church through baptism.
- **Surveys, questionnaires, mailers.** The spiritual interest questionnaire is an excellent way to start a conversation with someone, because it is usually not threatening to the person taking the survey. It is also a good way to get younger people involved in evangelism. I have seen very effective questionnaires with as few as three questions.
- **Missing member outreach.** Missing members often want to return but, because of their long absence and perhaps their lifestyle, are too ashamed to take that first step. An invitation to an event at which other missing members will attend may initiate a welcome opportunity for them to return to the fold.
- **Visitors' log.** The guest book is an invaluable source for contacts. Your sending a thank-you note, along with more information about the ministries of your church as well as upcoming events, can often create a good impression with them. They may even welcome a personal visit by the pastor or Bible instructor team and accept Bible studies.
- **Church banners** are ideal for heralding an event and attracting attention.
- **Welcome bags**. Deliver "welcome to our church" bags filled with gifts and information about Seventh-day Adventists, the local congregation, and online and TV programming at least once a year throughout the community and to those new in the neighborhood.
- **Information tables, stands, and kiosks.** Setting up a booth-style table at community events will give your church a professional

look that will attract people and interest them in what you are all about and the Bible study course being offered.

- **Brochures and door hangers** are a good way to introduce the community to your church and tell them about the services you offer. They are convenient to give to friends and distribute throughout communities.
- **Church bulletins and inserts** can be inspirational with eye-catching, thought-provoking themes, exciting the reader about the outreach life of the church. They can serve to enhance the church members' experience at their place of worship and increase motivation to invite others.
- **DVDs and CDs.** If a particular message or performance has touched your life, you will be inspired from hearing/seeing particular sermons and performances on DVD or CD, and to pass them on. You can share them with others as gifts or friendly gestures.
- **Special events and programs.** Sponsoring events and programs of community value throughout the year in conjunction with other follow-up activities for the primary purpose of outreach can be a major contributor to church growth. For example: book clubs, cooking/nutrition classes, Vacation Bible School, small-group Bible studies, yard sales, exercise classes, tutoring, etc.
- **Phone contacts.** The phone ministry team gets to talk to people one on one without actually seeing them. For that reason it is nonthreatening and a cordial method of connecting with families in the community. It is also a personal way to extend the love of Jesus to the world and make neighbors aware of upcoming events.
- **The ministries of the church** are all-inclusive—children, youth and young adult ministries; men and women's ministries; prison ministry; other social ministries, including choirs; and so on—allowing the church's discipleship process to expand. Such ministries equip, encourage, and grow members in their relationship with Christ and toward those in their sphere of influence.
- **Brainstorming sessions.** Here's where members of the church come together to list every name they can think of: family, friends, past and present coworkers, vendors, databases of contact names, etc. Often those facilitating the brainstorming will distribute a sheet listing such questions as Who was your last supervisor? or

Who sold you your last car? They can develop hundreds of names, and it's the members' task to secure addresses, phone numbers, and e-mail addresses. They become a database for sending invitations to church events and evangelistic series, Bible study interest cards, e-mails, etc. I worked with members through whom several of their coworkers, family members, and friends began Bible studies using this method and attended the upcoming evangelistic meetings, and many were baptized.

- **Television, cable, YouTube.** Mass media is a growing avenue for spreading the gospel and community follow-up. Churches use door hanger and flyer announcements to announce such media as Hope TV and Breath of Life broadcasts. Many become fans of key speakers and are delighted to attend evangelistic series featuring such individuals. Also, door hangers and flyers can similarly create interest in watching a church's live streaming on Sabbath morning and other special programming.
- **E-mail and Facebook campaign (social media).** Word gets around instantly using such Internet resources. You can easily spread announcements, invitations, questions and answers, and the like through Internet social networks. Every church member who has an e-mail address, a cell phone for texting, and/or is on Facebook can send information and ask the recipient to forward it on to their database of friends, who in turn will do the same. Such means hold great advantages and possibilities for evangelism.

Consider the case of the discarded door hanger. Mr. Stevens got out of his old Chevy truck and headed to do some maintenance in the facility where he worked. As he was picking up some tossed paper around the place, a door hanger caught his attention. It was a Hope Channel promotion offering free Bible study guides. Thinking about whether or not he should enroll, he tore off the mail-in section, tucked it into his pocket, and at the end of the workday took it home to show his wife. He had recently begun delving into genealogies in the Bible with a coworker, which had sparked an interest in the Word of God. Now he thought that perhaps the study guides might enhance his overall Bible knowledge. After all, they were free. Filling out the card, he dropped it into the mail. Instead of sending the guides through the mail, I showed up at his door to follow up on the mailed-in request, and met Mr. Stevens' wife. She got on the phone to him, and we made arrangements to start Bible studies that would last several months and culminated with their attendance at a major citywide evangelistic series. At the end of the meetings the couple was baptized and joined the local Seventh-day Adventist church.

God uses not only ordinary people to witness to others but the smallest efforts of each volunteer to reach people. No doubt someone had either discarded the door hanger or a volunteer distributing them had dropped it. Either way, Mr. Stevens and his wife found Christ. Only God knows the details. It was still nothing short of a miracle for the card to land right in Mr. Stevens' path and be there for him to pick up at the very time in his life when he had seriously begun to search for a better understanding of God's Word.

Such stories indicate the power and influence of everyone who make themselves available to the Holy Spirit for ministry. Christ's ministry was not limited to spiritual teaching. Besides healing and counseling and restoring the outcast, He fed hungry crowds and did much, much more. Jesus was an administrator and a team player and a servant to all. Always there for people, willing to take time with them and be sensitive to their needs, He is our perfect example of what it means to be a Bible instructor.

"And there are also many other things which Jesus did, the which, if they should be written every one, I suppose that even the world itself could not contain the books that should be written. Amen" (John 21:25).

If you have tended to isolate yourself from people, ask God to work a miracle in your life and begin expanding beyond your areas of connection. Through the strength that God will surely give, start being the person you know you must be for Him to use to bless others. If you continue to have difficulty being friendly and available, don't give up; it will come with persistence.

No one could be more shy than René, a fan of the It Is Written telecast. When Shawn Boostra, the program's speaker, brought It Is Written to Los Angeles and ran a major evangelistic series, she was thrilled and determined not to miss a night. Because the meetings were closer to her job than to her home, she left work each night, drove to the parking lot, and sat in her car until the sessions started. Although she enjoyed every meeting and hardly missed a one, not until she had attended the local Seventh-day Adventist church for nearly a year, along with receiving more Bible studies, was she finally baptized. Her husband came to church with her from time to time, but not until after the next evangelistic series and months of more Bible studies did he too accept baptism. In addition, one son and his family began attending church, and soon he was baptized as well. Making Christ available, and the path to salvation as accommodating as possible, is the mission of the church. Individuals will come in their own time and way. Happier than they've ever been, René's family members are serving Christ through the ministries of their local congregation and could not be more thrilled to be a part of the family of God, all because the It Is Written telecast and the patient follow-up of diligent Bible instructors opened the way to Christ.

Witnessing can occur in countless ways. Pray that God will show you your niche—for certainly you do have one (or more). It may even be something new that no one has thought of before. It's not really about you; it's about leading people to a Christ-centered life that they did not know existed. So pray for people. Soon you will see how God has changed your life for the better and is using you to be a part of the rebirth process of others.

Chapter Activities

1. Discuss each of the outreach programs described in this Chapter and determine which department of your local church could effectively implement each one and tell why.
2. If any of the programs would be a challenge to start, explain why.
3. Why do you think it took so long for René and her husband to join the family of God? In your opinion, could their journey have moved faster? If so, how?

Evaluating the Outcomes

There is always room to improve the effectiveness of every aspect of outreach. The Bible instructor coordinator and the evangelism team should take the lead in developing the tools and resources to evaluate the various types of outreach ministries and their methods. Taking the time to do so is the fastest way to improve results.

Bible instructing is truly both an art and a science. As an art, it's having a vision and developing objectives. It's drawing up the intricate details on how outreach shall be done—when, where, and why—and refining them with creative marketing strategies. Then you need to identify proven techniques to implement such important fine points as approaching people, greeting them, communicating with polish and distinction, and reaching out to all classes and diversities in the most amiable manner. You must keep analyzing what you are doing to see where you need to change to improve your results.

And as a science, it's doing the research to gather the best resources and find the best practices. Take the time to identify, evaluate, and analyze each strategic plan in each ministry of the church. Such research will indeed reveal gaps, and conflicts and thereby stimulate changes and improved coordination of effort.

It's about ensuring the most "bang for the buck" when it comes to the ratio of expense to delivery at every level and every stage of implementation. You need to determine appropriate timing and the best use of the training dollar. Consider, for example, the issue of accommodations. I have known Bible instructors to be housed in storage rooms, in houses where cats were allowed to roam freely, or where they had no place to store food or hang clothes. Some had to share their room with intruding children or vacate the premises with all their belongings to accommodate visiting friends of the family. Others had to park their car a considerable distance from the house. At the other extreme is the Bible instructor residing in a hotel for weeks, driving a rental car for months, and daily eating out. The denomination needs to do much to better coordinate housing for workers who leave the comfort of their home to give themselves completely and sacrificially to evangelism. Such things truly reflect the level (or absence) of respect and appreciation for the dedication and professionalism of the Bible instructor.

Bible instructing as a science includes how you present God's Word in the home. Analyzing what you have done in the past will help you to improve your strategies and methods in the future. For example, the Bible instructor team should seek to ensure that they have the resources to do the needed ongoing research and to receive continuous training. You should have ready access to Bible scholars, pastors, evangelists, and other types of Bible and social counselors. With more forethought and access to resources within the congregation, it may be possible to make better living accommodations for the instructor staff with greater financial savings.

Furthermore, Bible instructing as both an art and a science means developing and utilizing various tools to evaluate every aspect of how evangelism is done and its effectiveness on the widest scale possible. You should feel a sense of responsibility for being a part of the process by being willing to participate fully, by providing informative input, and by incorporating new and/or improved methods.

Evaluating and analyzing is an evolving process. Since every endeavor is unique, the ideal shifts like the seasons of the year. However, you must constantly ask many hard questions (before, during, and after the evangelistic events) to improve the methods and outcome of Bible work, such as:

- How do you motivate people to want to take the Bible studies as a result of what you say or do at the door?
- How do you encourage more church members to become involved in Bible instruction (and for the right reasons)? What can you do to reduce member attrition?
- How can you increase your ability to develop from a traditional doctrinal approach in Bible teaching the stirring principles necessary to captivate the mind and the heart with the love of Christ? How can you more effectively flow the principles that you teach through the filter of the love of Christ?
- How can you ensure through improved teaching techniques that the Bible study student will go beyond doctrine to personal application?
- Should the Bible instructor team provide more training in such areas as the conversion process and the point baptism should take place; marketing methodology; social psychology and counseling; themes in Daniel and Revelation; and Seventh-day Adventist doctrinal beliefs?
- Every member should be a Bible instructor. What would have to change to bring this goal within the realm of possibility?

Chapter Activities

1. Develop a brainstorming sheet of questions that will jog the memory for contact names.
2. Share what you feel is your niche for witnessing.
3. Discuss the merits of evaluating and analyzing aspects of local church evangelism.

---

* E. G. White, *Evangelism*, p. 431.

CHAPTER 6

AVAILING PRAYER CURRENTS

Behind the success of every evangelistic program is the power of praying saints. Just as underlying forces cause powerful and dangerous ocean currents, likewise, hidden forces can hinder a decisive response to the wooing of the Holy Spirit. As a result, God's people must cry aloud to Him in behalf of the sinner whose heart truly wants to be set free.

During a short evangelistic series (four to eight weeks), the evangelist will call for decisions nightly, some more subtle than others. You will find yourself often pleading with God for those about to make eternal decisions. "When we take hold of the work and wrestle with God, saying, 'I must have souls; I will never give up the struggle,' we shall find that God will look upon our efforts with favor."[1]

"In times past there were those who fastened their minds upon one soul after another, saying, 'Lord, help me to save this soul.' But now such instances are rare. How many act as if they realized the peril of sinners? How many take those whom they know to be in peril, presenting them to God in prayer, supplicating Him to save them?"[2] As Bible instructors we should want to stand up and shout, "I have those that I must see saved and safe in God's kingdom!"

Personal Communion With God

To live by the Word of God means surrendering to Him the whole mind, heart, and life. You will feel a continual sense of need and dependence, a drawing out of the heart after God. Prayer is a necessity. Family prayer and public prayer have their place, but it is secret, sacred communion with God that sustains the life of the soul.

Communion with the Lord also includes meditating on the Word of God as did David:

"My meditation of him shall be sweet: I will be glad in the Lord" (Ps. 104:34).

"Give ear to my words, O Lord, consider my meditation" (Ps. 5:1).

"Let the words of my mouth, and the meditation of my heart, be acceptable in thy sight, O Lord, my strength, and my redeemer" (Ps. 19:14).

The apostle Paul repeatedly admonished the saints to meditate on what they had been taught (and you should do the same with your Bible study students) and then let those thoughts transform them:

"Meditate upon these things; give thyself wholly to them; that thy profiting may appear to all" (1 Tim. 4:15).

"Having therefore these promises, dearly beloved, let us cleanse ourselves from all filthiness of the flesh and spirit, perfecting holiness in the fear of God" (2 Cor. 7:1)

"And be not conformed to this world: but be ye transformed by the renewing of your mind, that ye may prove what is that good, and acceptable, and perfect, will of God" (Rom. 12:2).

Jesus is our example, and it was His custom to spend all night in communion with God:

"And it came to pass in those days, that he went out into a mountain to pray, and continued all night in prayer to God" (Luke 6:12).

We could say much more on the value of taking time daily to know God (Ps. 46:10) through meditating on His goodness, His promises, His love, and then listening to His still small voice. It is said that prayer is God listening to you. Meditation, however, is you listening to God. If your prayer life does not include at least 15 to 20 minutes per day in scriptural meditation, why not begin adding this calming element to your day. Here is some scriptural counsel to consider:

"For as he thinketh in his heart, so is he" (Prov. 23:7).

"Casting down imaginations, and every high thing that exalteth itself against the knowledge of God, and bringing into captivity every thought to the obedience of Christ" (2 Cor. 10:5).

"Having therefore these promises, dearly beloved, let us cleanse ourselves from all filthiness of the flesh and spirit, perfecting holiness in the fear of God" (2 Cor. 7:1).

Paul reminds us of the constant struggle going on for the mind (Rom. 7:22-24). Our carnal mind wants to be in control (Matt. 7:21-23) and constantly wars against what Scripture lets us know is the mind of Christ (1 Cor. 2:16), given us at conversion. That conflict affects everything you do, including your work as a Bible instructor. Prayer and meditation are essential antidotes for the battles of the mind.

> "A good man out of the good treasure of his heart bringeth forth that which is good; and an evil man out of the evil treasure of his heart bringeth forth that which is evil: for of the abundance of the heart his mouth speaketh" (Luke 6:45).

In Jeremiah 17:9 the prophet reminds us, "The heart is deceitful above all things, and desperately wicked: who can know it?" The heart fuels our thoughts, which then influence our behavior. To keep your thoughts focused on our Savior and Lord, why not meditate on what Philippians 4:8 counsels us:

"Finally, brethren, whatsoever things are true, whatsoever things are honest, whatsoever things are just, whatsoever things are pure, whatsoever things are lovely, whatsoever things are of good report; if there be any virtue, and if there be any praise, think on these things."

Before God can use you as a Bible instructor, you must examine your own heart, and then recognize and overcome through the power of God anything that would hinder your ministry. Spiritual renewal comes only with time spent in Bible study and with God in prayer and meditation. You will definitely come to acknowledge how humbled and blessed you are that your communion with God has made your attitude much more positive. Even more, you will find perspective of increased faith and peace. This is the mind-set you want to take into the homes of those seeking the light and love of Jesus Christ.

> "Stand in awe, and sin not: commune with your own heart upon your bed, and be still" (Ps. 4:4).
>
> "Thou wilt keep him in perfect peace, whose mind is stayed on thee: because he trusteth in thee" (Isa. 26:3).

Select a passage of Scripture that you would like to reflect on while you sit prayerfully and relaxed, with your eyes closed, in a quiet place. Then offer a brief prayer asking God to calm your mind. Soon you'll be eager to use idle times in meditating on God's Word, such as when standing in lines or sitting in waiting rooms. They may also be good opportunities to memorize scriptures you'll use during your ministry in homes. Here are 10 favorite scriptures for starters to memorize. Reflect on what they say as you repeat them slowly:

"So shall my word be that goeth forth out of my mouth: it shall not return unto me void, but it shall accomplish that which I please, and it shall prosper in the thing whereto I sent it" (Isa. 55:11).

"Thou wilt shew me the path of life: in thy presence is fulness of joy; at thy right hand there are pleasures for evermore" (Ps. 16:11).

"Delight thyself also in the Lord; and he shall give thee the desires of thine heart" (Ps. 37:4).

"For the Lord God is a sun and shield: the Lord will give grace and glory: no good thing will he withhold from them that walk uprightly" (Ps. 84:11).

"Peace I leave with you, my peace I give unto you: not as the world giveth, give I unto you. Let not your heart be troubled, neither let it be afraid" (John 14:27).

"And we know that all things work together for good to them that love God, to them who are the called according to his purpose" (Rom. 8:28).

"I can do all things through Christ which strengtheneth me" (Phil. 4:13).

"But my God shall supply all your need according to his riches in glory by Christ Jesus" (verse 19).

"For God hath not given us the spirit of fear; but of power, and of love, and of a sound mind" (2 Tim. 1:7).

"Blessing, and glory, and wisdom, and thanksgiving, and honour, and power, and might, be unto our God for ever and ever. Amen" (Rev. 7:12).

Recommended longer passages of Scripture to memorize include the Lord's Prayer in Matthew 6:9-13; the Beatitudes in Matthew 5:3-12; the salvation of our children in Isaiah 43:1-7; the fast that God has chosen in Isaiah 58:6-12; Psalm 23; and the benediction in Ephesians 3:14-21.

"If the happiness of man consisted in doing nothing, the Creator would not have given Adam his appointed work. Man was to find happiness in labor, as well as in meditation."[3]

"Meditation upon holy things will elevate and refine the mind, and will develop Christian ladies and gentlemen."[4]

"Those who will put on the whole armor of God and devote some time every day to meditation and prayer and to the study of the Scriptures will be connected with heaven and will have a saving, transforming influence upon those around them."[5]

"But let it be the hidden man of the heart, in that which is not corruptible, even the ornament of a meek and quiet spirit, which is in the sight of God of great price" (1 Peter 3:4).

The Fast

Choose a day for fasting—systematic days of full surrender to God. In addition, consider a fast on days preceding, during, or following certain key events: that is, prior to and after outreach ministry endeavors, opening night of the evangelistic series, and nights in which *testing truths* (doctrines that will challenge current belief systems) will be preached. They should be times that you have surrendered everything and that nothing comes between you and your Savior as you intercede as a colaborer with Christ and all of heaven on behalf of those seeking, in their own way, God and deliverance from the bonds of sin.

There are many types of fasts. For example, you can eliminate something that you have been struggling with or you can add something spiritual you have been seeking to incorporate into your lifestyle. The former may entail removing all meat or dairy products or even a total fast of all foods and drink, with the exception of water.

You may keep the length of the fast always the same, or you might vary it according to the occasion, from eight or 12 hours to weeks. Pray about it each time and go with what the Spirit of God leads you to do. If it is a group fast, join in with what the group decides as a minimum. You may even decide to involve others.

> "Workers can never attain the highest success until they learn the secret of strength. They must give themselves time to think, to pray, to wait upon God for a renewal of physical, mental, and spiritual power. They need the uplifting influence of His Spirit. Receiving this, they will be quickened by fresh life. The wearied frame and tired brain will be refreshed, the burdened heart will be lightened."[6]

The Subject of Intercessory Prayer

Intercessory prayer is vital, and you need to understand its true purpose. "Prayer is not to work any change in God; it is to bring us into harmony with God. When we make request of Him, He may see that it is necessary for us to search our hearts and repent of sin. Therefore He takes us through test and trial, He brings us through humiliation, that we may see what hinders the working of His Holy Spirit through us."[7]

> "Again I say unto you, That if two of you shall agree on earth as touching any thing that they shall ask, it shall be done for them of my Father which is in heaven" (Matt. 18:19).

Pray for the fields of labor. "The Lord will provide ways and means for those who will seek Him with the whole heart. He desires us to acknowledge the divine superintendence shown in preparing fields of labor and in preparing the way for these fields to be occupied successfully."[8]

Pray before opening the Word of God. "Howbeit when he, the Spirit of truth, is come, he will guide you into all truth: for he shall not speak of himself; but whatsoever he shall hear, that shall he speak: and he will shew you things to come" (John 16:13). The Spirit of truth is the only effective teacher of divine truth. How greatly God esteems the human race, since He gave His Son to die for it and appoints His Spirit to be its teacher and continual guide!

Personal prayer to understand Bible truths. "Jesus saw Nathanael coming to him, and saith of him, Behold an Israelite indeed, in whom is no guile. Nathanael saith unto him, Whence knowest thou me? Jesus answered and said unto him, Before that Philip called thee, when thou wast under the fig tree, I saw thee" (John 1:47, 48). And Jesus will see us also in the secret places of prayer. Angels will be with those who in humility of heart seek for divine guidance.

> "If ye then, being evil, know how to give good gifts unto your children, how much more shall your Father which is in heaven give good things to them that ask him?" (Matt. 7:11).

Pray with/for those convicted by the truth. In addition to your continuous efforts to meet and pray with those you are seeking to reach, the pastor has a responsibility. "Let ministers and evangelists have more seasons of earnest prayer with those who are convicted by the truth."[9]

Pray for harmony and unity among the Bible instructors, the evangelists, and the ministers and others involved in the evangelistic series. Remember our greatest battle is not with flesh and blood, "but against principalities, against powers, against the rulers of the darkness of this world, against spiritual wickedness in high places" (Eph. 6:12).

"Acting under divine guidance and sustained by the prayers of their more experienced fellow workers, they [we all] may do a good and blessed work."[10] Always remember, "we are labourers together with God" (1 Cor. 3:9).

"Take the word of Christ as your assurance. Has He not invited you to come unto Him? Never allow yourself to talk in a hopeless, discouraged way. If you do, you will lose much. By looking at appearances and complaining when difficulties and pressure come, you give evidence of a sickly, enfeebled faith. Talk and act as if your faith was invincible. The Lord is rich in resources; He owns the world. Look heavenward in faith. Look to Him who has light and power and efficiency."[11]

You are never alone while working for the salvation of others. "Angels are helping in this work to restore the fallen and bring them back to the One who has given His life to redeem them, and the Holy Spirit is co-operating with the ministry of human agencies to arouse the moral powers by working on the heart, reproving of sin, of righteousness, and of judgment."[12]

Those who do not put their confidence in their own gifts but who work in simplicity, trusting always in God, will share in the joy of the Savior. Their prayers will bring others to the cross. Heavenly angels will respond to their self-sacrificing efforts. By the power of the Holy Spirit, Jesus will move upon hearts, working miracles in the conversion of sinners. For it is "not by might, nor by power, but by my spirit, saith the Lord of hosts" (Zech. 4:6).

Chapter Activities

1. Discuss the strategy behind calling for decisions throughout an evangelistic series.
2. Discuss the implications of the spiritual battle for human minds.
3. Discuss why there is so much emphasis on prayer in Bible instruction work.

---

[1] E. G. White, *Evangelism*, p. 294.

[2] E. G. White, *Gospel Workers*, p. 65.

[3] Ellen G. White, *Confrontation* (Washington, D.C.: Review and Herald Pub. Assn., 1971), p. 11.

[4] Ellen G. White, *Christian Education* (Battle Creek, Mich.: International Tract Society, 1893), p. 109.

[5] E. G. White, *Testimonies*, vol. 5, p. 112.

[6] Ellen G. White, *Education* (Mountain View, Calif.: Pacific Press Pub. Assn., 1903), p. 260.

[7] E. G. White, *Christ's Object Lessons*, p. 143.

[8] E. G. White, *Gospel Workers*, p. 65.

[9] *Ibid.*

[10] E. G. White, *Testimonies*, vol. 9, p. 119.

[11] E. G. White, *Christ's Object Lessons*, pp. 146, 147.

[12] Ellen G. White, *Testimony Treasures* (Mountain View, Calif.: Pacific Press Pub. Assn., 1946), vol. 2, p. 497.

CHAPTER 7

STACKING THE DECK

When it comes to distributing names of attendees to Bible instructor team members for follow-up home visits, the team should expect a "stacking of the deck" in which you will seek every reason for why the team should visit a person and establish a relationship with them. No lifestyle or environment can provide an excuse for not locating the individual and making the contact. No name will get rejected. God values everyone, and the team should treat them as such, and that principle will always stack the deck in the favor of the attendee.

- It is vitally important that every non-Adventist attendee fully register and that their information be clearly recorded.
- You should see each individual as divinely placed in your hands for salvation and spiritual growth. You are first of all accountable to God for your diligent care of each person you accept for visitation.
- A copy of the registration card for each attendee should be made available for assignment to a Bible instructor.
- The team should keep a form on each interest. It should track the visits, lessons covered, the progress in interest (A-B-C), family members in the home, and profile information. Only the evangelist, head Bible instructor, or designated person assigns who will visit an individual.
- While each Bible instructor will receive names to contact, two individuals together should make the actual visitation.
- Only the evangelist, head Bible instructor, or designated person should make any changes in assigned names, so that families do not get visited by more than one team or neglected under the assumption that another team has already contacted them.
- Make assignments nightly following the meeting and/or during regularly scheduled observational review sessions.

- Make assignments with respect to geographic location, sorted by zip codes.
- Give first preference of an assignment to the Bible instructor who is already visiting the attendee, originally invited the person, or is working with the person's family.
- Take into consideration when assigning visits such special circumstances as age; housing conditions such as questionable locale, or stairs; working hours; gender; or anything else that might cause hesitation in sending a certain Bible instructor team.
- Volunteer Bible instructors who have full-time jobs or other work obligations should take only the number of names that they can handle responsibly.
- You should log the information from the attendance, quiz, or decision card and then return it to the lead Bible instructor with your name and the date received written on the back.
- You should retain a master list of your assigned interests and a profile sheet detailing such information as name, address, contact information, age range, information about family, job, attendance record, lessons missed, and visitation record. Most of this information gets gathered over time as you visit the attendee. Request only vital information at registration.
- The Bible instructor coordinator will keep a copy of the profile sheet and updates of the attendance record, along with other vital information, for each attendee.
- You should be willing and prepared to give a detailed report on any attendee assigned to you whenever asked. One of the main reasons for using Bible instructors is to keep up with each attendee and guide the process to baptism.
- You should never feel free to share information about your assigned attendees. However, information about an attendee and/or anyone else in the attendee's household must be made readily available to the evangelist, team leader, and the Bible instructor team if deemed appropriate by the evangelist (or team leader).

Once you step into the life of an individual as a Bible instructor, few circumstances should ever prevent you from continuing with the studies. Whatever the reason, it should not be because of discouragement, impatience, or inconveniences without every effort having been made to arrange for the studies to continue with someone else. Even when the person wants to stop the studies, you can call on the power of prayer. A personal crisis may warrant the need to solicit another Bible instructor to take over the studies, but you should always keep praying for the student. Because it is important to maintain continuity, if it becomes impossible to meet your commitment to a Bible study student, even if only for a short period, ask your Bible instructor partner, or another instructor, to take over the studies until you can resume. If you know that you may have to drop out, it is imperative that you handle the student with great care and consideration. It is fully your responsibility to arrange for the continuance of the studies and to check from time to time to ensure that all is going well.

Going through interest cards one day for any uncompleted Bible study series, I came across Danielle's name. It appeared that she had been visited awhile back, perhaps months earlier. But it wasn't clear how many lessons she had received, nor who had been responsible for her. (That is why good recordkeeping is important.) Her phone was disconnected, so I decided to pay her a visit. After several attempts to catch her at home, I finally met Danielle. Later we determined that two young men, neither of whom still lived in the area, had brought her the Bible study guides she had ordered. They gave her 12 Bible study guides, but she never saw them again. She still had the lessons and was happy for our visit. Having completed most of them, she assured us that she would have the rest of them done when we returned. Although she kept her word, we needed to slow her down and review the many lessons she had already finished. We enjoyed many wonderful studies together, my partner entertaining the two little ones while I engaged Danielle in the lessons. The incident had been a case of outright neglect. No one told anyone about her, and no one should have given her 12 lessons all at once. Nor had anyone made arrangements for follow-up. Not even a note appeared on her interest card. Fortunately, we salvaged the case, and Danielle began attending church with her children. It could have turned out much worse.

Examples of reasons you may find yourself forced to rethink your commitment to a Bible study student and release the name to another Bible instructor include:

- health crisis or death in the immediate family
- conflict with new work or school schedules that make it impossible to coordinate a day and time to meet
- gender relationship issues

- transportation challenges because of a distant relocation of residence
- the Bible study student demonstrating a lack of interest, such as seldom being home at the designated time and never completing the Bible study guides (but there always exists the possibility that the person may relate to another instructor differently)
- obvious competition with the Bible study student's pastor, church members, or family
- rude and argumentative Bible study student

Personal negligence on your part is answerable first of all to God, and then to the Bible instructor team. If a visitation problem does surface, let the team leader know as soon as possible. The Bible instructor team is to be supportive and should develop a solution to it or any other problem with an attendee. It would be far better to give up a name when you feel their care falls short of what is needed than to hang on to it knowing that you cannot for whatever reason provide the level of care necessary.

Chapter Activities

1. Go down the list of suggestions for distributing names and discuss the merits of each recommendation.
2. Why is the way that you distribute names an important process?
3. Discuss the obligation that you acquire when accepting a name for visitation.

CHAPTER 8

KEEPING TRACK

The Bible instructor team should plan to meet with the evangelist and/or Bible instructor team coordinator on a regular basis. Such sessions may meet daily during an evangelistic campaign and weekly otherwise, usually for one or two hours at a time. In the meetings, revisit what has been done, measure its effectiveness, and strategize what to do next. In all that the team does, the members must evaluate their work in a quantifiable manner that asks the right questions for the right reasons to effect the best methods. Thus a coming together on a periodic basis and being willing to discuss details honestly is an imperative that must take place in a nonthreatening, encouraging atmosphere. The meetings may include:

- a devotional
- period of intercessory prayer
- intervention observations
- the assigning of names for visitation
- receiving gift materials to give to attendees
- a detailed update on the spiritual growth, possible challenges, and potential threats that each interest is encountering
- addressing personal questions and/or concerns and challenges
- ongoing training
- strategic procedural planning
- directives and announcements

Do not regard such observational reviews as optional, intimidating, or threatening. You must be willing to admit failings, mistakes, errors, and shortcomings as well as achievements, spiritual growth, etc., in your work with attendees. Never forget that you are in a real spiritual battle and will likely meet tremendous challenges. Be willing to accept and value constructive corrections/opinions when useful and appropriately share the same.

Chapter Activities

Discuss the following questions:

1. What are some ways to measure the effectiveness of field work, i.e., outreach ministries and Bible instructing?
2. What are the advantages and disadvantages of reporting details of field work?
3. How can you inconspicuously obtain profile information from a Bible study student?

Unity Among Staff

Comments should never involve gossip, bring dissention, or demean. The Bible instructor team must constantly be on the alert lest the spirit of Satan find even the smallest entering wedge. Again, you are in a battle for the salvation of precious souls and must constantly remain alert to the importance of keeping Christ at the center of your motives, as well as your thoughts, feelings, and attitudes toward each other, the leaders, the attending believers, and the non-Adventist the attendees that God has placed in your spiritual care.

A major responsibility for you as a Bible instructor is to do all that you can to generate and maintain a cohesive spirit. It is not about competition for numbers but being filled with the Holy Spirit to help transform lives. The entire focus must always remain on those waiting to hear the gospel. Do not let anything distract you during an evangelistic series. Permit no bickering, jealousy, or personality clashes.

You should demonstrate professionalism at all times. You must be willing to find ways to work with and support the diversity of leadership styles and personalities, appreciate individual gifts and talents, be flexible, and cooperate with requests, assignments, and changes. If anyone creates dissension within the team, the team leader must take them aside for special prayer and counsel.

Constructive criticism (with ideas for solutions) has its place. Corrective remarks and concerns should be caringly brought to the attention of those who have the authority to address them. If it appears that your criticism did not get acted upon in the way you thought would be best, pray that the Holy Spirit move upon your heart and those involved to bring peace to the situation and the people affected. Also pray that God will show you and others the way He would have things continue. God will answer your sincere prayer. However, if the disruptive ones persist, the leader should ask them to return their assigned names and no longer attend the observational reviews or consider themselves a part of the Bible instructor team.

> "The success of our work depends upon our love to God and our love to our fellowmen. When there is harmonious action among the individual members of the church, when there is love and confidence manifested by brother to brother, there will be proportionate force and power in our work for the salvation of men."*

Chapter Activities

1. List some of the ways disunity among workers can affect the success of an evangelistic series.
2. What are the advantages and benefits of having regular observational review meetings?
3. How can you avoid disunity among evangelistic team members?

---

* Ellen G. White, *Testimonies to Ministers and Gospel Workers* (Mountain View, Calif.: Pacific Press Pub. Assn., 1923), p. 188.

PART 2

PREPARING THE FIELD

HFTH-3

CHAPTER 9

WALKING THE CITY

> "Christ's method alone will give true success in reaching the people. The Savior mingled with men as one who desired their good. He showed His sympathy for them, ministered to their needs, and won their confidence. Then He bade them, 'Follow Me.' "[1]

Once the evangelistic team has identified individuals and families who have expressed interest in receiving Bible studies through community or citywide interest card distribution, community surveys, etc., arrange an unannounced home visit as soon as possible for introductory purposes and to deliver the first of the series of Bible study guides. People are much more likely to respond positively to a stranger they can visibly see at their door with a pleasant smile and Bible in their hand than to someone who tries to convince them by phone to arrange an appointment to deliver Bible study guides.

Two by Two

> "After these things the Lord appointed other seventy also, and sent them two and two before his face into every city and place, whither he himself would come. Therefore said he unto them, The harvest truly is great, but the labourers are few: pray ye therefore the Lord of the harvest, that he would send forth labourers into his harvest" (Luke 10:1, 2).

It is best to go two by two, male and female, or female and female. Least preferred would be male and male, or a male or female working alone. Unfortunately, men can appear threatening, especially if dressed casually. Most elderly and females alone at home will hesitate, or even refuse, to open their door if they see two unknown males. A team of two males is far more likely to have success if wearing dress shirt and tie or full suit.

If you are visiting by yourself, you should not enter alone the home of a person of the opposite sex. It would be far better to talk on the steps or porch. Also keep in mind that a woman alone in a house who opens her door and allows a man, or a team of two men, to come in could create the wrong impression. You would be amazed at how many neighbors know everything going on in their community. On occasion I have been stopped by people and questioned about why I've been seen visiting a neighbor. And word gets around. It's good in a sense, because it becomes a means of gaining the support and/or respect of neighbors. (However, it can turn on you if the potential Bible student doesn't want the studies.) Recognizing the potential for an unintended impression and/or volatile experience, teams of two men should dress appropriately and carry a visible Bible and by all means sit at a respectful distance from the student in the home. It is an area in which men especially must be most cautious. For the sake of their integrity, we strongly encourage male Bible instructors to have a female partner, rather than working alone or working with another male. And if this is not possible, be discreet in how you dress and where you sit in the home.

Henry was one of our new, young, and energetic Bible instructors. Because he had some experience as a literature evangelist, we assigned him a territory to follow up alone. He did a very good job initiating Bible studies, but soon he felt the need for a partner. Once the evangelistic series started, one of his young female Bible study students now seemed upset. To make a long story short, she accused Henry of using her to end a relationship with another young woman in the church. After we questioned her, we discovered that he had been alone to her apartment only twice, yet she was convinced that he wanted a relationship. After the second visit he felt uncomfortable with her and wisely turned her name over to a married couple to continue the studies. However, he was cordial to her when he saw her during the evangelism series. He doesn't know how she arrived at such thoughts, since he had merely sought to introduce Cassandra to other young women in the church. He had no personal interest in any of them. Such situations are not uncommon, especially for young single Bible instructors and males more specifically, since females request most Bible studies. Learning to be discreet in demeanor, in dress, in body language, and in focus is an essential for all Bible instructors, particularly males.

That is not to say that men should be discouraged from becoming instructors. On the contrary, we need many more men, and they make outstanding and powerful leaders. Some go on to conduct successful home meetings and larger evangelistic series, and even become pastors. Like women, however, men must be aware of certain cautions similar to the challenge they must overcome in being elementary school teachers. Male Bible instructors are some of the most effective and helpful members on a team, and that is one of the reasons they face more social challenges than women. Women in the home can be intentionally seductive. The team must do all that is possible to safeguard the male staff.

Hang in there, men—you are needed on the team. Just be as cautious as women working alone, especially in questionable, high-crime areas and after sunset. As a matter of fact, it is unfair to male Bible instructors for female Bible instructors to request that they accompany them into dangerous areas after dark. It is really not fair to put men in threatening situations that no one should be in. Give more consideration to the safety and care of male Bible instructors.

Chapter Activities

1. Discuss the picking of a partner for visitation.
2. Discuss the challenges for male Bible instructors.
3. Discuss places and times that could pose a danger to you as a Bible instructor.

Mapping the Visitation Route

During the premeeting marketing, which includes door-to-door Bible study interest cards of some kind, interest lists can quickly grow toward, and often more than, 100 homes for each Bible instructor. You will need to visit those homes as soon as possible once they have shown interest in Bible studies. The longer the wait, the greater the possibility that the person, or family, will change their mind. With good organization, a Bible instructor should be able to contact each home and deliver the first Bible study guide within two or three weeks at the most (preferably with a trainee). To save time and fuel, we recommend the following procedure:

1. Map out the route for the next day's visitation schedule.
2. Schedule the first visit to a home after 11:00 a.m. During the visit, arrange to stop by earlier (or in the evening) to review the Bible study guides and to provide the next one.
3. List the names in the order you will visit them, based on the route mapped in step 1.

4. Find and mark all addresses on a city street map, road atlas, online map, or preferably a handy global positioning system (GPS) instrument.
5. Get specific directions to each address. Either write out turn-by-turn directions from the city street map or road atlas, look up the addresses on the computer in Mapquest or another similar Web site and print out the directions, or enter addresses and save them on your GPS.
6. On the trip, have your city map and/or GPS available to find the addresses as quickly as possible and to move through the visits in the most efficient manner.
7. Keep a record each day of mileage in a mileage record or receipt book in case you need it for tax purposes or reimbursements. I have found that a simple columned recording of date, mileage, and fuel cost with the number of gallons jotted down whenever you purchase fuel works well. Even a small receipt book would serve this purpose sufficiently along with an envelope for receipts each month.
8. Focus on specific zip codes and city sections in the visitation route each day, and route the visits in an efficient manner.
9. Bible instructors who have experience in arranging introductory visits by phone may suggest to the Bible student the days and times the instructor is available to visit in the student's area. It won't be foolproof, but it does help.

Although some students will not be available during the day because of work schedules, few people work seven days per week, so it is a matter of determining their day off. Once you have made the rounds of visitation, you will be able to determine who is available during the day and whom you must see in the late evenings or on the weekends (note: during the evangelistic series, weekends could include visitation on Sabbaths).

The evening visitation schedule should begin about 5:30 p.m. and last no later than 8:00 p.m. Efficient visitation routing is just as important for evenings as it is for the daytime visits. Taking the time to meticulously ensure that you are not wasting precious time ricocheting back and forth across the city will reduce frustration and allow you to contact more homes. Also, take note of risk management concerns. Your safety as a Bible instructor is paramount. Arrange with the attendee for the safest manner to visit them. They might need to give instructions regarding parking, entrances, what to avoid and be aware of, etc. I remember arranging visitation with a family by calling when I arrived. Either the husband or teenage son would come out and escort my partner and I to and from their apartment. We waited in the car until one of them arrived, and they saw us off at the end of the Bible study. Not surprisingly, Mr. James became a wonderful deacon in the local church.

Once you have determined which day of the week you will focus on each zip code or city section, begin to arrange with your Bible study interests to visit them according to your schedule, recognizing that there will often be those whom you cannot see on the preferred day. For them, you can either seek to schedule at the beginning or end of your visitation day, on the weekend, a day designated just for special scheduling, the off night of the evangelistic series, or, if absolutely all other efforts fail, as a last resort you may have to find another Bible instructor willing to meet them on the day and at the time that they require.

A decision whether or not to retain a name during an evangelistic series will reflect a completely different set of circumstances than prior to the start of the meetings. Once the series starts, you may be challenged to care for the often dozens of names that you must see at least once or twice during the week to answer questions and keep them coming. Thus it would be better to reassign a name that presents an irresolvable visitation challenge to someone already working the area on the required day than not provide the care the person deserves to receive.

Other factors may play into such a decision, such as how distant a person may live, how many interests you are visiting during that day, or whether a night visit in a difficult access apartment is the case. You can work out most questionable housing situations by meeting in a mutually agreed upon location, such as a library, restaurant, park, or other public place convenient to both. Of course, your preference should be to work out a visitation arrangement as far as possible with each of the interests assigned to you while not accepting more than you can handle.

Bible Studies by Phone

Certainly, the phone is not the preferred method of giving Bible studies, but in some situations to do so as a temporary arrangement can be quite effective. A few times I found that a full review by phone worked well in unique cases. With Geraldine, we would spend as much as an hour reviewing a lesson over the phone when she would not be disturbed.

Sometimes the studies would take place late at night and other times early in the morning as we scheduled around her two jobs. I would slip the Bible study guide in the mailbox to avoid their ferocious dog. And she felt free to phone me whenever she got stuck and couldn't understand a question or answer, with the understanding that if I was busy, I would return her call as soon as possible. Geraldine called me often to ask questions. She visited the church for a couple events and finally to receive her certificate of completion.

I also studied with another individual by phone whose husband was gravely ill and whose hospital bed and equipment was set up in the living room. Because he was in constant discomfort, Helen could not study with me during his waking hours, so we arranged times that it was convenient for her to do so by phone. I delivered the Bible study guides to her in her front yard. We often reviewed some points while I was there, and I answered any questions she had. But it was late in the evening when we actually studied the lessons together by phone. She too thoroughly enjoyed the studies and called me whenever she needed help. With the permission of her husband, she began attending church. It was something she had been missing out on for some time. After learning of and accepting the Sabbath, she attended church with me as often as it was possible.

Those were unique cases, but if a person is seriously interested in the Bible studies, you must do all you can to work out the most unusual situations. One woman wanted me to continue studies in the hospital with her. Feeling it such a blessing to study God's Word and learning so much, she didn't want to discontinue our lesson reviews. We even added the singing of hymns and testimonies. More than anything else, you must keep in mind that your work is first and foremost a divinely appointed ministry.

Chapter Activities

1. Compare finding 10 addresses using a GPS, Mapquest, and a city map. Then purchase a GPS (look online for the best deal).
2. Discuss the pros and cons of visiting homes before 11:00 a.m. and after 8:00 pm.
3. Discuss the advantages and disadvantages of phone Bible study reviews.

Why Strangers Accept Bible Studies

It very likely will not be because a Bible instructor, or volunteer solicitor, was so eloquent at the door that Bible study enrollees accept them in their home. They probably allow strangers to enter their home and accept study guides filled with information that may possibly conflict with their religious beliefs for deeper reasons. You should try to discover the motivation during the very first meeting, and then keep it in mind throughout the series of studies.

It would not hurt to probe a little in your initial conversation at the door. You may discover dissatisfaction with current church or spiritual life. The person may want to discover how to connect with God or begin to understand the Bible. A family crisis with children or spouse may have arisen. Perhaps they needed prayer and didn't know how to do it. They may have experienced personal losses or challenges, such as health conditions. The more life-changing events the prospective student encounters, the more apt they are to accept Bible studies. And the more distant individuals feel they are from God or the more deeply they sense a need for change in their life and/or circumstances, the more open they will be to an offer to study the Bible. It may be possible for you to discover an overwhelming personal challenge in conversing at the door and then offer Bible studies as a way to bring order and peace back into their life, or at least help them to cope.

Such was the case at one house. After knocking on the door and waiting a bit, we heard a gruff voice from inside the house. "Who is it?" We responded with our names in the most cheerful manner we could muster, and briefly explained the reason for our visit. "No, thank you" came the response. Quickly imagining that the woman could not come to the door most likely for a health reason, we tried to gain entrance again. "We just came by to assure you that God wants to do more for you than you can ever imagine. He loves you with an awesome love and will never leave or forsake you. Do you believe that?" We were yelling through a window located in the other direction from the door. "Who did you say you were?" she responded. We told her again and offered her prayer. "Not now, I'm in bed." Before leaving, we assured her that we would keep her in our prayers, and we also got permission to return. She also said that we could leave some literature in the doorway. This went on for several visits—talking encouragement and quoting scriptural promises, praying with her through the window, and leaving inspirational literature.

Finally to our delight, we went to visit with Ms. Margaret one day, and her adult son answered the door. Visiting from Chicago, he had plans to stay with her indefinitely. Apparently she had been telling him about us, and he appeared pleased to meet us. We conversed with him for a while and found him to be a very spiritual person. When we expressed our pleasure to meet his mother, albeit through the window, we learned from Jimmie that she had once been quite active in church. Loving to sing, she had been in the choir, but now, with her health condition and weakness, she had become depressed and refused to go out of the house or have anything more to do with church. We told her son about the Bible study guides and how they would help her regain a positive spirit. He became so excited about the lessons that he not only offered to encourage his mother to get into them but also accepted our invitation to take the studies himself. Although we never got into the home, we were able to engage Jimmie in wonderful studies, and he in turn involved his mother. On one visit we learned that Ms. Margaret had been in and out of the hospital. After her return, Jimmie reported to us again, as he had done on several occasions, that his mother's attitude and condition were improving thanks to our prayers and the biblical information he was passing on to her.

Here was a person whose deteriorating health prevented her from even expressing her need of spiritual and emotional help. As long as a person does not end the conversation and is dismissive, continue to pursue the contact. Bible instructing is about people. It's about finding them where they are and not leaving them there. Do not be satisfied until they feel the touch of God's love. But to do that, you must be patient with their resistance. Breakthroughs will come in time. Bible work is about ultimately winning the battle for the hearts of others. And it is about being available for God's purposes, even ones that may not be what you had in mind.

Some will tell you right away the reason for their interest in accepting Bible studies. Judy and Andre were considering marriage. They had been friends for a few years now. It would be the second marriage for both of them. We eagerly convinced them that there couldn't be a better way to begin a serious relationship than by making God the center, and explained how it would make a great difference. They talked much about their individual, and each other's, need of the Lord. Soon Bible studies began in the home with the two of them. They were such a joy to work with and full of humor. As they gained respect for us, they promised to attend our church one day. It was truly exciting when that moment came. Our pastor married them in a small wedding ceremony of a few church members and some family. Having been unchurched when we met them, they could not have been more delighted to actually have what they dreamed of and had only hoped could be possible—a church wedding. And you can imagine the joy on baptism day. Relationships begin at the door. If it does not, there may never be a relationship.

While many will eagerly welcome Bible instructors into their home merely because they "look" and "talk" like sincere Christians, others will strongly resist. Some will not even recall filling out the enrollment card or taking the survey, and others will deny filling them out. And still others will say that someone else enrolled them. And that very well may be the truth.

Thomas accused his ex-wife of filling out the card with his name and address. When he gave us her phone number, we called her. After talking to her a while, she too became interested in the Bible study guides. She now lived on the other side of town but welcomed us. The divorce had turned her life upside down, and she was at an emotional crossroad, trying to determine her future without Thomas. Although Thomas avoided us, JoAnn and her mother, with whom she now lived, actually accepted the lesson studies. Had it not been for Thomas, we would not have met JoAnn and her mother.

At first Trinity didn't know how her name had ended up on an enrollment card. Then she recognized her daughter's handwriting. Andrea, a high school teenager, had enrolled her mother and, as we later discovered, her mother's sister. The mother accepted the Bible study guide and made sure we left one for her daughter—as pay back. When the sisters discovered that they had both accepted the lessons, they decided that all three should get together weekly for the Bible studies. Even though they were not always consistent, we enjoyed wonderful, though sometimes challenging, studies (they asked many very good questions), and the Lord eventually reaped the harvest of two families.

You should expect resistance. Some people will even be insulted that the Bible study guides did not come through the mail and refuse to consider home visits as an option. One approach we tried would often break through to such individuals. After building up the privilege we enjoyed of meeting those who enrolled for Bible study guides, we would then ask them how they would feel about us coming by weekly to review the lessons with them. Those showing obvious reluctance we would give the option of taking the studies by correspondence. For those who decided to do that, they had at least had the advantage of meeting us. After they mailed back the sixth lesson, we would return with a gift book and again promote the benefits of home Bible studies. If resistance continued, we again offered them the opportunity of continuing by correspondence. Most switched to home visits after the twelfth lesson because of their increasing difficulty. The twelfth lesson in the Search for Certainty Bible study series is on the doctrine of the Sabbath.

One of the primary attributes of successful Bible instructors is the ability to forge around, or through, resistance. The more one confronts and embraces it, the better one gets at navigating it. It is best to seek to understand what motivates such reluctance while keeping the conversation going and to ask the Holy Spirit for guidance on how to reach the heart. I would encourage you to use every incident of resistance to sharpen your skills in moving the individual past the initial opposition to a position of acceptance. This is a skill that every Bible instructor must develop to be successful.

Often it is simply that such individuals are very involved in their own church but feel insecure in their Bible knowledge and are embarrassed for anyone to know. Assure them that many take the studies to sharpen their knowledge of spiritual concepts, Bible history, and doctrines. You'll meet those who know about Seventh-day Adventists and already recognize the differences they have with our doctrines. Ensure them that the studies will either strengthen their beliefs or challenge them, and either one is a good thing. Many "ministers" of other churches take the lessons to increase their Bible knowledge. In some traditional churches you merely declare your calling and preach a very brief sermon to be ordained a minister. They require no additional education. As a result, such individuals will accept the lessons to receive an official certificate of proof that they have gained some biblical education. In fact, some have taken several series offered by Seventh-day Adventists and have even switched faiths as a result. We have all heard of first-day pastors, rabbis, and other ministers who have brought their entire congregations with them. Only God knows how far and wide the seed of the truth of the gospel of Jesus Christ from the hand of a faithful Bible instructor will spread.

Always insert into the solicitation the fact that it was not by coincidence that they enrolled in the Bible studies. It was the Holy Spirit's leading. Ask, "Do you believe in the power and influence of the Holy Spirit?" Thus it is no coincidence that you are the one that should meet them that day.

Also ask, "Do you feel that God has an interest in you personally?"

The Lord chose you, and He chose them. Because we both love God and are loved by Him so much that He cares about our spiritual well-being, He brings circumstances and people together to fulfill His divine will and purpose.

Here is another type of question: "Would you agree that God is always preparing us for His bigger plan and next move in our lives?" Then point out that He has a blessing for them in the Bible study guides that they cannot afford to miss out on.

Here is a statement of fact: "Whenever there is a focus on the study of God's Word to be drawn closer to Him in one's Christian walk, God begins to open doors that no person can shut—doors of opportunity, doors from which blessing will flow." When you state it with passion, it will encourage people to respond affirmatively.

Then to close, hand them the initial lesson (if you haven't already put it in their hand at the beginning of the conversation) and say, "Let's begin with the first lesson and go from there." The power of suggestion tends to move people in the direction of what you expect of them. After they agree, arrange a schedule of meetings with them.

The above is an example of someone convinced to accept the Bible study guides despite their initial resistance. Perhaps they only agreed to get rid of the Bible instructor. But whatever the reason, the Bible instructor should keep in mind that this is a very tenuous case that may require a great deal of patience. The easy part is obtaining an agreement to accept the first lesson. The challenge begins with the follow-up if they feel "buyer's remorse" after you leave them. Hopefully the Holy Spirit will instill in them the benefits you stated in your solicitation appeal. Here is where your prayers come into play—a major part of what Bible work is all about. Remember, this may be your one opportunity to get into the home with Bible studies. The point is to keep the conversation going until the person either accepts the Bible study guides or emphatically declines.

Chapter Activities

1. Discuss the kinds of things that could impress the person at the door to accept Bible studies.
2. Discuss what could cause the person at the door to reject the Bible studies.
3. Role-play, soliciting interest in accepting home Bible studies with someone who resists taking them.

At-the-Door Field Work Follow-up

When individuals come to the door, they should see someone cheerful and full of expectation that they will accept their Bible study guide. You should speak to them as though you have been acquainted for years and this is merely another occasion to get together and enjoy each other's company. Be congratulatory and excited about your new friend for eternity, and in turn they will feel the excitement and very likely move toward your indicated expectation. After the introductions, I want them to know that they are to be applauded for their decision to begin a course of Bible study.

I try to place the first lesson in their hands as I talk, thus giving them a moment to peruse the lesson. As I provide a little information about the lesson, I point out some of the features that might interest them. They may not remember signing up for the lesson. Perhaps they may not want the lesson or someone coming to their home. Others may be suspicious of our intentions, know nothing about Adventists, nor even have a Bible. A surprising number may not read or write well, and some may be controlled by an addiction. None of that deters me—I still seek to enlist their commitment to regular Bible studies because I know how much God loves them and how close they are to their deliverance.

Carefully study the following approach when delivering Bible study guides at the home of someone who mailed in an interest card:

1. Knock on the door, or ring the doorbell, at least three times before concluding that no one is home.
2. Stand back from the door each time so that you do not startle whoever opens it.
3. Speak up so that you can be heard.
4. Congratulate the individual for registering their interest in the beautiful, full-color Bible study guides.
5. Show them the interest request form and ask them if they are [the name on the request form]. It is important that you show the *original* interest card to the interested person who filled out the card to confirm its authenticity and the legitimacy of the visit.
6. If they confirm it, let them know that you have come to deliver the Bible study guides that they have requested.
7. Introduce yourself (and your partner).
8. If asked what organization you belong to, proudly let them know and continue with the fact that it is a community-wide project sponsored by your organization and how excited you are to take

part. Again, thank them for enrolling to receive Bible studies and for taking advantage of a worthwhile community project that will hopefully enhance their own spiritual growth.

9. Place the lesson in their hand and allow them to examine it. Let them know how honored you are to be the one to deliver it to them, and how happy you are that they have shown interest in receiving Bible studies. If they are willing to accept it, they will very likely not want to be rude and return it.
10. Cite some aspect about the first lesson that may encourage them to read it.
11. Open the lesson (without taking it out of their hand) and explain that it should only require about 30 minutes or so to complete the questions. Explain that the lessons are in a question and Bible answer format, enjoyable, yet challenging. They will discover new Bible facts and brush up on current knowledge.
12. Ask if they have a Bible (needed to look up scriptures).
13. Entice them with the thought of receiving a certificate upon completion of the series and that they will then have an entire set of Bible study guides free of charge for future review and sharing.
14. Let them know that you will return next week to review and correct the lesson and given them their next Bible study guide(s). Arrange the best day and time by suggesting two options (for example: "Would Monday or Wednesday be better for you? Are you normally home during the day, or would an evening time be better?").
15. Intermittently, while you are striving to secure the next appointment, ask questions to get the person to tell you a little about themselves. They may volunteer information in the course of conversation, after which you may also share a little about your family and how much you enjoyed meeting some of their neighbors. (Seek to show that they are not the only ones in the community taking the Bible studies.)
16. Take note of any other obvious needs. Perhaps God sent you to this home for other reasons. Don't be so focused on giving the study guides that you miss out on ministering to the family. The person might mention a family crisis that calls for special prayer support, some immediate need that requires your help to find resources, transportation and/or child care may be necessary when the evangelistic meetings start, etc.

17. Exchange contact information (write yours on the first lesson) and sincerely encourage them to call you with any questions that come up during their study. By all means, ask them for their phone number and let them know you'll be phoning to confirm future appointments.
18. Introduce yourself to anyone else in the house and seek to invite them to also accept the free Bible study guides.
19. When convenient, request to have prayer with them. If they are speaking with you through a screen or a latched door, or if there are other disturbances in the house, it may not be appropriate on the first visit.
20. If they are definitely not interested, let them know that they can begin the lessons by correspondence—by mailing in the completed lesson to a central address and in return receiving the next lesson, along with the corrected one in the mail.
21. Should they still show no interest, thank them for their time and leave.
22. Take notes about the visit and return arrangements once you return to your car or by day's end. Index cards or a dedicated notebook are sufficient for this purpose.

You may have to visit homes several times on various days and at various hours of the day until you find someone at home. Make your rounds, and then repeat them some hours later, and then again, until the day runs out or until someone is home for the first visit. It may require returning a number of times before you actually meet the potential Bible student for the first time.

When you show the enrollee the Bible study guide, try to place it in their hands and let them know how much they will be blessed to participate in a citywide Bible study project to increase the Bible knowledge in the community. Use a little salesmanship to sell the idea of participating in the home Bible studies. Questions such as the following usually appear in the first lesson and are designed to help spawn interest:

- Have you ever wondered how you can have peace in uncertain times?
- Have you ever wondered if we are really nearing the end of earth's history?
- Have you wondered why it seems as though God is not doing anything about human pain and suffering?

A little encouraging will perhaps convince them to take the studies. If the targeted person is not home or does not indicate interest in receiving their first Bible study guide, make conversation with whoever comes to the door. Be cordial and learn their name, sharing with them your own. Always be alert to the real reason that God chose you to be His messenger at that particular door—to solicit interest in the study of the Word of God.

Once you have introduced yourself to the potential Bible student and delivered their first study guide to them, return to such topics as signs of the times, the need to go back to the Bible for answers, etc.

It is up to either the evangelist or to you whether you will visit once or twice a week. Take into consideration how much time the Bible student will have to complete the lessons before the meetings convene. It is not imperative that they be finished, however. Studies can continue during the evangelistic meetings, but completing them should be a goal. Some evangelists prefer a large graduation at the beginning (to get Bible students to the meetings) and at the end of the evangelistic series (to keep them coming).

If you encounter an objection to accepting the lesson, put on your salesman approach and try to be convincing. With a big, friendly smile, remind them that they enrolled in a community project and you are making it as personal as possible. Ensure them that there is no cost or obligation. At the end of the lessons they will have the entire series of guides free of cost for future reference, and in the meantime they will enjoy their studies. They have nothing to lose. It is a win-win invitation for them. Also, let them know that you are willing to assist them in finding Bible answers to other questions on which they've always wanted clarification. The lessons call strictly for Bible answers, not opinions or theories. It is truly a wonderful and rewarding opportunity to have regular, personal Bible studies.

Chapter Activities

1. Role-play with three people, one to answer the door and two Bible instructors.
2. Switch the positions in number 1.
3. Discuss the challenges and list possible strategies for obtaining positive responses.

Organizing Profiles of Interest

Various types of marketing may have produced the names for cold call introductions. Requests for free Bible study guides may come through It Is Written, Breath of Life, Voice of Prophecy, and Hope Channel telecasts, and/or from community interest surveys, special church- or community-sponsored events, etc. Set up a simple database and file to keep track of all activity related to each interest card. While the Bible instructor receives the original card, the data entry person should have a copy with the name of the instructor assigned to it written on the back. Type the information on the interest card into a database system (or card file) and place the paper copy in a file folder arranged in the most convenient categorical order depending on how you may access them at some future time: i.e., by date received, zip code, last name, or name of Bible study guides. The database can include such information as:

- complete name
- complete address
- home phone and cell phone
- e-mail address (optional)
- bible instructor's name(s)
- date assigned
- date of each interaction (or failed attempt) by visit, phone, correspondence, etc.
- whether the interaction was by way of drop off, sit down, phone, or correspondence (including e-mail) (we discourage text messages, especially for new Bible study interests)
- next visitation day and time
- name of Bible study guides being used
- the number of the last lesson completed
- other Bible study guides taken and completed
- literature/books received
- prayer requests
- others in the household
- Sabbath service attended (date, sermon subject heard)
- church-related event attended (date, event type)
- evangelistic series attendance (dates, list of sermon subjects heard)
- notes/comments/concerns

You should record the profile information listed above on each Bible student in your own personal records. At some point, return the original interest cards to the data entry person to place on file with the retained copy. Again, it is important that you show the *original* interest card to the person who filled out the card in order to confirm its authenticity and legitimacy of the visit.

Chapter Activities

1. Discuss how you might obtain various profile items inconspicuously.
2. Discuss how the profile items may become useful at some future point.
3. Discuss some ways to find the Bible students at home.

Throwing Out the Net

Don't be discouraged if you find no one at home on your initial visit, or if the person rejects the opportunity to receive Bible study guides. Finding those sincerely waiting for someone to help them better understand God's Word can be an arduous task. Your patient determination and prayerful persistence will pay off with Bible students with whom it will be a joy to share the Word of God. Many times it has been my experience after returning to a home several times that the Lord sends me back just in time to meet the actual one(s) that needed the visit. Often they are not even those who made the request for Bible studies but rather a family member and/or friend, or both. Family members often sign up relatives and/or friends. Spouses and ex-spouses sign up each other. And sometimes addresses intentionally lead to dead ends. I have also returned to a home just in time to meet a neighbor who readily gives me more information about the person I've been seeking and the best time to find that individual at home. I call them angels. If you are patient and determined, God will intervene with those angels.

You may seem to encounter more failure than success in continuing studies after the first session, but prayer and persistence is all you can do. If the Bible student does not cooperate by being at home, answering or returning calls, etc., you may consider reaching them through another Bible instructor team. After explaining the details of the challenges you've been having with the enrollees, pass the name on to them. It's not uncommon that the second team can successfully take up where yours left off and be able to continue the studies. Who knows why? Different personalities and backgrounds may touch a trait that you did not have. Be thankful it happened, even though it was through someone other than you. However, if that too fails to secure a consistent Bible study student, respect the person's right to refuse and wait a few weeks or months, and then have another team call on them when circumstances for them may have changed and they are finally receptive.

Never use force or appear frustrated or upset. Timing is everything, and it just may not be the right moment for them to begin. Sometimes they may share with you their reason, and other times they may demonstrate their objection by consistently avoiding you. Try to be prayerfully understanding and patient, but don't waste precious time and energy on people who really are not interested. It can be a difficult call to make as to when to cease your visits and calls, but God will lead you. Being as unbiased as possible, discuss the challenges you have been having with the Bible student with the head Bible instructor or evangelistic team, and make a prayerful decision with their affirmation.

Remember to record all attempts and interaction with the interest in the Bible instructor files and report them to the data entry person and during regularly scheduled meetings with the evangelist, pastor, or lead Bible instructor.

> "In humble dependence upon God, families are to go forth and settle in the unworked places of His vineyard. As the reward of their self-sacrifice in order to sow the seeds of truth, they will reap a rich harvest. As they visit family after family, giving Bible studies, opening the Scriptures to those in spiritual darkness, many hearts will be touched."[2]
>
> "Consecrated men and women are needed to stand as fruit-bearing trees of righteousness in the desert places of the earth. In fields where the conditions are so objectionable and disheartening that many workers refuse to go to them, most remarkable changes for the better may be brought about by the efforts of self-sacrificing lay members. These humble workers will accomplish much, because they put forth patient, persevering effort, relying upon no human power, but upon God, who gives them His favor. The amount of good that these workers accomplish will never be known in this world."[3]
>
> "The work we have to do calls for consecrated energy. It demands the whole heart, the faculties of the mind, and the physical powers. The truth of God must be presented with soul fervor. Not much can be accomplished without it. Let enthusiasm be kindled in the church, and let her God-given powers be roused to activity. But a small proportion of her intellect or wealth is enlisted in active effort for the glory of God.

There is enough to do in places where the truth has not been preached. As you look at the cross of Calvary, work, O, work with burning enthusiasm. This enthusiasm means the fullness of divine inspiration, a consecration of the whole soul to the work.

"Beholding the life of Jesus, His self-denial and sacrifice, His matchless love, man becomes transfigured, uplifted, filled with the fullness of God. To be an enthusiast in Christ's work is to be a partaker of the divine nature. The Holy Spirit has taken possession of the soul; the Sun of righteousness has shone into the chambers of the mind and heart, and all-absorbing truths have sanctified the mind. Let none fear this, but pray for it most earnestly, and live for it perseveringly. It will make you strong as workers together with God. With such laborers, the church will arise and shine, for her light is come, and the glory of the Lord is risen upon her."[4]

The task of securing Bible students through cold call introductions may seem daunting, but remember, "there is joy in the presence of the angels of God over one sinner that repenteth" (Luke 15:10). As far as possible, you should do all you can to enroll someone in the household. Regard everyone you speak to as possibly having an interest in what you have been sent there to offer. In addition, as time allows, why not prayerfully walk the neighborhood (or apartment units) of the targeted home, knocking on doors and surveying other neighbors in the same locale. You might find others in the same area who will gratefully accept Bible studies.

Chapter Activities

1. List some reasons the Bible study enrollee might decline the succeeding lessons or having home Bible studies.
2. Discuss what you can do to increase the chances of the Bible studies continuing after the initial introduction.
3. Discuss the advantages of working the community around the home of your contact.

The Bible Study

You will find any number of Bible study guides available for preevangelistic series studies: Search for Certainty, Amazing Facts, End Times Like These, Good News for Today, Prophecies of Hope, Focus on Prophecy, In His

Word, Real Truth, in addition to numerous versions for children and youth. The evangelist chooses the Bible study guides to use both before and during the evangelistic meetings. In addition, the evangelist may determine the order, number, and timing of the lessons.

You should prepare in advance a set of personal lessons that you will be sharing in the home. It is important that you have your own set of Bible study guides. Then you can complete and study each one so that you are quite familiar with each lesson and each scripture. Having your own Bible study guides also gives you the opportunity to make notes after the questions to be discussed, cite other references and scriptures, and mark areas for emphasis.

It is always helpful to those instructors in training also to have reference tools and role-play training on how to share Bible study guide content with a student. You should not take it for granted that merely because someone is a member of the Seventh-day Adventist Church they know how to present the lesson topics. Through presentation, teaching methodology and techniques, and role play, there are many means by which the new Bible instructor should be afforded the opportunity for interactive training on each topic. The open discussion and role play will reinforce the wonderful truths of the gospel. Certainly the group studies will raise the confidence of the church members who have enlisted to share God's Word and even add to the ranks those who may have been previously hesitant to be instructors.

The Holy Ghost was to teach the disciples all things, by bringing all things to their remembrance that they had heard from their Lord (see John 14:26). The Holy Spirit is the memory of "the new man." Here is the true secret of remembering the right scripture at the right time. For at the time you need a scripture (provided you have made studying the Bible a serious habit, thus giving the Holy Spirit something to work with), surely God will not disappoint. Scriptures, themes, testimonies, understanding, and scriptural interpretation will come during a study as needed to draw the Bible study student into the love of God. Notice that I didn't say to win a debate or argument involving differences in interpretation or points of view on a subject. As a Bible instructor you are an ambassador for Christ, not a debater.

> "Therefore if any man be in Christ, he is a new creature: old things are passed away; behold, all things are become new. And all things *are* of God, who hath reconciled us to himself by Jesus Christ, and hath given to us the ministry of reconciliation; To wit, that God was in Christ,

> reconciling the world unto himself, not imputing their trespasses unto them; and hath committed unto us the word of reconciliation. Now then we are ambassadors for Christ, as though God did beseech you by us: we pray you in Christ's stead, be ye reconciled to God" (2 Cor. 5:17-20).

Here are 20 guidelines, or teaching techniques, that you can apply in most home study situations for presenting a Bible study by using Bible study guides:

1. Briefly engage the Bible study student in small talk before getting into the lesson. We will discuss this later.
2. Begin with a prayer for open hearts to hear the voice of God through His Holy Spirit and to receive the Word of God.
3. Introduce the subject title for the Bible study guide.
4. Read or give a brief overview as an introduction to the lesson.
5. The lesson may have been given to the Bible study student to study in advance, prior to reviewing it with the Bible instructor, or the lesson may be gone over first and then handed to the Bible study student to complete by writing in answers during the upcoming week. Both ways have their advantages and disadvantages. It is usually up to the Bible instructor which method they feel more comfortable with. Typically, instructors provide the lesson study guide in advance of its study in the home so that students can prestudy and prepare questions.
6. Ask at least one leading question before the study begins, to determine the level of knowledge on the subject.
7. Make a brief statement that will create curiosity, interest, and enthusiasm about the topic.
8. Do not assume the Bible study student knows anything about the subject, even if they completed the lesson already. Many times Bible study students will merely write down the texts without thinking about their meaning or practical application. Therefore, they receive a certificate for writing texts rather than for experiencing conversion. That is why it is a great advantage to study with the Bible student rather than merely picking up the lesson guides and handing out or dropping off the next one.
9. The Bible study guides will begin with subject matter that the students can feel comfortable with and then present a doctrinal tenet that they may find challenging to their currently held beliefs.
10. Before getting into the point of the lesson, paint the big picture of

God's eternal plan through the given scriptures. Such a deductive approach will help them grasp the overall theme of God's love as presented through the subject before they embrace the topic itself. It is something that you must become very good at—presenting how casting Lucifer out of heaven actually displays God's love. Show His love in ensuring humanity of an antidote to sin and how His love shines forth through the judgment, the Second Coming, the law of God, the Sabbath, the health principles, etc. You want people to embrace and serve God from hearts of love rather than from fear.

11. Move through the Bible study guide, asking the provided questions, looking up the supplied scriptures. (This is what determines whether to give the Bible study student the guides in advance of the study or not. If you prefer the lessons to be already completed, hand them out in advance. But if you would rather go over the lesson first, allow the Bible study student the week to review each text and write in the answers, then study the lessons first without incorporating the answers.)
12. Engage the Bible study student. Many times Bible instructors hurry through the lesson or are pressed by time to the extent that the students have no opportunity to say anything but perhaps read a text from time to time. That is poor teaching and poor Bible study. It is the responsibility of the instructor to ensure that (a) the student can interpret, or explain, the texts read, (b) can apply the scriptures using their own examples (most adults will willingly share life experiences), (c) is in agreement or in harmony with the points of each scripture, and finally, (d) demonstrates a desire to obey God's Word as studied. If the Bible study student is not doing these four things, it will certainly not come automatically at the conclusion of studying 27 to 34 lessons. A, B, C, and D must happen with each and every Bible study guide.
13. Never ask a question that you have no idea of how to answer. Merely throwing questions out to the Bible study student without an answer lowers confidence in you as the teacher. Always ask ones that will clarify, or spotlight, points in the lesson. Why ask, for example, Do you think it's a good idea to pay tithes on the gross or the net income? All you can give is perhaps your opinion because you have no sound scriptural answer. If you have no

clear, thought-through point to make, don't raise an issue. Give an additional pamphlet and/or references on the subject and ask the student to study and report on them.

14. Always work toward "conceptual overlap" as you progress through the study guides. Become aware and utilize every opportunity to help the student integrate the new knowledge with what they already know. For example, one can incorporate health principles into the student's knowledge of how meat is prepared, the Sabbath into how they already worship, or the state of the dead with the student's desire to see loved ones again. The more difficult it is to gain such integration, the more challenging it will be for them to actually begin applying their new understanding and acceptance of Scripture. Information that conflicts sharply with their previous understandings will take even longer, if it happens at all, or for any length of time.
15. Moving too quickly through points of the lesson interferes with conceptualizing its content. It would be far better to talk through some questions and scriptures and spend more time on fewer texts than to rush through many questions and scriptural answers without fully engaging the student. Most Bible study students will not tell you candidly that they feel rushed or that they do not grasp the information clearly. They may merely agree with a nod and not challenge the Bible instructor when they actually don't understand at all.
16. Be careful how you handle mistakes or errors that the student may make. Whether it's the misinterpretation of a text, wrong answer to a question, etc., gently acknowledge their response as an interesting point (or a good thought), and then suggest that they read the scripture again before explaining it, or tell them that "the Bible may be saying something a little different. Let's explore it in more depth." In some way, assure them that they are okay, and then help them visualize what the passage is portraying. Most of all, never allow the student to feel stupid, embarrassed, scolded, etc., but rather given an "ah-ha" moment of discovery in the Word of God. Break down the scripture into small chunks and give applicable examples and even a personal testimony. Make new learning a delightful eye-opener.
17. When you know the subject will directly conflict with already held

beliefs, pray for wisdom in the delivery. Study the topic thoroughly and search for the best approach for that particular individual. Go into the home with a positive spirit, believing with all your heart that your student will receive the Word of God with gratitude. Your attitude is crucial, because it will pervade the entire presentation, either creating negatives or dispelling them altogether.

18. Always acknowledge the viewpoints of the student in some positive manner. Keep in mind the adage "The customer is always right." It works just as effectively in Bible work as it does as a business principle. For example: "I can see what you're saying, but would you mind my sharing another perspective?" or "That's an interesting way of thinking about ___. Let's take another look at what the Bible has to say about it." "I can see why you would look at it that way, but here's what I was thinking. The Bible says in ___." Seek to understand the Bible study student and their perspective from their background in the Word before you seek their understanding of you, or the scriptures you present, and always allow the Spirit of God to lead.
19. Explain the main points to the student from more than one angle or perspective. For example: "For the living know that they shall die: but the dead know not any thing, neither have they any more a reward; for the memory of them is forgotten" (Eccl. 9:5). You can take such a text apart piece by piece. Discuss "die" in terms of death as a sleep, the decaying process, a return to dust, without life or memory, and so on. Providing more than one perspective helps the Bible student experience conceptual overlap and move away from long-held beliefs on the subject.
20. The use of media to present a lesson has many advantages. Many adults love it, and you can reinforce media presentations with sit-down studies. Such media can include slide (or PowerPoint) presentations, DVDs of other speakers presenting the lesson or some aspect of it, programmed instruction, inviting the Bible study student to tune into a special presentation on television, books with pictures, or reference material on the subject. They can be very effective in providing confirmation of the legitimacy of the Bible study guide material and your knowledge on the subject, and might even be the turning point for the student's acceptance of truth.

Such techniques for presenting the Bible study guides will certainly make a difference in the outcome as you walk your students through a series of lessons. You will find other important suggestions about how to conduct oneself in the home outlined throughout this training manual.

Beverly's experience provides a typical example of individuals who read the Bible but do not understand it. Beverly was not a strong reader. In fact, she struggled with reading and stumbled in her pronunciation of words. As soon as I noticed her difficulty, I politely let her know that I didn't mind reading if she didn't mind listening and being ready to tell me something about how the scripture blessed her. Here she struggled too, so after each text I sought to paint a picture in her mind by either using a metaphoric example, related proverb, contrived parable, or brief personal testimony, and often she would add her own (the demonstration of understanding that I needed to hear from her). Visualization worked very well with her. Soon she became engaged and started doing the same. She shared many life experiences that rightly illustrated the point being made. We enjoyed wonderful times together in the Word, and all of us (my partner and I along with Beverly) learned so much from the Word of God through visualization and conceptual overlapping.

Using Ecclesiastes 9:5 let me present a scenario to illustrate my point. Let's pick up the subject with the two forces that comprise the soul—the body plus the breath (Gen. 2:7).

We interjected the question, What is the breath? Then we explained that it is God's special essence that gives everything life and makes everything the being that it is. Job 33:4 says: "The Spirit of God hath made me, and the breath of the Almighty hath given me life." Acts 17:28 tells us that it is in God that we live, move, and have our being. Jesus said that without Him we can do nothing (John 15:5). Without the spirit (or breath) of God in our being, we can literally do nothing. (Note: This is the beginning of shattering the notion that the dead are active in heaven or hell.)

What God spoke into existence at Creation He meant to remain forever, but sin entered the world and waylaid His plans for a forever relationship with humanity. It was like an exciting vacation on a train, riding through the beautiful mountain scenes of nature, when suddenly a warning call comes to the engineer to switch tracks immediately or all will be lost. (Note: The Bible study student should feel the peace of heaven jolted by the introduction of sin.) The sin of Adam and Eve instantly switched God's perfect plan temporarily onto another track. (Note: At this point, the Bible study student should gain an association with and appreciation for the plan of salvation.) The wages of sin is death (Rom. 6:23), but thankfully God temporarily switched tracks. He defied sin and Satan and immediately provided the gift of salvation that we can actually begin experiencing right now when we give our heart to the Lord. However, when Jesus comes again, He will switch us back to the original track. Only then will we realize the fullness of God's presence throughout the ceaseless ages of eternity. (Note: Again we lead the Bible study student away from the notion of going straight to heaven in death.) I think you get the picture of the benefits of using visualization.

Employing such illustrations with important points wedged in helps the Bible student put past beliefs aside to truly understand God's Word. They can visualize the Bible truths that they probably have never read before and gain a more acceptable perspective. At this point it is much more painless to inform them sensitively that all those who are dead are resting in peace in anticipation of the switching of the tracks. None have gone ahead to heaven. All await that glorious day when Christ shall return with the entire heavenly host of angels and take His faithful children home. Emphasize what a glorious day that will be. Gently stress that no doctrine should take away this long-hoped-for event. And then conclude with a brief discussion of 1 Corinthians 15:51-57:

"Behold, I shew you a mystery; We shall not all sleep, but we shall all be changed. In a moment, in the twinkling of an eye, at the last trump: for the trumpet shall sound, and the dead shall be raised incorruptible, and we shall be changed. For this corruptible must put on incorruption, and this mortal must put on immortality. So when this corruptible shall have put on incorruption, and this mortal shall have put on immortality, then shall be brought to pass the saying that is written, Death is swallowed up in victory. O death, where is thy sting? O grave, where is thy victory? The sting of death is sin; and the strength of sin is the law. But thanks be to God, which giveth us the victory through our Lord Jesus Christ."

There are many ways to create visualization. This is merely one example. Notice the focus was more on the love of God and His reunion with humanity rather than on death. Here is where the focus should be with each and every lesson presentation. While it takes time, forethought, and experience to become natural at this, it is something that has proven successful.

Chapter Activities

1. Identify and discuss each of the visualization and/or conceptual overlaps introduced in the abbreviated Bible study above.
2. Discuss how metaphors, illustrations, testimonies, etc. help you understand concepts better.
3. Role-play a Bible concept using metaphors, illustrations, testimonies, and the like.

Around the Table

Once in the home, after a few minutes of complementary small talk, begin the lesson. Remember you are on the business of the King of kings. Let the student know in advance, with the greatest respect, that you would prefer nothing to eat or drink except perhaps water. Sharing such things can distract from the lessons.

If the television or radio is on, hopefully the Bible student will volunteer to turn it off. If not, perhaps a little but not too obvious body language might bring attention to the disturbance. If that doesn't work, a very polite request may be needed.

As you advance through the lessons, always keep your objectives uppermost in your thoughts, words, and actions:

- to build rapport with the Bible student
- to spend quality time with them (being sensitive to other needs)
- to create a level of respect and confidence in you as a Bible guide/teacher and spiritual friend and who looks forward to the studies together
- to gain finally a decision for Christ through smaller ones in the affirmative on each topic
- to break through barriers to accepting truth and engender a response of love to God and humanity
- to take advantage of every opportunity to prepare the Bible student to question deviations from Bible truth, to test what they hear for agreement with God's Holy Word, to affirm a desire to obey God's Word, and to apply God's Word to the daily life even though change may be necessary
- to help meet objections from friends, family, and especially their church and pastor
- to create a hunger for more knowledge and greater understanding that will recognize God has a bigger plan and purpose for their life

- to transition the candidate mentally, then physically, from the home to the public evangelistic meeting place

Bible instructors have no power of themselves to guarantee success in any one of the preceding objectives. While God uses Bible instructors to minister to those searching for truth (Heb. 1:14), it is the work of the Holy Spirit to guide into all truth and to convict of sin (John 16:8, 13). As a Bible instructor you have the privilege of partnering with God for the salvation of others. Only through earnest prayer and a genuine and growing relationship with Jesus Christ can you be fit to colabor with God for those who shall potentially be heirs of the kingdom of heaven. Therefore, it is not by force, but by love; not by demanding, but by carefully addressing objections and excuses; not by impatience, but by patiently forging various avenues to the heart; not by overtalking or outtalking, but by a spiritual ear to hear and respond, is Christ lifted up and people are drawn to the Savior.

You are on your way to an exciting time with your Bible students during the evangelistic series if you accomplish all nine objectives prior to the opening night.

Chapter Activities

1. Role-play shifting from small talk to the Bible study.
2. Role-play handling the resistance of a student reluctant to continue the studies. Discuss when it is time to discontinue efforts to work with someone.
3. Discuss your opinion of the value of each of the teaching techniques in this Chapter for presenting a series of Bible study guide lessons to a student.

---

[1] E. G. White, *The Ministry of Healing*, p. 143.

[2] Ellen G. White, "Words to Lay Members," *Review and Herald*, Aug. 26, 1902.

[3] Ellen G. White, "Stony-ground Hearers—Continued," *Review and Herald*, June 14, 1892.

CHAPTER 10

ARMED AND DANGEROUS

When you engage with all your heart in evangelism, you are closely allied with the angels of heaven as colaborers with Christ. It brings you a little closer to heaven and Jesus. "Are they not all ministering spirits, sent forth to minister for those who shall be heirs of salvation?" (Heb. 1:14). Therefore, dedicate yourself to soul winning with all your energy.

May the Spirit that was in our divine Lord rest upon each Bible instructor. That Spirit is the Spirit of love. "Love one another, as I have loved you" (John 15:12). Jesus' love was salvific, and thus the Bible instructor's love must be a yearning for the salvation of others that no other pursuit can satisfy. Jesus' love for lost humanity called for the sacrifice of His life. Our love for lost souls requires a selfless effort that will make sacrifices beyond the mere call of duty, especially during the course of a major evangelistic series.

The hours involved in visitation can become long, especially when the Bible students are a challenge to connect with on a consistent basis. Dealing with disappointment can be difficult at times. Every day presents its own problems and excitement. Traversing the city can become a wearying ordeal. But as long as you keep the big picture in view, you'll be able to understand readily the battle going on—the conflict between Christ and Satan raging around the work of God. You must move forward consistently and persistently, ever resisting the temptation to withdraw or become discouraged.

Chapter Activities

1. Discuss the implications of colaboring with Christ and angels.
2. List some of the joys and challenges that come with the daily work of a Bible instructor.

3. Discuss some things that the you can do to resist discouragement as a Bible instructor.

Your Personal Testimony

"Strive to arouse men and women from their spiritual insensibility. Tell them how you found Jesus and how blessed you have been since you gained an experience in His service. Tell them what blessing comes to you as you sit at the feet of Jesus and learn precious lessons from His Word. Tell them of the gladness and joy that there is in the Christian life. Your warm, fervent words will convince them that you have found the pearl of great price. Let your cheerful, encouraging words show that you have certainly found the higher way. This is genuine missionary work, and as it is done, many will awake as from a dream."[1]

Seventh-day Adventists have a message to tell to the world. It is one of love and is to be given in love. In body and in spirit we reflect Jesus to the world. "To know the love of Christ, which passeth knowledge, that ye might be filled with all the fulness of God" (Eph. 3:19). Your unique experience in coming to Christ and your life since accepting Him can be effective tools in communicating the gospel to others. God has given them to you individually, and no one can take them from you. Your personal testimonies of the times God revealed Himself unquestionably to you, particularly in moments of crisis, become your weapons of mass destruction against the strongholds of Satan.

Certain testimonies you can carefully adapt to either a group situation or a casual one-on-one conversation. Others will be spontaneous, spoken with confidence and sincerity to affirm and encourage someone facing a challenge similar to ones you have endured. Still others will be the testimony of a biblical character or the sharing of an experience that you in turn have heard from or witnessed in others. All should be well chosen, biblically accurate, and appropriate for the situation. With personal testimonies you are armed and dangerous to the wiles of the enemy, armed and powerful against his attempts at discouragement. They will be effectual in breaking down the strongholds of unbelief.

The love story of a Deity who would not let you go should be the theme of our testimony. Out of the depth of love, our God, who would not leave us to our own destruction, walked away from His majestic home in heaven to give His life to redeem us from our wretched, hopeless state. He was treated the way we deserve—death, the wages of sin—so that we could be treated as He deserves—honor, glory, power, and an inheritance that includes eternal life.

> "For all have sinned, and come short of the glory of God" (Rom. 3:23).
>
> "For the wages of sin is death; but the gift of God is eternal life through Jesus Christ our Lord" (Rom. 6:23).

A good outline for an effective testimony generally includes three parts: what your life was like before you accepted Christ, how you received Him, and how your life is different as a result. I refer to it as the Before/How/After format. This same format can work with personal testimonies of other types: what was happening in a challenging situation, how the intervention of God transformed it, and how things have been since God made the change. Your testimonies should be brief but powerfully lift up the love of God, recounting His goodness and wondrous works in your behalf. It is vital that a personal testimony apply directly to the situation being discussed. In addition to the testimony, be sure to add an attention-getting introduction and a brief concluding thought that expresses from the heart the plan of salvation.

> "For ye know the grace of our Lord Jesus Christ, that, though he was rich, yet for your sakes he became poor, that ye through his poverty might be rich" (2 Cor. 8:9).
>
> "For God so loved the world, that he gave his only begotten Son, that whosoever believeth in him should not perish, but have everlasting life. For God sent not his Son into the world to condemn the world; but that the world through him might be saved" (John 3:16, 17).
>
> "Eye hath not seen, nor ear heard, neither have entered into the heart of man, the things which God hath prepared for them that love him" (1 Cor. 2:9).
>
> "Then shall the King say unto them on his right hand, Come, ye blessed of my Father, inherit the kingdom prepared for you from the foundation of the world" (Matt. 25:34).

As you prepare your thoughts, keep in mind the following quote from *An Appeal to the Youth*:

"Our sins caused Jesus to die a shameful death, that through His sufferings and death we might receive pardon. Can we receive the forgiveness of sins before we feel that we are sinners? and before we realize the sinfulness of sin? I think not. When we repent before God of our sins sincerely, we shall feel that without the pardoning blood of Christ we must perish. If we cast ourselves in our wretchedness wholly upon the mercy of Christ, and feel that unless He saves us we perish; when we yield our own will, our own way, and plead for Jesus to control our will and actions, then we come into a position where we can receive and appreciate pardon and the forgiveness of sin."[2]

As you prepare your testimony, follow these steps:

1. Ask the Lord to guide your thoughts and written words. Then trust Him to do so. Remember, your story can bring glory to Him and also be inspiration for the salvation of others.
2. Write as if you were sharing with just one person.
3. Keep it short: three minutes (about one and a half to two pages typewritten double-spaced).
4. Consider using a theme (see second sample testimony). A theme is a phrase or idea that you state in the introduction, weave throughout the body of the testimony, and then restate in the conclusion. It helps to keep the testimony on track and aids in the listener's understanding and retention.

> "We should adapt our prayers and testimonies to the occasion and to the company present. Those who cannot do this are not needed in such meetings. There are themes that Christians may at any time dwell upon with profit, such as the Christian experience, the love of Christ, and the simplicity of faith; and if their own hearts are imbued with the love of Jesus, they will let it shine forth in every prayer and exhortation. Let the fruits of the sanctifying truth be seen in the life, in a godly example, and it will make an impression that no opposing influence can counteract."[3]

When Christ has set an individual free, the sooner they tell friends the better. While some may try to discourage them or even give a scornful put down, others will be amazed at their new joy and want to know more about their experience with God. Read the following four New Testament passages that clearly encourage and affirm new members witnessing to friends, loved ones, and community:

The story of the demon possessed man who was healed by Jesus:

"Howbeit Jesus suffered him not, but saith unto him, Go home to thy friends, and tell them how great things the Lord hath done for thee, and hath had compassion on thee. And he departed, and began to publish in Decapolis how great things Jesus had done for him: and all men did marvel" (Mark 5:19, 20).

The parable of the lost sheep:

"And when he cometh home, he calleth together his friends and neighbours, saying unto them, Rejoice with me; for I have found my sheep which was lost. I say unto you, that likewise joy shall be in heaven over one sinner that repenteth, more than over ninety and nine just persons, which need no repentance" (Luke 15:6, 7).

The parable of the lost coin:

"Either what woman having ten pieces of silver, if she lose one piece, doth not light a candle, and sweep the house, and seek diligently till she find it? And when she hath found it, she calleth her friends and her neighbours together, saying, Rejoice with me; for I have found the piece which I had lost. Likewise, I say unto you, there is joy in the presence of the angels of God over one sinner that repenteth" (verses 8-10).

The woman at the well after her encounter with Jesus:

"The woman then left her waterpot, and went her way into the city, and saith to the men, Come, see a man, which told me all things that ever I did: is not this the Christ? Then they went out of the city, and came unto him" (John 4:28-30).

Such stories and parables encourage not only new members to rejoice with friends when they receive Christ as Lord of their life but also any Christian in which God intervened in a trying experience that is cause for uninhibited praise. We must not overlook the blessings of God or hide under a basket His great mercies toward us, especially when He answered beyond whatever we could ask or imagine. Instead, we must share the good news of God's goodness toward us and our loved ones. Praiseworthy testimonies are healing words—they are salvific.

"Our confession of His faithfulness is Heaven's chosen agency for revealing Christ to the world. We are to acknowledge His grace as made known through holy men of old; but that which will be most effectual is the testimony of our own experience. We are witnesses for God as we reveal in ourselves the working of a power that is divine. Every individual has a life distinct from all others, and an experience difference essentially from theirs. God desires that our praise shall ascend to Him, marked by our own individuality. These precious acknowledgements to praise of the glory of

His grace, when supported by a Christ-like life, have an irresistible power that works for the salvation of souls."[4]

The wonderful acknowledgements of divine intervention and the grace of God toward us in times of personal crisis make for potent personal testimonies that the Holy Spirit will bring to our remembrance. They can have a powerful impact when woven into our conversations and our Bible studies with those whom God is loving through us. In addition, we have the biblical record of the lives of Saul of Tarsus in whom there was so much fear among the Christians that God changed his name to Paul the evangelist when He transformed his life (Acts 9), the female fortuneteller who became a follower of Paul (Acts 16:16-18), the blind beggar (Luke 18:35-43), and the leper (Mark 1:40-45). They are merely examples of the numerous stories recorded and unrecorded of those who experienced a life-changing encounter with God that became their powerful, effectual personal testimony. Each of them told what they knew, what they had seen and heard, and what they had felt of the power of God. Entire communities responded to the gospel as a result.

Jesus painted picture stories through such experiences that have touched lives for centuries. In the present world we may never know their full impact. Many times people have approached me to tell how they remember a testimony or experience I shared and how timely it was, or how God used it to bless their lives. Appropriate, well-stated personal testimonies guided by the Holy Spirit should become a natural part of the Bible instructor's ministry.

Always remember to keep testimonies detailed but brief. Ask God to give you wisdom and guidance in your sharing.

Chapter Activities

1. Share your testimony of coming to Christ.
2. Share an unforgettable experience since coming to Christ.
3. What is the potential impact of a sincere testimony shared with passion?

---

[1] E. G. White, *Testimonies*, vol. 9, p. 38.

[2] Ellen G. White, *An Appeal to the Youth* (Battle Creek, Mich.: Seventh-day Adventist Pub. Assn., 1864), p. 67.

[3] E. G. White, *Testimonies*, vol. 4, p. 565.

[4] Ellen G. White, *The Desire of Ages* (Mountain View, Calif.: Pacific Press Pub. Assn., 1898), p. 347.

CHAPTER 11

THE SUM OF ALL THE RULES

If you were to summarize all the rules of Bible work in two words, they would be "building relationships." The goal of everything that you do as a Bible instructor is to create relationships both between God and people and among people. It is vital that the instructor pursue amiable relationships everywhere, anytime, always, and especially with Bible students as quickly as possible. Once established, you will need to maintain a respectful relationship at all costs. Ask God to fill your spirit with His love for others and to enable you to be inclusive to new faces and cordial to all. Quickly notice something complementary, discover some interests you may have in common, find some way you can be supportive in their quest for truth, and learn to empathize with their challenges. Be quick to note God's goodness, mercy, and power in nature, personal circumstances, and Bible prophecy. All that takes serious focus. It requires much prayer and having an ear to hear the promptings of the Holy Spirit. Relationship building is paramount to the your ministry as a Bible instructor.

Here are some important points about building relationships that you should consider:

1. It is more important to be a good listener than always the one talking. In listening you give the person opportunities to open up to you more and more about themselves, their challenges, and where they are spiritually.
2. Arrive a few minutes early, or at the very least, be on time to all appointments. If you cannot make an appointment on time, call ahead and apologetically let the person know what is happening.
3. Always speak in a pleasant tone, even should disagreements arise. Never let yourself be abrupt, rude, inconsiderate, angry, argumentative, unpleasant, or using body language to express

disgust. You are always an ambassador for Christ—represent Him well under all circumstances.

4. Refrain from getting too personal, i.e., asking question after question about a matter when students do not volunteer information.
5. Go out of your way to demonstrate kindness—for example, pick up the newspaper on the front porch; bring gift books and supplemental materials from time to time to go along with the lesson; and when your partner is presenting the Bible study, volunteer to care for the children.
6. Cordially invite others in the home to join in the Bible study rather than ignore them.
7. Invite your Bible students to church-sponsored events (if appropriate before the evangelistic series starts). However, note that if you do, you may be opening the door to be invited to their church-sponsored events as well, and if you are, you should probably try to attend.
8. After the first visit, begin calling your Bible student a day before the next arranged study to ensure that they are going to be home. Ask them if they have any questions.
9. Be of support during a time of crisis or need. Find ways to show you care.
10. Before praying for the family, ask for any prayer requests (and don't forget to mention them in your prayer). When you pray in the home, the prayer should be clearly heard, include any requests, and be brief.

I remember going along with another Bible instructor to the home of a man for an introductory visit, and after we complemented him on the art in his home, she began asking a litany of questions about his marital status. He was divorced, but he and his ex-wife still had a congenial relationship because of the grandchildren. My partner was flabbergasted to learn that the two lived next door to each other. The Bible instructor I was with was outraged and strongly expressed her opinion about his relationship with his ex-wife. Aghast, I quickly changed the subject. Bible instructors are in the home for one reason and one reason only—to lead others to a saving relationship with Jesus Christ. Bible instructors are not marriage counselors, psychologists, physicians, or nutritionists. If the family shares the need for some type of counseling, you have the responsibility to refer that need to the pastor or Bible instructor coordinator.

You must take full responsibility for any recommendations, suggestions, counsel, or referrals offered in the home. Remember, Satan will take advantage of every opportunity to waste time on subjects that have nothing to do with the Bible lesson. If you find yourself off track, immediately return to the reason for your visit. Unfortunately, once the Bible student finds you are willing to discuss other subjects and talk about whatever they are interested in, they will seek to enjoy your time while knowingly avoiding the subject at hand.

Chapter Activities

1. Discuss the merits of each of the recommendations for building relationships.
2. Discuss the problems created by deviating from the purpose of the home visit.
3. List the drawbacks in offering recommendations, suggestions, counsel, and even referrals to a Bible student.

Presenting the Study Guide Topic

As you study with the student, review the lesson in such a way that the student feels comfortable with the presentation. Needless to say, you must be thoroughly prepared to teach each subject covered in the study guides. It may be necessary to take certain lessons slowly, piece by piece, in more than one session. That is always preferable to rushing to complete a lesson at each session.

You will find that a mere assent to what is being discussed does not necessarily mean the student understands or is experiencing spiritual growth. You must prayerfully read your student's attitude toward a lesson, learning to ask the right questions (without being obnoxious or insulting) in order to determine the level of reception. And by all means, do not present difficult topics until you are reasonably sure the person has had a conversion experience. Keep in mind this Ellen White statement: "When they surrender heart and mind and will to God, they are then prepared candidly to weigh evidence in regard to these solemn, testing truths."[1]

Depending on prior religious experiences, the students will normally receive such topics as those involving the plan of salvation, signs of the last days, the Second Coming, the judgment, the Sabbath, clean and unclean meats, tithes and offerings, baptism, and some of the prophecies of Daniel and Revelation without much conflict. They are good, inspirational subjects that can be quite enjoyable to study together. However, I have found that such issues as the state of the dead (whether the dead go straight to heaven or hell), the location of hell, the rapture of the saints, whether the millennial period is before or after the Second Coming, the tribulation period, who is Michael the archangel, time prophecies, America in Bible prophecy, the mark of the beast and seal of God, and other Daniel and Revelation subject matter can be very challenging to present.

A *testing truth* is any doctrinal belief that challenges people to interpret the Word of God from a completely different perspective than they were previously taught. Because God alone gave all Scripture by inspiration (2 Tim. 3:16) as the testimony of Jesus Christ (John 1:14) and only the Holy Spirit can teach it correctly (John 16:13), you must believe that scriptures do not conflict with one another, nor with the character of Christ, no matter how specific texts are worded. The truths of the Bible are so interrelated that the misinterpretation of one doctrinal belief will likely have a domino effect that flows over into other aspects until it reaches the character of God Himself. Satan works to bring confusion into the human mind regarding the divine character, and by so doing to engender conflicts with the Word of God as a whole. That is why you must start early to feel out and identify from the expressions of your Bible study students those misinterpretations of Scripture that you must prayerfully confront before they can fully embrace the love of Christ.

Testing truths can make or break a decision for Christ. In Gena's belief system, the Sabbath was a part of the Ten Commandments done away with at the cross of Christ. For her, it was a testing truth. Because of the interrelationship of doctrinal beliefs and the gospel of Jesus Christ, testing truths can quickly halt all progress in a series of Bible studies, and Gena had reached that point. Even though we more or less agreed to disagree temporarily until we could complete more research on the subject of the Sabbath and review it, the topic continually wedged its way into each Bible study (either intentionally by me, or by Gena).

It is always a good idea to present a topic from various perspectives. You never know which viewpoint will result in an aha moment for the Bible student. One evening when I arrived at the home of Gena for our regular Bible study, in the living room sat her pastor along with three other ministers from her church. Their grins assured me that they were waiting and ready to scripturally eat me for dinner on the subject of the Sabbath and the law that according to their beliefs had been done away with under the "old dispensation." I was alone that evening (my partner could not be with me, but I'd been in a similar position many times before). Rather than back away from the potential battle, I felt the assurance of the Holy Spirit that Jesus, the Word, would prevail.

So that we would not wind up arguing over scriptural differences, we set the ground rules. They would make their presentation first, and then I would follow with my mine regarding the law and the Sabbath. When both sides had finished, questions could be asked and answers could be given uninterrupted. I must say, we stuck to our rules very well until the end of the debate. Well, to make a long story short, like Elijah on Mount Carmel I encouraged them to go first. What ensued was at least an hour of them hollering at me very few scriptures and lots of opinions and interpretations regarding the fulfillment of the law, what was done away with at the cross, the old and new dispensations, Pentecost being on Sunday, the resurrection of Christ inaugurating Sunday as the day to keep by faith, and the doing away with the Jewish Sabbath as the day one kept as works. They argued that we are no longer under works but faith, and being saved by grace not works, and so on. *No wonder people are totally confused about the law of God and the sanctity of the Sabbath,* I thought to myself.

Nervous, I wasn't sure I could readily come up with the scripture to defend the cause of God. That is why as a Bible instructor you pray for the infilling of the Holy Spirit before home visitations, and also why you do them with a partner who remains in prayer during the study. By the time it was my turn, I was only hoping I could survive the experience without being a total embarrassment before my Bible study student. She sat quietly in a chair away from all the yelling and pacing and finger pointing. Before I began I requested that we pray. I have no problem praying fervently, and that I did unashamedly. It was calming, although I only had an idea of where I would start—the words of Jesus in John 14:15: "If ye love me, keep my commandments." Then I talked about the love of God expressed by the two great laws of God in Matthew 22:37-39 and sought to paint a picture of the principle of love by which God operates and by which He desires to relate to humanity.

Next I emphasized that by throwing out the law of God, it changes completely our perception of His character and how we will view His relationship to the human race. I continued on with this theme—how the

Israelites actually assumed they could keep the law, but like all who think they can obey it by their own resolute determination, they utterly failed. Rather than do away with the law, since the cross, Christ has not only put them in our mind and written them in our hearts (Heb. 8:10) but has fulfilled His promise of a Comforter to guide us into all truth (God's law is the truth [Ps. 119:142]). After continuing this line of thought regarding the law, I began in Genesis 2:1-3 with the Creation story, stopping in such books as Exodus (the Ten Commandments was the only law written with the finger of God) and Isaiah (in which the Sabbath was not only for strangers but for all those who desire to ride on the high places of the earth), Ezekiel (how God identifies His people), and Jeremiah (in which God makes a promise to put His law in our inner parts where the Holy Spirit resides, removing it from works to anointing). Next I stopped a few places in the New Testament, such as Matthew (where Jesus breaks the commandments down into the two great laws of God), Luke (Jesus sets the example), John (in which God identifies His disciples as commandment keepers), Hebrews (if Jesus had given us another day, He would have spoken of it, for God covenanted again, as He did in the book of Jeremiah, to give us power under the anointing of the Holy Spirit only, not by the works of human determination), and ended in Revelation 22:14: "Blessed are they that do his commandments, that they may have right to the tree of life, and may enter in through the gates into the city." At this point, the ministers could not contain themselves another minute. They ranted and raged until they tried to get me to consent to baptism in Gena's bathtub. That's when I demanded to have prayer and headed for the door.

By now I felt beat down as though I had been in the boxing ring with Mike Tyson. I thought for sure Gena would not want me to return. Not able to sleep, I knelt in fervent prayer for her, her ministers, and for myself. I prayed that my feeble efforts to present the love of Jesus had been acceptable to Him and then, empowered by the Holy Spirit, I prayed for the Spirit of God to make their night restless and to contemplate what they had heard. I prayed that the spirit of rebellion would succumb to the Spirit of God. On and on I prayed for much of the night.

The next day Gena and I spoke by phone, and to my amazement, she was thoroughly upset with the way her ministers had treated me and apologized profusely. She felt impressed with my calm spirit in contrast with the one that they displayed. Touched by my simple approach as opposed to the yelling, finger pointing, and pacing, she saw the light through the scriptural picture I had painted and was ready to begin observing God's Sabbath. Soon she and her children were baptized. Although I wouldn't want any Bible instructor to experience what I had endured that night, I praise God for the experience and especially for the outcome.

Remember, you are not there to debate Scripture. Give additional research assignments on the subject and perhaps plan special sessions to discuss it. If necessary, agree to be in disagreement on the subject for the time being, and move on. The seeds of truth have been planted. Now you must pray that they have fallen on good ground that the Holy Spirit can water for an abundant harvest. Relationship must be first and foremost. At all cost, you certainly don't want to be asked to leave the home and never return, as many well-intentioned Bible instructors have been.

Study each subject thoroughly and prayerfully. Review scriptures that would be appropriate to address objections. Write them, if necessary, on a small piece of paper and insert them in your Bible and have them ready when needed. I use Post-it notes placed in the front and/or back of my Bible to list scriptures I may want to remind myself of. Most important, ask God to take you deep below the superficial to the cisterns of the love of Jesus that the doctrines open up. That is what the student is to receive and accept. If they can feel and experience the love of Jesus as it shines through the doctrine, they will ask, "What must I do to be saved?" "If you reveal the love of Christ to them, you may lead the hungering, thirsting ones to Jesus, and He will give them the bread of life and the waters of salvation."[2]

As a Bible instructor you must understand that the Holy Spirit convicts and converts, and no one else. It is one of the main reasons it is important to go into the homes two by two. One of the two should be inconspicuously in constant, fervent prayer that the students will receive the power of the Holy Spirit into their hearts and that the Holy Spirit will work in the heart of the instructor making the presentation. The prayer may be that the love of Jesus will shine through in word, attitude, and deed.

The enemy will bring about all sorts of distractions to hinder the Word of God from reaching the heart. I sat down in one home, and the cat entered the room just about the time we were getting ready to pray and begin the Bible study. The animal started meowing louder and louder as it walked back and forth along the sofa where we were sitting. My Bible study student tried in vain to quiet the cat. Finally she put the cat in the next room and shut the door. Not surprisingly, the creature continued its meowing even louder. Finally I suggested that we pray for it to become silent. Kneeling in prayer, we asked God to take control of the meowing cat so that our study could go on. God answered our prayer, and we never heard the cat again during the entire study. The devil can use even pets to hinder a Bible study, as well as children, spouses, etc., but the Spirit of God will prevail.

Another one of my Bible study students had to be rushed to the hospital for the first time in her life. Margaret ended up receiving a pacemaker and remained in the hospital for many days. We had had only a few studies, and now the hospital stay and the succeeding home recovery threatened to interrupt them. I was able to visit her daily in the hospital, encourage her spirit with texts from the Bible, and pray with her. It came to my attention that her nephew was taking Bible studies with another instructor. Right after her release from the hospital, guess who I saw walking through the door of the evangelistic meetings? None other than Margaret. I had spoken a few times to her nephew about her, and he promised me that he would provide her transportation to the meetings. He had kept his word, and soon she came regularly. We were able to continue the studies, and she was baptized. The devil will not hesitate to attack health, finances, transportation—anything to block attendance.

Learn the many promises of God's Word so that you can address Satan in the way Christ did during His wilderness battle. Jesus constantly referred to "it is written," and you must do the same. Revelation 12:11 declares: "And they overcame him by the blood of the Lamb, and by the word of their testimony; and they loved not their lives unto the death." As time marches toward the second coming of Christ, you will be ever more aware of the fact that you can win such battles only in the strength of our Lord Jesus Christ and through the enormous power of the Holy Spirit.

> "Therefore rejoice, ye heavens, and ye that dwell in them. Woe to the inhabiters of the earth and of the sea! for the devil is come down unto you, having great wrath, because he knoweth that he hath but a short time" (Rev. 12:12).
>
> "Finally, my brethren, be strong in the Lord, and in the power of his might. Put on the whole armour of God, that ye may be able to stand against the wiles of the devil. For we wrestle not against flesh and blood, but against principalities, against powers, against the rulers of the darkness of this world, against spiritual wickedness in high places. Wherefore take unto you the whole armour of God, that ye may be able to withstand in the evil day, and having done all, to stand. Stand therefore, having your loins girt about with truth, and having on the

> breastplate of righteousness; And your feet shod with the preparation of the gospel of peace; Above all, taking the shield of faith, wherewith ye shall be able to quench all the fiery darts of the wicked. And take the helmet of salvation, and the sword of the Spirit, which is the word of God: Praying always with all prayer and supplication in the Spirit, and watching thereunto with all perseverance and supplication for all saints; And for me, that utterance may be given unto me, that I may open my mouth boldly, to make known the mystery of the gospel" (Eph. 6:10-19).

Once you have completed the study in that home and prayed together, when you return to your car, or before you and your partner depart for the day, stop and thank God for the privilege to wrestle against the powers of the darkness in the name of Jesus, praise Him for His presence and power, and claim God's promise over all that was said and done as found in Isaiah 55:11: "So shall my word be that goeth forth out of my mouth: it shall not return unto me void, but it shall accomplish that which I please, and it shall prosper in the thing whereto I sent it."

The Spirit of God will continue working on the heart of the student long after the Bible study is finished that day. His activity, in fact, has only begun. The enemy of souls will seek to bring contradiction and discouragement to the Bible student, hoping the seed has fallen on stony ground. Many times I've received reports from my students that their pastor came by for a visit or a relative had something to say that questioned the beliefs of Seventh-day Adventists. In the midst of such a battle, do not hesitate to begin fasting and praying that the seed has fallen on good ground and will spring up and increase to the glory of God.

Chapter Activities

1. Share experiences during which it was unmistakable that the devil was hindering Bible studies and how you or someone else handled it.
2. Discuss the importance of tactfully asking questions to affirm understanding and acceptance of Bible teachings.
3. Discuss why some subjects act as testing truths and others do not.

Giving Special Assistance

As a Bible instructor you must be particularly observant on the first few visits. It may be that your student lacks the reading, writing, or comprehension abilities to focus on a whole lesson. If they haven't finished the lesson upon your return, assure them that you can complete it together. Use body language to beckon for the Bible student to get the lesson and then move to the table (if convenient) or sofa to go through it with them in a cordial manner. Assure them that it's all right if the Bible study guide was a challenge to complete, stating that it was a little more advanced, and that they will be just as blessed by doing the lesson together with you. However, remind them that one of the benefits of the Bible study guides is to encourage a routine of studying the Word of God at a specific time each day.

While it takes longer to do the lessons in this manner, remember they are merely a means to an end and not an end in themselves. The instructor or the partner may even have to do the reading and writing. But it is more important that the Bible student is engaged, understands the subject matter, is able to answer questions as you move through the lesson, and indicates agreement with its spiritual and biblical points. The time you spend with your students should be one of prayer, sharing, teaching the lesson's Bible principles, affirming conviction, and gaining decisions of agreement and personal application. It should not be a stressful push, but rather methodical encouragement in a relaxed manner.

Knowing that the lessons will be done together, the instructor should determine in advance which questions may be most challenging for the student, which ones will need special emphasis, and which will lead to a decision on the subject of the lesson. It is at your discretion either to study the lesson before turning it over to the student to complete it during the week, or to merely provide an overview of the salient points first with the student and then allow them to finish it. Either method seems to work well.

If the students lack the ability to find scripture passages, assure them that that is why your partner is with you. He or she will aid them in locating the text. If they lack Bible understanding and cannot identify the answers when they see them in print and then discuss them during the study, show them the answer in the Word of God and let them talk about it. Throughout the process, handle the Bible study student with great care, reassurance, and humble respect. Completely overlook their inabilities by focusing on the points of the lesson. Complement their comments whenever possible. With each lesson they should get better at identifying the answers to the Bible questions and finding the scriptures. If they at any time feel demeaned, belittled, or embarrassed, they may avoid contact with you in the future.

If the little child is precious in God's sight, certainly the disadvantaged are also. You must make them feel as though you are one from whom they can receive welcome help. They should quickly be able to recognize your sincerity. As they come to appreciate your friendly spirit and helpfulness, they will look forward to your visits and be willing to stop everything they may be doing to participate in Bible study with you.

Even when the Bible study student has all answers filled in, along with notes in the margin or in a notebook, do not take it for granted that they fully grasp what the texts say. Very often they do not. Wanda was like that and even took notes while we walked through the questions and her answers. By lesson 12 she made a strange request. "Can we review the lessons again, starting from lesson 1? There is so much I didn't understand." She had been merely filling in the answer with scripture. It is important to take an interactive approach to the Bible study. The student should be able either to voice the answers to the questions without rereading the scripture or to explain the scriptural answer after reading it. So I suggested to my partner to have her begin reading the scriptural references for the questions, but write the answer in her own words based on those references. It was a struggle for her at first, but this method challenged Wanda to pray over the text more and allow the Holy Spirit to be her teacher. As a result, her understanding of the scriptures that she read improved greatly.

As you move through the lesson, always remember relationship comes first. Use the lessons not merely to answer the questions, but take advantage of the question to bring out thoughts designed to fortify love for God and obedience to His Word. Also, use the Bible study guides to address potential objections due to cultural or traditional beliefs. One of the major objectives in utilizing them is to begin making love for Christ first, last, and best in the life as early as possible, and gingerly and prayerfully to help the student face traditional thought on specific subjects with truth from God's Word.

As you highlight and place emphasis on certain parts of the lesson, stop along the way and ask questions to test their understanding and attitude toward what is being taught. Don't assume their conflicting responses or questions are a sign of indifference. It may merely be an indication of frustration in not understanding the Word of God. Remain patient and calm at all times. Reassure them that things will become clearer the more they get into the lessons and through our reviews when you stop by.

Sometimes it may be necessary to present an additional text or two to increase clarity or to give a further biblical example. Here is also when a parable, short story, or testimony may help explain a point or diffuse any negative feelings toward the subject being presented. Short stories and personal testimonies have a calming effect and provide a mental picture. The Bible student will remember the lesson better and have an easier time making applications when they can visualize the concepts, their importance, and ways to put them into practice. Keep the love of Jesus for them the central theme of each lesson. Stories can be powerful tools in clarifying a point while strengthening your relationship with them.

Example Bible Study Presentation: Baptism

For example, the subject of baptism may be presented to someone who was sprinkled at birth. Give examples of the many ways people are baptized. Talk about the meaning of the word itself. To *baptize* is "to immerse, submerge, dip, or make very wet." Acknowledge that only one way truly qualifies as baptism. Lead the discussion to how Jesus was baptized. Talk about how glorious it was. The very atmosphere of His presence was holy and awe-inspiring. John the Baptist and those witnessing the event could perceive the purity of His character. Explain how humbled John the Baptist was to perform the service, yet Jesus insisted on baptism by immersion to fulfill prophecy and leave an example for the Christian church. "And Jesus answering said unto him, Suffer it to be so now: for thus it becometh us to fulfill all righteousness. Then he suffered him" (Matt. 3:15). The word translated in the King James Version as "suffer" means in the original Greek "to send forth." Jesus persisted that His request for baptism by immersion be honored immediately, and He "suffered" John or gave him the freedom to do so *right now*.

Paint a mental picture of the glorious scene—the Holy Spirit descending on Jesus' shoulder like a dove and the audible voice of God the Father. "And lo a voice from heaven, saying, This is my beloved Son, in whom I am well pleased" (Matt. 3:17). "Upon coming up out of the water, Jesus bowed in prayer on the river bank. A new and important era was opening before Him."[3] And it is the same with each one who is baptized according to the example that Jesus left us.

Finally, tell about your own baptism experience, the meaning of its symbols (Rom. 6:3, 4), and the need to receive the baptism of the Holy Spirit (John 3:5) as one embarks upon a new Christian walk. Keep the end in view—agreement to baptism, not because they are being pushed, but because they understand the need for the water baptism experience (whether it is the first time or rebaptism) and are willing to go all the way in giving their life to Christ.

As you advance through each presentation, stop along the way and make sure they agree with what they are learning. Take time to clarify when necessary. At the end of the study you should carefully and sensitively call for a decision of acceptance. If it does not come, find out where the question or confusion lies. Should the concerns not get cleared up in a timely manner, they can become the topics for the next study. Give assignments, encourage the use of the question-and-answer box if they are attending an evangelistic series, and let the evangelist address the issue.

Chapter Activities

1. Role-play helping someone who is a poor reader and doesn't write well.
2. Role-play entering into a discussion of the lesson on a front porch with someone who has not done their lesson.
3. Role-play calling for decisions of agreement and acceptance on aspects of a lesson.

Patience With the Nonresponsive

As you return faithfully each week and are stopped at the door, continue to encourage a little time to sit down together to review the study guides. At some point the Bible student should see in you someone in whom they can comfortably and confidently share their home and time with. It may happen on the second visit, or it may take longer. Certainly by the fourth visit they should not be still avoiding you or not inviting you in. If they are, assume that there exists a bigger challenge with letting you enter the home, such as an embarrassing home environment, they think you may belong to the Jehovah's Witnesses denomination, their pastor or family may have intervened, or there may be a fear that you are coming only to change their religious faith. Distinct signs of a wall of apprehension include:

- Never home or not answering the door when you know they are home, or even going inside the house when they see you coming. Worse yet, sending their spouse or child to the door to let you know they are not home or available (usually sick).
- Not returning calls when you leave a voicemail message or note in the door, not answering the phone once they recognize your phone number, or even hanging up when they realize it is you on the other end of the phone line.
- Continually putting off appointment dates for whatever reason.

- No matter how many times you visit them, call them, or encourage them, they have not begun to complete a lesson.
- Constantly talk about their pastor, fondly believing them to be their Bible authority and admitting that they have been counseled against further studies.
- The pastor, family, or friends are there when you arrive after which time they cease communication with you. Note: If guests are in the home, the person you came to see may not want to be rude and ask you to leave; therefore, voluntarily dismiss yourself—do not stay. Let your student know you will call them later to arrange another time.

You cannot write off anyone, recognizing that God placed in their spirit the original desire to receive Bible studies. Until they request that you not return, pray that the seed sown by the Spirit of God fell on fertile ground. Weeks after one of our students informed my partner and I that she wanted to discontinue the studies for the time being (she was under much pressure from her aunt who was also her pastor), I received a desperate call from the woman wanting prayer to overcome an addiction. She did not feel free to talk about her situation with her pastor, family, or friends, but she felt she could trust me and so appreciated the prayer I gave in her home. I arranged with her to pray together every morning at 8:00 for two weeks. At the same time we also talked and continued to build a relationship. Unfortunately, the Bible studies did not resume, but I believe the seeds sown over the phone strengthened her relationship with God. Here are additional approaches you can consider to handle situations in which the person who enrolled for the Bible studies avoids you for some reason:

- Let perhaps two or three weeks go by and try again to make contact just to talk and most of all listen and listen and listen.
- Recognize that God may be sending you to the home to invite another person in it, or even a neighbor, to receive Bible studies. That happens quite often.
- Learn by listening about things for which the person may desire prayer. Try to take advantage of any opportunity to pray in the home or with the person by phone. As I have already shared, I've received calls from people who never followed through with Bible studies with me but wanted me to pray with them. God works in miraculous ways to reach hearts through our prayers with and for people. We may not know until we see them in the kingdom of God how our powerful prayer seeds set them on the path for eternity.

- Reiterate the benefits of taking the Bible studies:
  - Having actual scriptural references on hand that affirm Christian beliefs.
  - Having a knowledgeable Bible teacher to whom one can direct questions and receive sound, biblical answers.
  - Gaining the habit of taking time each day or week for the study of God's Word.
  - Having something meaningful to study, rather than mere random Bible reading.
  - Drawing closer to God, which increases faith and trust in Him.
  - Growing spiritually as a result of better knowledge and understanding of the Word of God.
  - Combining Bible study with prayer and faith to see God make desired changes in the life and home and other circumstances.
  - Increasing Bible knowledge and understanding of God's Word.
  - Becoming a better witness for God.
  - Becoming a more spiritual person and family example.
  - Overcoming in areas of weakness and sin.
  - Finding a church home that offers spiritual growth and opportunities for outreach—thus meeting one's spiritual needs.
- Pray without ceasing and watch so that as God begins to give breakthroughs, you don't miss those opportunities to intervene with love.

> "Praying always with all prayer and supplication in the Spirit, and watching thereunto with all perseverance and supplication for all saints" (Eph. 6:18).

- Be bold for God, listen to His Spirit, and slip in lessons of doctrinal quality even when you cannot give a Bible study. Remember, a Bible study may not always be by way of a sit-down session. It can happen during the course of conversation, through a story of moral and spiritual value, through a personal testimony, or even as the answer to a question asked. Lessons of moral and/or spiritual merit come with the wisdom that only the Holy Spirit can give. Pray for it, and use it often.

Knowing the lesson we were to cover, I have often wedged into front porch conversation questions and factoids on the subject. Not being able to sit down with a person to have a Bible study should not hinder us from talking about the subject if they haven't completed the study guide. I remember a woman who never seemed to have her lesson completed or even know where it was. Since she was home and would come out on the porch, I would merely start talking about the content of the next lesson and pose questions of interest. We covered many lessons like that and gained many decisions. Sometime later another Bible instructor invited her to church, and she came. Whether you do it through formal or informal sessions, nothing can deter Bible instructors from their objective—to build relationships between God and human beings and person to person.

Remember too that the greatest Bible study that you may be able to give is your life, your cordiality, your patience, your testimonies, your obvious love and caring concern, your prayers of healing and hope, your listening ear, and your support in their times of need. May they see Jesus in you in such a way that their deepest desire is for the Jesus in you to become the Jesus in them. This too is the mystery of the plan of salvation.

> "To whom God would make known what is the riches of the glory of this mystery among the Gentiles; which is Christ in you, the hope of glory: Whom we preach, warning every man, and teaching every man in all wisdom; that we may present every man perfect in Christ Jesus: Whereunto I also labour, striving according to his working, which worketh in me mightily" (Col. 1:27-29).
>
> "Seeing then that all these things shall be dissolved, what manner of persons ought ye to be in all holy conversation and godliness, Looking for and hasting unto the coming of the day of God" (2 Peter 3:11, 12).

Chapter Activities

1. Discuss why building relationships is paramount to the ministry of Bible work.
2. List ideas on how to reach an avoider of the gospel with Bible studies.
3. Share your own experiences with building relationships through ministering to others.

---

[1] E. G. White, *Evangelism*, p. 485.
[2] *Ibid.*
[3] E. G. White, *The Desire of Ages*, p. 111.

CHAPTER 12

IN SYNC WITH THE PACE

"And they that be wise shall shine as the brightness of the firmament; and they that turn many to righteousness as the stars for ever and ever" (Dan. 12:3).

Do not expect everyone to demonstrate the same conversion experience. Always remember that it is Jesus, through the power of the Holy Spirit, who impresses the heart and gives to the sinner a new birth to a new life in Christ. It's just that simple. There may be "no violent conviction, no soul rending, no remorseful terrors." Like the children of Israel during their wilderness journey, when "they looked upon an uplifted Saviour; they lived. They saw the soul's need; they saw the Saviour's sufficiency and His claims; they heard His voice saying, 'Follow Me,' and they rose up and followed Him. Their conversion was genuine, and the religious life was just as decided as was that of others who suffered all the agony of a violent process."[1] "And I, If I be lifted up from the earth, will draw all men unto me" (John 12:32). What happens following their conversion experience with Christ—how it is captured, nurtured, and cultivated by the Bible instructor and the church family—is what will make a lasting difference.

"When truth is held as truth only by the conscience, when the heart is not stimulated and made receptive, only the mind is affected. But when the truth is received as truth by the heart, it has passed through the conscience, and has captivated the soul with pure principles. It is placed in the heart by the Holy Spirit, who reveals its beauty to the mind, that its transforming power may be seen in the character."[2]

You must study the strengths and weaknesses of your students, how they think, and their spiritual background and teaching, so as to establish a learning pace comfortable for them. Do not expect the Bible student to grasp everything presented the first, second, or even the third time. Rushing the process could cost a person's salvation just as surely as moving too slowly and not encouraging them. Always pray that God will give you the sensitivity to apply pressure when necessary, and when to stand back and approach from another perspective until your Bible students are in sync with the pace you are moving them through the studies.

"Though we cannot see the Spirit of God, we know that men who have been dead in trespasses and sins become convicted and converted under [His] operations. When we see . . . the evidence of [His] work on the heart and on the changed character"[3] of sinners come to Christ, it is the Bible workers' responsibility to be by their side to encourage, pray with, reassure through the Word of God, and prayerfully, patiently, sensitively lead step by step through the conversion process of belief and obedience. "With one hand the workers would take hold of Christ, while with the other they would grasp sinners and draw them to the Savior."[4]

What does the expression "Ye must be born again" mean? Should the desperate one look for a miraculous experience, a distinct sign of a changed heart, have a spiritual response that is visible and physical, hear the sound of a voice from heaven? Many are perplexed in regard to conversion. "Some have lived in sadness for years, waiting for some marked evidence that they were accepted by God. . . . They dare not profess Christ, because they fear it would be presumption to say that they are children of God. They are waiting for that peculiar change that they have been led to believe is connected with conversion."[5]

Some try to think back and attach a date to the very moment of their conversion encounter with God, not considering "that they were adopted into the family of God before that time. God accepted them when they became weary of sin, and having lost their desire for worldly pleasures, resolved to seek God earnestly. But, failing to understand the simplicity of the plan of salvation, they lost many privileges and blessings which they might have claimed had they only believed, when they first turned to God, that He had accepted them."[6] That is the point that you must learn how to reveal to your students as you seek to move them forward from principle to application of the truths they are learning.

As a Bible instructor you must not set up barriers to spiritual growth by presenting a checklist of must do's before God will accept the one weary of sin. Let the path be one of coming out of darkness into His marvelous light, not into the heat of judgmental legalism. Be very tender, encouraging, and positive with the progressing Bible student, assuring them of God's favor and acceptance all along the way. It appalls me to hear Bible instructors tell their students that they are going to hell or will be lost if they don't start following some belief they themselves hold as paramount. Such language is uncalled for under all circumstances and cannot be tolerated. No Bible instructor should ever be heard predicting excommunication of anyone for whom Christ gave His life because the Bible student has not yet grown to the level of fully embracing some doctrine. The steps to salvation may be ever so gradual for some. Their feet are unsteady, and they need your patience, further instruction, and your prayers. The life you portray and the counsel you give may become either a major incentive or a destructive barrier to their making that final decision to follow Jesus.

Bible students can fall into another more dangerous error. They are governed by impulse. Their sympathies stirred, they regard this flight of feeling as evidence that they are converted. But the principles that govern their life have not changed. The evidences of a genuine work of grace on the heart do not appear in feeling, but in the life. "By their fruits ye shall know them" (Matt. 7:20). The Bible study guides when used properly can help by presenting God's greater plan and purpose for their lives. If employed in a salvific, rather than a rushed and legalistic, manner, the lessons can clarify beliefs. When the Bible student is ready, review the specifics of the Second Coming, for example. Give guidance on how to keep the Sabbath day holy, help them identify the clean and unclean meats, develop a reference library of selected Ellen G. White and other devotional materials, establish God's standard of modesty, and guide them with suggestions for witnessing to family and friends.

These are some of the things that should happen in the course of your relationship with the Bible student, before, along with, and continuing after their attendance at evangelistic meetings. Regard each tenet as a conversion experience that may require a major lifestyle change and thus must be handled with much prayer, patience, and tender persistence. Take nothing for granted. Near the end of each Bible study, ask questions that review previously studied subjects and provide scriptural answers. That is the way to assure yourself that your Bible students are keeping pace. When they need more clarification, provide it through a variety of means, for example, give an assignment, offer other literature, review the scriptures or even the lesson, or address specific questions.

You will also come across those individuals who sincerely expect some irresistible force, over which they have no control, to overpower them. They overlook the fact that the believer in Christ is to cultivate their own salvation with fear and trembling (Phil. 2:12). Persons convicted of their sins must act their part. They must believe that God accepts their repentance, according to His promise. "Without faith it is impossible to please him: for he that cometh to God must believe that he is, and that he is a rewarder of them that diligently seek him" (Heb. 11:6).

While God accepts sinners when they first turn from sin to their Savior, "the work of grace upon the heart is not an instantaneous work. It is effected by continuous, daily watching and believing the promises of God. The repentant, believing one, who cherishes faith and earnestly desires the renewing grace of Christ, God will not turn away empty. He will give him grace. And ministering angels will aid him as he perseveres in his efforts to advance."[7] "All that the Father giveth me shall come to me; and him that cometh to me I will in no wise cast out" (John 6:37).

Chapter Activities

1. Discuss how you can tell when a Bible study student is not keeping pace.
2. Role-play reviewing a Bible doctrine in less than 10 minutes.
3. Discuss how Bible instructors can be too judgmental in their approach and how to avoid such pressuring.

---

[1] E. G. White, *Evangelism*, pp. 287, 288.

[2] Ellen G. White, "The Truth as It Is in Jesus," *Review and Herald*, Feb. 14, 1899.

[3] Ellen G. White, "Operation of the Holy Spirit Made Manifest in the Life," *Review and Herald*, May 5, 1896.

[4] Ellen G. White, "The Work Before Us," *Review and Herald*, Sept. 10, 1903.

[5] E. G. White, *Evangelism*, p. 286.

[6] *Ibid.*

[7] *Ibid.*, p. 287.

PART 3

LET THE EVANGELISTIC SERIES BEGIN

CHAPTER 13

OFF TO THE FINISH LINE

Nightly Pre- and Postintercessory Prayer Intervention

Once an evangelistic series starts, the weeks will race by quickly. Timing is everything in moving an individual from where they are to a decision to follow Christ. The goal, of course, is to see it happen with as many as possible during the few weeks the meetings last. To watch a person approach the foot of the cross is a solemn and awesome experience that cannot be taken for granted.

Never trust yourself to do God's bidding based on any human ability. Allow for time with God before the nightly evangelistic meeting to ensure that you are Spirit-led just as you would before you enter a home to meet with a family. During your personal meditation and nightly prayer commit the evangelist to the moving of the powerful, bold Spirit of God along with the entire evangelistic team. Pray for harmony and unity among the believers and an urgency to make guests feel welcomed and in a safe and friendly place. Cover the meeting place with the power of the Holy Spirit and the protection of God's ministering angels. Ask that they hold back the winds of strife in the hearts of the people and in the environment outdoors—that they will remove darkness on the subject being presented and that each attendee will receive the light of truth with thanksgiving.

Some will be wrestling with whether or not they will attend the meetings. Pray for the Spirit of God to win the battle raging right then in the hearts of many in their homes and those walking or driving by. Pray that every seat be filled. And above all, pray that salvation comes to the meeting place each night.

During the meeting you should not engage in casual conversation with other Bible instructors, but rather you should remain in a prayerful mode. Prayer power is always needed for spiritual breakthroughs. The enemy of souls will never willingly give up one over whom he has had control.

Some will be attending the meetings for the very first time, having missed previous nights. Others will be hesitant about being there and about all that they are hearing. God has given us the privilege to be a part of the royal priesthood reconciling the world to Him. Let us utilize our privilege to the fullest during such times.

> "And all things are of God, who hath reconciled us to himself by Jesus Christ, and hath given to us the ministry of reconciliation; To wit, that God was in Christ, reconciling the world unto himself, not imputing their trespasses unto them; and hath committed unto us the word of reconciliation" (2 Cor. 5:18, 19).
>
> "But ye are a chosen generation, a royal priesthood, an holy nation, a peculiar people; that ye should shew forth the praises of him who hath called you out of darkness into his marvelous light" (1 Peter 2:9).

As part of relationship building, welcome your attendees as they enter before the meeting starts and as you move with them to their seats. Walking into a place filled with unfamiliar faces, they may experience some apprehension from night to night. They will be looking for you, your smile, your cordiality. If they are already seated and the meeting hasn't started yet, greet them with small talk, perhaps asking how they have been enjoying the meetings thus far. It may even be convenient for you to sit next to one of your attendees from time to time, perhaps a different one each night. While not an imperative, they may see it as a caring gesture, especially if they are alone or need special assistance.

I have utilized the few minutes before the meeting convenes to introduce myself to attendees I haven't been able to catch at home, and besides relationship building, have successfully gained appointments. One individual was often out of town, but once I met her before the meeting, she was delighted to have me come to her home. She had many questions and had already made some decisions with regard to doctrinal differences. One of the major purposes in making unannounced introductory visits is so that a person will not prejudge Bible instructors before the person has actually met them. Meeting your attendees at the site of the evangelistic series also accomplishes that purpose.

At the end of the session Bible instructors should make sure everyone has a ride. If you brought people, try not to have them wait very long while you greet others before you take them home. That would be rude. Some nights the evangelist or head Bible instructor will call for a short meeting with the team, and, therefore, you may get delayed in leaving. If detained, let the guests you brought know that you were summoned to a meeting that shouldn't take long and make sure that it is OK with them—and try not to be long. See that they are seated and comfortable as they wait. If it is necessary for people you brought to leave immediately, excuse yourself from the meeting and take them to their destination. Relationship building comes first at all cost.

On the way home, talk about some of the highlights of the meeting or inquire whether they have questions that you can discuss at your next visit. Of course, you want to be as positive about the meeting as possible and about their having attended. Since it is all about relationship building, you certainly don't want to get into any negatives or disagreements with the presentations. Arrange a home visit to discuss any concerns they might have. Now that you know what the concerns are, you can be better prepared to make the appropriate clarifications.

Any available Bible instructors and/or the prayer team should plan to meet for the purpose of intercessory prayer as quickly as possible once the meeting place has emptied of people. It is vital that you spend time at the conclusion of each session to entreat the power of the Holy Spirit to embed the gospel into the hearts of the people. It is a time to pray not only for acceptance of the Bible teachings presented but also for the great peace that comes with a desire to obey the will and voice of God. Also, pray for angels to surround each one in attendance for a safe arrival at their destination and for the safety of their homes in their absence. Pray for the infilling of the Holy Spirit for the Bible instructors. And pray that they will be imbued with fresh clarity and wisdom as they review their notes of the night's sermon if they will need to explain anything further when they visit the homes of attendees.

The Most Important Role of Church Members

Following the nightly session, as far as possible the Bible instructor team should greet people, introduce themselves, and bid the guests a good night with the hope of seeing them again at the next meeting. Encourage every church member to do the same. It is always good to have the church members arrive early to welcome attendees and demonstrate friendliness toward new faces. Making new friends of guests will flow over into a vibrant church.

No talk about the Adventist Church should take place until directed by the evangelist. Just be friendly. Follow the example of Jesus with Nicodemus (John 3:1-7) and with the woman at the well (John 4:7-29), and that of Paul with Lydia (Acts 16:13-15). Such biblical examples demonstrate how friendliness can lead to the salvation of others. Because our great commission is to share the gospel throughout the world in an effort to usher in the second coming of Christ, Seventh-day Adventists should be the friendliest people on earth. Everywhere we may find ourselves should present to us a fresh opportunity to be friendly and cordial. We have a message to bring to the world, friends to make and bless with the love of Jesus. As people of God we should not hesitate to be welcoming.

The evangelistic series is an ideal place and time for all church members to grow and strengthen this virtue. God will use it to draw people to Himself. If there is one thing I truly believe church members can do to support the evangelist, one thing that will make the biggest difference in evangelism, enhance the quality of the meeting, swell the attendance and baptisms, and have the greatest influence in sustaining new believers, it is friendliness. It is critical that the church members understand and embrace the importance of the part they can play—friendliness among themselves and, putting self aside, friendliness toward every new face coming to the meeting and to the church. It will truly make a difference in the outcome and in the assimilation of new believers and visitors.

> "A man that hath friends must shew himself friendly: and there is a friend that sticketh closer than a brother" (Prov. 18:24).

Hopefully the friendliness of the membership will lead to greater support of the needs of the evangelistic series (e.g., transportation for guests, staffing various posts, and consistent attendance). And, of course, as new members join the congregation, friendliness will help make their incorporation much easier and their commitment to God more steadfast. How delightful it is to hear such comments as "Wow, people here are so friendly" or "We enjoy the people as much as the presentations."

The second most important involvement of the general membership of the churches involved in the evangelistic meetings after a welcoming environment is to ensure that the attendees have the very least amount of hindrances to hearing the gospel of salvation and receiving Christ as their Savior. The members can ease the journey to salvation by being actively attentive and involved in a number of ways, from the parking lot to ushering, from greeting to performing, from caring for the children to providing technical support, by coming early and not leaving until the end of the meeting, and much more. When the nightly meetings do not run smoothly, the obstructions and distractions actually become obstacles to the salvation of the attendees.

Friends and family are considered the A list for invitations to an evangelistic series. They already know much about what members believe through observing their lifestyle. Thus attending the meetings may indicate an interest in learning more. Therefore, members should:

- Contact friends and family members early on. Be excited about the sessions when around friends and family.
- Enlist friends and family members' interest in Bible studies, even if someone else actually conducts them.
- Make sure friends and family are aware of the upcoming meetings.
- E-mail (or snail mail) a copy of the announcement regarding the series to all they know.
- Ensure that friends and family receive several printed copies of the flyer. They may be willing to share them with others they know.
- Invite friends and family to all premeeting events.
- Make sure transportation is not an issue—bring friends and family or find them rides.
- Encourage friends to tell their friends and family about the upcoming meetings.
- Bring friends and family on special nights when members will receive a gift for having first-time guests.
- Refer their questions either to the evangelist's question-and-answer box or to a Bible instructor. It will encourage their return to hear the answer, or to be more open to a visit.
- Seat them close to the front, where there are fewer distractions.
- Be ready to give up their seat if seats run out, or a family wants to sit together.
- Help with small children and babies of friends/family members to prevent them from being a distraction. Also, keep their own children from being a disturbance.
- Park a little farther from the door of the meeting place if they can. It can be quite discouraging to a guest to have trouble finding a parking space.
- Be cordial and accommodating to all in attendance.
- Provide follow-up support to new members, not by giving counsel

and correction, which should be referred to the pastor or Bible instructor, but by welcoming, speaking cordially to the new members and visitors, touring and/or directing them around the church, inviting them to dinner and other church-related events, providing transportation, and attending to other needs as they arise. General friendly interest and concern goes a long way to making people feel comfortable in a new environment.

Encourage members to cooperate as far as possible in joining one of the important ministries actively operating during an evangelistic series. It takes many hands to make it a success. The more dedicated and faithful people involved, the better. The meetings will need help in many areas, such as:

- prayer team
- registration team
- greeter
- usher
- musician
- choir, group, and soloist performers
- parking attendant
- security
- crowd control
- money management team
- technician: computer, media, PA system
- platform management
- decorations
- flyer distribution
- interest gathering

Members can participate on a rotational basis if not available nightly. A director or coordinator should ensure that each auxiliary above is working at optimum efficiency and effectiveness, and should take corrective action when necessary.

I have included a chapter on the involvement of church members, because Bible instructors need to understand their role. They must focus on developing and following up interests, getting into the homes, and giving Bible studies. That is their responsibility. Certainly the members should assist in creating interest, but the work of the instructors is to lead individuals to Christ. Overextending oneself usually will cause something to be compromised. The safest approach is to stay in your lane as a Bible instructor.

Chapter Activities

1. Discuss the importance of the two crucial roles of church members during an evangelistic series.
2. List those who would be on an A list for inviting to the meetings.
3. Discuss ways to get church members to be actually friendly.

Dress for Success

First and foremost, Bible instructors *are ambassadors for Christ.* It is very important that their dress be recommended by the evangelist or Bible instructor coordinator, who may not feel a uniform is necessary. In contrast, some evangelists do prefer a uniform style for Bible instructors for the entire length of the series or, at the very least, on occasion. The most formal uniforms have included black suits and white blouses/shirts with the same coordinated style of scarf/tie and often with white gloves.

Grooming should be conservative (e.g., no big decorative pins, lavish hairdos, headdresses, or heavy makeup). Shoes should be comfortable, yet stylish. Always entertain the thought that you represent the King of kings foremost, putting selfish interest and self-aggrandizement out of the picture. The ushers and greeters should never dress in the same uniform as the Bible instructor. It gives the attendee a sense of comfort when they notice the presence of their instructor, and a distinctive style for that position helps the attendee to spot them more easily.

When we do not recommend any uniform during the hours of the meeting, dress should still remain conservative, appropriately fitting, and stylish. Shoes should also be stylish. Business casual would be appropriate for men and women, since we are on God's business. Avoid jewelry, tennis shoes, and tightly fitting clothes. Neat and modest apparel is the counsel of God's Word. Bible instructors should never give the impression that they are shabby and needy, or that they are attracting unnecessary attention to themselves. There have been times I've had to turn my head when my Bible instructor partner bent down with a low, loose neckline or short skirt. Always evaluate the possibility of dress being a distraction, or worse, an embarrassment. It would be far better to choose a few appropriately fitting outfits and wear them only during the hours of the meetings. Always keep in mind that you model the way for those who are following you to the kingdom. Let your dress reflect the level of expectation you hope others will uphold.

> "In like manner also, that women adorn themselves in modest apparel, with shamefacedness and sobriety; not with broided hair, or gold, or pearls, or costly array" (1 Tim. 2:9).

Also carefully consider dress when visiting the home of an attendee for any reason. Bible instructors are first of all professionals, chosen by God to fulfill the highest calling given to humanity. For women, the wearing of slacks of any kind is at the discretion of the evangelist, as is the tie and sleeve length for the men. Dress in a manner that will not distract in any way from your special vocation. A rule of thumb is that the spontaneous response of the one being visited should never be a gasp, stare, or quick head/eye turn for any reason based on appearance. They should not be drawn to something you have on such that it becomes a subject of conversation. Dress should be modestly conservative, yet stylish. Business suits, slacks, shirts/blouses, dresses, or skirts of decent length for sitting are all appropriate for the home. Ties are encouraged for men but not always required. Remember, it's not about us—we are on assignment for the Lord.

Not only your dress but also your demeanor is important. You should conduct yourself in a humble, respectful manner. As a Bible instructor you cannot ever afford to be rude, impatient, or sharp tongued, but rather be patient in listening and helpful, polite, and reserved. All too often I've seen Bible instructors talking while chewing gum, wearing socks and tennis shoes with a dress (comfortable and stylish walking shoes would look much more professional), or with straw hats, jewelry, and low-cut garments (to name merely some of the inappropriate attire).

Following in the footsteps of Jesus who is your leader, you should season every spoken word with the wisdom and love of God. Even your demeanor is a witness that lifts up (or puts down) the name of Jesus. Your smile should tell of your joy in the Lord (always smile), and your voice should reflect His tender love (practice a kind way of speaking). How you walk should indicate that you walk with God, so walk like it. And your dress should indicate that you feel comfortable being created in the image of God.

Chapter Activities

1. Discuss dress ideas for men and women for the nightly meetings and for daily visitation.
2. Discuss your opinions about uniform dress for the nightly meetings.
3. Discuss candidly your opinion about the demeanor that should characterize the Bible instructor.

Be Visible and Accessible

Being as visible as possible by moving around the auditorium is a more subtle means of relationship building. People feel more comfortable and relaxed when warmly greeted and seeing a familiar face. A relaxed person, I think you will agree, is more apt to receive the Word of God with the right spirit than someone who is tense and apprehensive. Therefore, you would do well to prepare the audience for the evangelist's presentation by walking about cordially greeting individuals and taking time to chat with them before the meeting starts.

Be as accessible and flexible as possible during the nightly sessions (e.g., greeting guests, assisting with the distribution of any gifts or handouts, and being prepared to hand out and pick up decision cards and pencils). A genuinely warm and cordial welcome is crucial to the attractiveness and professionalism of any evangelistic series.

If you as a Bible instructor are not excited about the night's meeting, why should the attendees be? If you feel tired, overwhelmed, unsure, etc., give it over to the Spirit of God to remove and replace with the joy of knowing you are fulfilling your highest calling in Christ Jesus—the privilege of being a representative for Him. Open yourself up in prayer for the infilling of the Holy Spirit to touch lives through your life with the love of Jesus. Take some deep, relaxing breaths and ask God to fill you with His Spirit of love for each person, and an overpowering desire to see every person saved in the kingdom of God.

Attendees should regard you as a welcome sight as they enter the auditorium from night to night. As a Bible instructor you should consider yourself just as much a greeter as those designated for that role. As they get to know you better, they may often seek you out just because you are pleasant and it's so nice to be around such people at the end of a long day of work. Hopefully each night will have first-time guests who will be impressed by several warm greetings (in addition to the friendliness of Seventh-day Adventist members).

While the primary individuals you as a Bible instructor will look out for will be those assigned to you, you should treat everyone warmly. Be alert to signs of discontent or dissenting talk that you need to report to the assigned instructor, lead Bible instructor, or even to the evangelist. It is important to respond to concerns, issues, questions, comments, and emergencies as soon as possible. The Bible instructor should also learn the names of all the people, even if they are not on your assigned list.

Connecting with the guests provides opportunities to let them know how much everyone appreciates their attendance, and will get them excited about the night's subject. Make eye contact as you greet the attendee, and shake hands warmly. Encourage them to sit close to the front of the auditorium and even escort them (or place them in the care of an usher to do so) if they seem hesitant. It may be necessary to assist them personally in the signing-in process, securing the next lesson, and/or taking their children to the children's program. Also, it is always a good idea to determine whether they have any questions that they would like the evangelist to address. Help them with pencil and paper to write their question(s) and put them in the question-and-answer box.

Learn to move through the greeting process with each attendee as quickly, yet as cordially, as possible. You will not want to spend too much time with each one, because as others come in, you need to remain accessible. While not seeming rushed, move them along quickly. Should they want to talk at length, ask for a time in which you can discuss any issue that they want help on. If they seem to need it urgently, pull them aside and address the situation. Most preferred would be to arrange a home visit. Should their concern appear more pressing, inquire whether they have been assigned to a Bible instructor or visited by one. And if so, ask that individual to assist you with the attendee. But if not, lead them to a quiet area to hear the problem. It is always a good idea to have a second Bible instructor with you (and definitely if it is a person of the opposite gender). Should things start to get out of hand, which can indeed happen, you'll have help to keep the individual under control. As far as possible, keep the focus on the night's meeting. Ideally, other matters should be taken up at another time. Perhaps it may even be appropriate to invite them to meet with the prayer team for special prayer, or lead them quickly to a quiet area to pray together. If they have been assigned to another Bible instructor, assure them that you will pass on their concern to that person, who will follow up with the question or issue.

Chapter Activities

1. Review some of the ways you can be visible during the nightly meetings.
2. List some of the types of interaction you should have with your attendees and other guests during the nightly meetings.
3. Discuss how to handle feelings of exhaustion or discouragement during the nightly meeting.

Be Flexible and Responsible

Every Bible instructor must be flexible during the evangelistic meetings. Plan to arrive early and remain afterward until dismissed. Of course, an exception would be the need to transport guests (if at all possible, assign the task to others not on the Bible instructor team). Do not come in and sit like a guest. You should see yourself as responsible for the best possible outcome of each nightly meeting. If the series does not have enough volunteers, the instructors may find themselves asked (or volunteer) to assist at a contact station (greeter, helper at registration desk, or in another area that should be manned by those not part of the Bible instructor team) or to function somewhere behind the scenes.

Bible instructors may even need to participate on the program (lesson review, song service, pianist, soloist, opening/closing prayer, etc.). You may be blessed with special gifts of talent that would add much to the atmosphere of worship and learning. There is something for each Bible instructor to do. Do not wait to be called on. If you notice an area that needs support, as you are available and can step in, do so and do your best. But it would be preferable if you can find someone to handle the need, allowing you to remain at your post. As a Bible instructor, take full responsibility for ensuring the professionalism and smooth flow of the nightly meetings.

Strategic Seating

The instructor's full focus and responsibility during an evangelistic series is to support the evangelist's efforts to draw people to Christ. That means that you are their eyes, their ears, their mouthpiece, their feet, and their hands to accomplish this, not letting the needs of even one person who attends any meeting fall through the cracks by being overlooked. Use the following guidelines to be most effective in this role:

1. You may want to position yourself near the back or side of the auditorium so that you can see the people who arrive late, and make a note of what they have missed. Near the back, or back side, of the auditorium is also a strategic place for Bible instructors not only to observe who is in attendance but also to view the reaction of the audience to aspects of the message presented and appeals made. A good instructor learns to focus on the people as well as on the evangelist. Body language and how quickly people respond serve as pretty reliable indicators of the level of acceptance.
2. No more than two Bible instructors should sit together. Ideally

they should disperse among those attending. It is even permissible to sit with different people on your assigned list each night, but only if it is convenient. Be cordial and friendly, remembering to take advantage of every opportunity to build relationships, to break down any barriers, and to foster feelings of comfort with the presentation.

3. Always have whatever the ushers are passing out just in case someone near you needs the materials. In addition, always be prepared with supplies of decision cards and pencils each night.
4. Be alert to anyone who doesn't have a Bible, not merely to lend them your own, but to find the texts (assuming that there may be a reading problem, or the person does not know how to look for Scripture passages). Many evangelists now use graphics that display their texts on the screen and provide a presentation outline at the conclusion of the meeting. This is very helpful. Searching for texts and jotting down notes can be a major distraction for attendees.
5. Whenever you have a convenient moment to do so, greet those near you. Later, when you are not with them, jot down a few notes of what you observed or learned from them to help you remember some specifics when you see them again.
6. Make a note of those you noticed who showed obvious reactions during the sermon. Try to greet them after the service and inquire, "What did you think of the presentation tonight?" If they are positive, praise God with them. If they are despondent or negative in any way, encourage them to use the series question-and-answer box. Also, ask, "Has a Bible instructor contacted you to meet you and assist you with your questions?" If not, then ask them for their name and phone number and assure them that someone will be in touch with them. Thank them for attending the evangelistic series and let them know that the next presentation may clear up whatever their question is. Always end by using the power of suggestion, such as "I'll look for you tomorrow night."

Chapter Activities

1. Discuss the strategy of Bible instructors sitting along the side or in the rear of the meeting auditorium.
2. Discuss what you would do if you overheard someone speaking negatively at the meetings.

3. List some advantages of having a question-and-answer box during the series.

Good Note-taking

Bible instructors should take good notes each night of the evangelistic series, for two reasons: 1. If someone assigned to them misses a meeting, you will be able to study the presentation privately and then review it with those not in attendance. But remind them that hearing it secondhand is no substitute for experiencing the evangelist's presentation of the important subjects firsthand. 2. Good note-taking keeps you on track while reviewing the night's missed lesson with the attendee. Even have the evangelist or Bible instructor coordinator go over your notes prior to the home visitation so that you will know what points to stress.

During an evangelistic series, continually seek to strengthen the connection between the attendee and the evangelist. Under the power and anointing of the Holy Spirit, the evangelist initially directs the path to their salvation and calls for decisions for Christ. The instructor's role is to make that decision as natural and effortless an experience as possible for both evangelist and attendee. It happens most smoothly when attendees are present every night, visited often for intervention purposes, and given general support as they progress along the path of spiritual growth and assimilation. Before you can bring them to Christ, you must first win the hearts of the persons assigned to you by being warm and friendly, positive and supportive.

Making Contact at the Conclusion of the Meeting

At the end of each meeting, greet everyone. Encourage Adventists and non-Adventists alike to invite and bring guests. Praise those bringing others. Thank all for their attendance and always end with "I'll look for you tomorrow night" or "I'll see you tomorrow night." Refrain from discussing the topic of the presentation after the meeting. It could get lengthy or loud. Both could have a negative impact. It would be far better to meet with the attendee in their home to discuss any questions or concerns they may have.

If the person has concerns that you can easily address, do so. However, if they are of a more general nature, jot them down on the question card and place it in the question-and-answer box for the evangelistic team to address.

When you speak to your assigned interest after the meeting, be very cordial. Confirm your next home visit day and time, and express how much you are looking forward to reviewing briefly any of the presentations with them. If you are planning to bring a book or other supplementary materials, let them know that you will have something very special for them.

Chapter Activities

1. Discuss the benefits of note-taking each night during an evangelistic series. Develop a note-taking format.
2. Think of some disadvantages of sharing your notes with frequently absent attendees.
3. Discuss why the Bible instructor should take the conclusion of a meeting night very seriously.

CHAPTER 14

BACKSTORY

It is at the discretion of the evangelist when visitation should start once the meetings begin. In a six-week series, expect it to commence no later than the middle of the second week and as early as after the third night's presentation.

The evangelist will likely make an announcement to the audience about the presence of Bible instructors and their home visits. That way they will encourage a cordial reception on the part of the attendee. During an evangelistic series it is the responsibility of the Bible instructors to visit the homes of everyone on their list at least once during the week to encourage continued attendance, to review and make clarifications on the subjects preached, and to waylay any potential challenges. Visiting or phoning too frequently, however, could have negative consequences.

Staying too long in a home and giving too many proof texts are just as bad as visiting too often. It could turn off people from wanting you in their home, and in order to avoid you, they may not return to the meetings. Most individuals have their nightly scheduled routines, especially if they are working and/or have children. A break in their regular practices could cause them to give up on coming out nightly to the meetings. Keep the visit short (around 30 to 45 minutes) and simple (six to 10 texts). Know your purpose for the visit and seek to accomplish it sensitively and skillfully. Always leave the home on an inspirational note and after prayer.

While everyone has a backstory—a life story and distinct circumstances—you must be very careful not to pry. People will usually share as they become more comfortable with you. Allow them to do so at their pace, and do not dig so deeply or pose unqualified counsel to the extent that you disrespect privacy or insult or embarrass the individual. On the other hand, learning the backstory can contribute much to how and when you will present various aspects of the gospel. As you discover more about the person or family, feel free to share a few positive bits of information about your own life, such as where your family originated, something about your children or siblings, how much you enjoy what you do from home to home. It's all about building relationships.

Your efforts should also include getting to know others in the home. They could have a very definite impact on whether the Bible studies will continue at any given point. Their opinion can have anywhere from a positive to a devastating effect on your relationship with your attendee. Therefore, you cannot ever ignore or disrespect them in any way. On the contrary, I also make sure I cordially meet, greet, and give time and attention to anyone else I see in the home, and solicit their interest in attending the meetings and also to joining the attendee in the presentation reviews. It is also key to developing an interest to be followed up long after the conclusion of the evangelistic series.

JoAnn was eager to take Bible studies. She did not have a church home and knew someone that attended the local Seventh-day Adventist congregation. I noticed that she had two teenage children in the home. I always greeted them warmly before our Bible studies started. Their home was small enough for them to hear our Bible studies from their room. In fact, they appreciated the studies I was having with their mom. Every time we got together, I sought to coax the young people to help us find the Bible texts and give their opinion about them. One day I told them that I had brought something very special for them as I had promised at our previous meeting—their own Bible study guides. From then on they joined us, and we had wonderful times studying the Word of God together. We also discussed how to handle challenges they faced with peers at school, as well as helping with life choices. Although not baptized when their mother was, by summer they were ready. Others in the home are just as much potential candidates for heaven as the person targeted for the visit.

Note: Quoting from Ellen G. White or making statements that can be proved only from her writings are unfair to the new attendee and may make you and the entire evangelistic series appear cultish, or, just as bad, lead to a discussion that distracts from your purpose in the home.

Chapter Activities

1. Make a list of personal information that should absolutely not be shared with an attendee.

2. Make a list of personal information that would be relationship building to share with an attendee.
3. Discuss how others in the household could affect (positively or negatively) your relationship with your attendee.

Two Make a Team

"Calling the twelve about Him, Jesus bade them go out two and two through the towns and villages. None were sent forth alone, but brother was associated with brother, friend with friend. Thus they could help and encourage each other, counseling and praying together, each one's strength supplementing the other's weakness. In the same manner He afterward sent forth the seventy. It was the Savior's purpose that the messengers of the gospel should be associated in this way. In our own time evangelistic work would be far more successful if this example were more closely followed."[1]

"There is need of two working together; for one can encourage the other, and they can counsel, pray, and search the Bible together. In this they may get a broader light upon the truth; for one will see one phase, and the other another phase of the truth. If they are erring, they can correct one another in speech and attitude, so that the truth may not be lightly esteemed because of the defects of its advocates. If the workers are sent out alone, there is no one to see or correct their errors; but when two go together, an educating work may be carried on, and each worker become what he should be—a successful soul winner."[2]

In an evangelistic campaign each Bible instructor may be appointed a partner or allowed to select one. New partners can do a number of things to ensure their success as a team. We strongly encourage the following:

Become prayer partners. Set a time daily, preferably early in the morning, when you will have the least distractions and hindrances to praying together. Be flexible and sensitive to each other's needs, challenges, and responsibilities.

Become Bible study partners, especially if you are new at presenting the Bible study guides. Review the lesson material together to ensure that both are aware of the other's thoughts about various aspects of the lesson. It also provides an opportunity to make clarifications on the topic to be discussed in the home.

Become business partners. Work together to share responsibilities, such as who drives, fuel and other expenses, recordkeeping, organizing the route for visitation, and standing in when the partner cannot meet an appointment.

Become team teachers. When it is your turn to be the presenter, be prepared not only to review the lesson but to answer questions and meet objections from the attendee on the subject. As a partner, be supportive in the spirit of prayer and in assisting the family by waylaying potential distractions, helping to find scriptures or completing the lesson, looking up other Scripture references that may contribute to the discussion, etc.

Become friends. Relationship building is just as meaningful to Bible instructor teams as that between instructor and attendee. Learn to make every effort to function harmoniously with one another: be on time, be considerate, refuse to gossip or discredit, be patient and forgiving, and be benevolent and Christlike toward each other. Overlook the minor faults and learn to see the best in each other. If differences become intolerable, part in the spirit of love and seek another partner.

Be professionals. Learn to appreciate each other's talents, gifts, idiosyncrasies, and best effort. Always treat each other with respect and support, i.e., be cordial, work selflessly, and be sensitive to each other, especially when giving corrections. Remember, building relationship must be first at all costs.

The Bible instructor assigned an interest's name will do the introductions, lead the conversation, and conduct the review of the lesson. The second instructor should feel free to speak when impressed to do so, but never taking over the discussion. Both should refrain from correcting each other in the presence of the attendee unless absolutely necessary. You can discuss that later just between the two of you. Nor should partners debate differences of opinion or understanding of Scripture either in the home or when alone. It will alleviate differences if the pair have lesson studytime together prior to the presentations and do their research, including seeking help from the pastor or from a more experienced Bible scholar on the subject.

The focus must always be on the attendee, and you should not take for granted your knowledge of the subject. Rather you should personally study the lesson in detail, including possible objections and potential questions, as well as a review with your partner. If either of you have questions with regard to a lesson, you should meet together and go over them prior to the visitation. You should be professional and know with confidence the subject matter you plan to cover. One of your responsibilities is to make certain that you have thoroughly answered your own questions and that you have rehearsed your presentation beforehand.

The partner can be an important asset to the success of a visit. If you do not feel confident to present a lesson review, you should discuss it with your partner and allow them to conduct the study while you take notes. The home may have little ones who need to be distracted or even animals to restrain. Partners may run errands to the car to get supplies when necessary. They may assist the attendee in finding texts and make comments from time to time but must never take over the discussion.

Any note-taking should be appropriate. Never jot down something in the home that you would not want the attendee accidentally to read (e.g., comments about them, their home, or their children). If the attendee happened to pick up your notepad, they should be able to read your notes without embarrassment or disgust. A simple note that the attendee is going to need clothes to wear to church, the baby cries a lot, or the family needs food, while appearing innocent, could be insulting. Make such personal notes later in private and never take them into the home. Give the enemy no avenue that could possibly lead to jeopardizing your relationship with your attendee.

If for any reason you and your Bible instructor partner seem to be constantly in conflict, carefully evaluate the relationship. I've had the experience when my partner and I had completely different ideas on how to do things. For example, I didn't mind working long hours, but my partner didn't like to start visitation until the afternoon. It was important to me to return again to the homes of people who did not show up at the meetings, while my partner thought once a week was enough, whether the person was home or not. Sometimes I could work through two lessons with an attendee, although my partner felt that was being too aggressive. Other times my partner was ready to go home, but I still wanted to visit one or two more families. Finally we decided that perhaps we both needed a change in partners so that we could remain friends. Although there was nothing wrong with either of our views, it just makes for a more wholesome and workable relationship when the partners can be in comfortable agreement on decisions. It was not about us—it was all about the work God had entrusted to us.

Chapter Activities

1. Discuss each of the points on how to have successful teamwork.
2. Discuss possible ways my partner and I could have made our relationship work.

3. Discuss the importance of having a partner in Bible study ministry.

Organizing for the Visit

> "Not only is the truth to be presented in public assemblies; house to house work is to be done. Let this work go forward in the name of the Lord."[3]

Once the evangelist has given the OK to start visitation, you can begin making appointments. Setting the appointment for the home visit of one who is attending the meetings is a little different than with someone who enrolled to receive Bible study guides. No doubt the evangelist will have the Bible instructors stand or come up front and forewarn the audience that they will be doing visitation to provide individual support throughout the series by answering questions and making certain each topic is clear. Thus the evangelist will solicit the cordiality of the audience for any Bible instructor that comes by. This introduction always helps a lot in gaining entrance into the home.

In small towns it may be convenient to stop by the homes unannounced for the first visit to those who have been attending. In large cities, however, such an approach will likely not work well because of time consumed in heavy traffic, the distance between homes, and the number of people on your list to visit. Therefore, if the evangelistic meetings take place in a large city, you will usually set up appointments. If you feel comfortable talking with the attendee on the phone to arrange visits, that would be preferable. Because of the time it takes to traverse a city, it may be wise to make certain the person will be home.

Make appointments with a person before the meeting begins only if the individual doesn't seem to be in a rush to go inside and be seated and at the end of the meeting night only if the attendee doesn't appear to be in a hurry to leave. Some attendees arrive early, making it a good time to chat and set appointments. If the person is of the opposite sex, be sure your partner is with you so as not to give the wrong impression. The end of the night's evangelistic presentation is normally an ideal time to get with your attendee, greet them warmly, and set up a home visit.

By being creative and determined, you'll find many ways you can learn who your attendee is, such as:

Asking people their names when you greet them at the entrance as they arrive and exit.

The registration table can be quite helpful in identifying attendees by name, and those working there can point them out to you if you haven't met them yet. By giving them the person's name, they can be on the lookout for the individual when he or she signs in for the night's program.

Before the meeting starts, walk up and down the rows and aisles and become acquainted with those who appear to be non-Adventists.

Rather than an usher, the Bible instructor can collect decision cards/quiz cards from each row and quickly review the names.

Ask other Bible instructors about the name you are seeking. They may have met your interest already, or a family member or friend of the person.

Meet people in the parking lot, hallway, children's program, even the restroom, wherever guests might be.

If it is your first encounter, let them know how much you have been looking forward to getting to know them better and that the visit will be brief.

When speaking to an attendee to arrange a visit, the Bible instructor should already have in mind the scope of the city and which parts of the city will be visited on which days. At this point, each Bible instructor team will preferably have a good GPS or possess a city map of the targeted sites involved (much more cumbersome).

Organize the route either the night before or early in the day. Working in pairs, collaborate on whom to visit based on location. Map out the location of homes and decide on the route. It should definitely include appointments already set for that day. Record clear directions to each home. Homes located near each other should be first on the list. As the evangelistic series progresses, expect that your visitation schedule and route will change from day to day. Therefore, it is necessary to plan your visits carefully so that you will use your time most efficiently.

Visits should last no longer than 30 to 45 minutes. Bible instructor partners should know which study guide they will review in each home to ensure a united front prior to arrival. In addition, they should discuss what they will need at each place, i.e., the lessons to review, any supplementary items, and promised gifts, reference materials, and equipment if using some type of media. A visitation checklist sheet will help make sure all is prepared.

If no one is home, either have a note card that you can leave in the door that simply states that you came by and that you will look forward to seeing the person at the meeting, or contact them by phone to rearrange your visit. You can also develop various types of statements and print them on small cards for this purpose, such as:

- "Thank you for enrolling in [series name]. We have your special gift. Please call me at [phone number] to arrange delivery."
- "Sorry I missed you. I will give you a call later to arrange a short visit."
- "Sorry I missed you. I can be reached at [phone number] to arrange an introductory visit."
- "Your Bible study guide is ready. Please give me a call."
- "Sorry I missed you. I'll see you at tonight's meeting. Let's try to meet to arrange for the delivery of your gift."

Chapter Activities

1. Discuss some strategies for visitation when people are not home.
2. Discuss some of the materials and supplies that you should carry in the car used for visitation.
3. Discuss any benefits or drawbacks to leaving a note when the attendee is not home.

Setting the Appointment for a Home Visit

An approach may be: "It is our custom to give everyone who registers to attend the [name of evangelistic series] a short visit to welcome you and tell you a little more about the series and what can be expected. We won't be long at all. Are you home during the day?" [If yes:] "Would 11:00 or 11:30 a.m. on Thursday work for you?" [If not:] "Would 6:30 or 7:30 on Thursday evening work better for you?" Keep your promise not to be long but make the occasion as valuable as possible. And by all means, be on time.

The first visit should be short, with the attendee doing most of the talking in response to general questions—how they found out about the meetings, etc. You may ask questions about information that the person has volunteered if common sense suggests you would not be digging too deeply. It is extremely important not to probe. The first visit should be strictly to make sure that the attendee is excited about the meetings and will return. Let them know of the materials available to them nightly and that you will be checking in on them regularly to answer any questions or address their concerns. Ask them when will be the best time to get together to review the nightly subjects. Feel free to share very briefly general information about yourself as well. Always end with a brief prayer of God's blessing upon their home.

At-the-Door Evangelistic Series Follow-up

When the Bible instructor pair first gets into the car for visitation, they should pray together, preparing their own hearts to be moved by the Holy Spirit and then claiming a receptive spirit in the hearts of the people to be visited. If done sincerely, there is no need to stop and pray before every home. Decide who will present the lesson and who will maintain a prayerful spirit in the home. The presenter should actually be the one assigned the name of the person being visited.

Carefully review your notes on each person to be visited (e.g., names of those in the household, prayer concerns, and nights attended and missed). If anyone missed lessons, have extra ones organized in the car. Should they have skipped meeting nights, be prepared with sermon outlines or to highlight the points of the sermon and gain confirmation on the concepts presented. Always keep in mind why you are at the home. Ask yourself the following two questions: What is to be accomplished there? What supplies/materials will be needed?

Knock, or ring door bell, and wait patiently before repeating. Stand back from the door so that those inside can see you clearly. Have a warm expression on your face, confidently believing God is in charge and He will do something special through your ministry to the person. Remember, the battle is not yours—it's the Lord's. Discretely, not obviously, observe the outdoor surroundings as well as the indoor environment.

Home visits should never be for a casual purpose unless a member of the family asks you to attend some special occasion. You are a professional Bible instructor on a divine mission for one purpose only—the salvation of precious souls. Have a definite purpose toward some specific end when you enter a home. Recognize that once you are in the home, God may have a completely different agenda than the one you planned. Be careful to hear present needs and be sensitive to address them first, placing them ahead of your predetermined goal. It may be that a particular challenge consumes the meeting time. That's all right, because relationships come first. Try to weave into the discussion the main parts of the Bible concepts you had planned to present, and by all means have closing prayer together.

Chapter Activities

1. Make a list of what should, and should not be, taken into the home of an attendee.
2. Role-play arranging an appointment with an attendee under various circumstances (e.g., at the meeting place, in the parking lot, and on the phone).

3. Role-play introducing yourself to an attendee at the door.

Remember FORT

After the exchange of pleasantries, here are some starter examples that you can consider for safe questioning. They follow the acronym of FORT. Different questions work better in various situations. Pray that the Spirit of God will lead you to those questions that will build relationships. Also, remember that you do not need answers to all questions at the very first visit. As you continue to visit attendees and build relationships of trust, they will share additional information that will help in your ministry to their needs. Study these examples:

F—Family

Tell me a little about your family.
How is your family doing?
What are the ages of your children?
What school do they attend?
Are any of your children married?
How long have you been married?
How long have you lived in [city]?

O—Occupation

Do you work?
Where do you work?
What kind of work do you do?
What shift do you work?
Is it enjoyable?
How long have you worked there?
Have you been into [type of work] all your career?
Do you and your husband both work outside the home?
Are you both off on weekends?
Do you work overtime?

R—Religion	What is your religious background? Are you a Christian? How long have you been a Christian? Are you satisfied with your religion? Do you attend church regularly? What church do you attend? Does the whole family belong to the same church? Where is your church located? How did you first come in contact with [name of evangelistic series]?
T—Testimony	Share a personal testimony. Share general information about yourself and family, giving glory to God.

Below are suggestions on how to handle oneself in the home:

- The goal of FORT is to become acquainted with the attendees assigned to you.
- Use only two or three questions from each category.
- Don't give the impression that you are prying into their personal business. If you sense that they feel uncomfortable with some of the questions, back off quickly and share something about yourself.
- When it is appropriate, give some personal information about yourself as it relates to each question.
- Do not ask questions to which the answer is obvious.
- Make good use of spin-off questions. For example: "Are you married?" "No, I'm single." "Do you enjoy single life?"
- Make a mental note of important information gathered and write it down in private after you have left the home.
- If you sense that your interest is uncomfortable with the first part of FORT, make a quick transition to Testimony.
- Show genuine interest and concern for your attendee as you become better acquainted.

Chapter Activities

1. Study FORT. What part of it would you be most comfortable with asking or not comfortable with using?

2. Role-play FORT.
3. Discuss the benefits and drawbacks of "small talk" in the home of attendees.

Share the Advantages of Attendance

Assure the individual of the many benefits of attending and completing the free series that [name of evangelistic series] has brought to the community. Some of the more popular ones include:

- the qualifications of the Bible-based speaker/Bible teacher
- professional assistance to ensure a successful, spiritually rewarding experience
- free Bible study guides and/or subject outlines
- a free Bible
- a visit from the Bible instructor team at least once per week to review the subjects (an invaluable service at no cost to them)
- question-and-answer box for questions they've always had
- child-care services so parents can focus on the presentation
- transportation for those who absolutely need it
- nightly reviews of the previous meeting's subject
- a prayer team available to pray with them about their special challenges
- other wonderful materials, books, and gifts to reinforce and expand their learning and build their religious library
- an opportunity to meet neighbors and other Christians in their community
- exciting nightly experiences and a certificate at the conclusion when they have completed all the lessons
- no charges or fees for all this, though there may be items available at some point for purchase, but it will always be optional, never a mandatory part of the course

The features will, of course, vary from series to series and from evangelist to evangelist, so be sure you know exactly which aspects to mention. Encourage the attendee to bring friends and family. Most evangelistic series will offer gifts to those who bring guests. If not, it may be possible for you to privately give your attendee a special gift for doing that. Some evangelistic series provide special classes for the youth, along with child care, transportation assistance, and community resources for special needs. The question-and-answer box is also normally available for attendees to hear responses from the evangelists or associate pastors. If such things are offered, make sure your attendee is aware of them.

On the first visit your focus should be on developing a wholesome relationship, building a bond of trust, and gaining a commitment for nightly attendance. Don't try to dig so deeply that you turn off the attendee from ever returning. On the contrary, the first visit should have the objective of establishing confidence in the Bible instructors and the evangelist.

By getting further acquainted with the attendee, over time you may learn more about what you can anticipate as potential challenges from their family, friends, pastor, or even employer. Remember you only have a few minutes to make an extremely important impression. Stay focused and don't waste a moment of it. Be as though you are reuniting with a best friend. But do not attempt an in-depth Bible study on the very first visit.

To review, carry on a few minutes of small talk (family, job, how they learned about the meeting, what their expectations are). Then tell the attendee a little about the evangelist, remind them of some of the features of the series that may interest them, and encourage them to invite others. It is not necessary to do an oversell. The attendee will find out all they need to know during the course of the meetings.

Chapter Activities

1. Prioritize what to share with attendees on the initial visit.
2. Discuss how you as a Bible instructor can be just as much a listener as one who has much to share. Which is more important?
3. Role-play how you would get someone to invite others to the meetings.

---

[1] E. G. White, *The Desire of Ages*, p. 350.

[2] Ellen G. White, "The True Missionary's Dependence Is in God," *Review and Herald*, July 4, 1893.

[3] E. G. White, *Evangelism*, p. 431.

CHAPTER 15

HACK GOOD DIVOTS

During the series of meetings the evangelist, not the Bible instructor, is giving the Bible study. The sermons preached from night to night are the large-group public Bible studies. That is why it is so important that you as a Bible instructor do all you can to encourage regular attendance. It is so much easier to work with the families in the homes when they are attending the meetings faithfully. In fact, one of your most important responsibilities during an evangelistic series is to make sure everyone on your list of interests has as close to perfect attendance as possible. This cannot be overstated. They must participate in the nightly meetings. The experienced evangelist has strategically designed each night to fulfill some dynamic intended to move the audience along a journey toward fully surrendering their life to Christ. Any interruption in attendance becomes a break in the flow of dynamics that should occur in their evolving spiritual awareness. Their being there is crucial.

Very few if any Bible studies will need to be given in the home if the persons attend the meetings nightly. The only time you should have a study in the home is when questions arise that indicate a complete review or when there has been an absence. Since the evangelists are conducting the series, they should have the opportunity to answer questions that the attendee needs clarification on. It is not your responsibility as a Bible instructor to do the job of the evangelist by going into the homes and repeating the presentations already given. On the contrary, your main and most important tasks during the meeting are to (1) ensure clarity, (2) reinforce or obtain decisions on what was presented, and (3) keep the attendee coming night after night. A sidebar to this is to (4) always seek opportunities to increase attendance by inviting others in the home and in the community. Building attendance must be a given. The fifth and sixth crucial responsibilities come at the conclusion of the evangelistic series, and they are to (5) prepare candidates for baptism, and (6) ensure their assimilation into the family of God.

You must take very good notes nightly on the sermons. They become your review material. However, you should go over in the homes only what the evangelist has presented. You should not discuss subjects not yet dealt with, nor should you take up time in the home to answer unrelated questions to the extent that the previous night's presentation never becomes the primary focus of the visit. It is much easier and fewer challenges arise when you stick to the planned purpose for the visit.

As a Bible instructor during an evangelistic series you may have one and only one opportunity to work with a person. You should view it as a once-in-a-lifetime opportunity to partner with God to snatch a soul from the grasp of Satan. In golf a divot is both the turf scraped up and the hole left when you hit a golf ball. A good divot occurs when the hole comes in front of where the ball was at rest, indicating that the golf club struck the ball first, then the ground. If the divot starts behind the ball, the golfer has *mis-hit* the shot. In an instant, because of an insensitive word (or missed opportunity), unclear response to a question, or the negative results of an action, a mis-hit can occur that could have discouraging results or prolong the process needlessly. Moreover, a good word in due season—a good divot—will prove to be just what was needed to move the attendee to the foot of the cross. Like a conscientious golfer who repairs their divots when necessary, let's fix how we may have represented Him poorly and/or misrepresented God's Word with great care and prayerfully move the process of salvation forward.

The question-and-answer box is a great tool to keep your interests returning to the meetings night after night. Great for clarifying mis-hits, it can especially shed greater light (or reinforce the light) on both the subjects presented and to respond to questions unrelated to your visit. Encourage the attendee the next time they come to a meeting to write down their questions and place them in the question-and-answer box. It is better to have them submit their own question than for you to take the question and then forget to submit it. Also, quite naturally, they must be in attendance to submit a question. Let the attendee know that their question is appreciated. If you feel the question is not one for the question-and-answer box because the subject will soon be part of a forthcoming sermon, let them know that the evangelist will cover it on a future night. You can use such questions to encourage continued nightly attendance so as not to miss the very evening that will address their question.

Keep in mind that during an evangelistic series Bible instructors will likely have several homes from both partner's lists to visit each day, therefore they must use time their effectively and efficiently. Some attendees may be available only on the weekend and/or the off night of the meeting. If you miss them, another whole week could go by before you can visit with them again. Here is another reason nightly attendance is crucial. If you miss the attendee during your home visits, hopefully you'll be able to touch base with them during the nightly meeting. Have your well-thought-through questions ready for them so that you can ascertain how they are responding to the presentations. Perhaps you will create a desire on their part to be more motivated to meet with you. Some principles to keep in mind:

- After you've made an appointment, be on time.
- If you are dropping by, make it a habit to be brief, so that the attendee will look forward to your visits and still have time to prepare to attend the meetings.
- Before your brief prayer at the beginning and end of your visit, always ask whether they have a prayer request that they would like included in your prayer. And don't forget to pray for it. Such prayers are an important part of relationship building.
- It is the instructor's responsibility to know the subjects that the evangelist will present during the evangelistic series. They should be listed and kept at hand.
- Take good notes at each the presentation. If you miss a night, get the notes from another instructor and study them carefully.
- Study your notes and highlight the aspects that you will focus on in the home. It's a good idea to write out your own review questions to lead the discussion.
- Stay on the subject. Because you cannot visit the same people every day, you will need to plan on using questions and answers to briefly review no more than one subject each time, only going into detail on subject presentations that they missed or need more clarification on. Know the subjects and the review questions you'll be asking before the visit.
- Use the evangelist's name often as you refer to what they said in their sermons to build confidence in the speakers.
- Remember, it's not your Bible study—you are merely highlighting the evangelist's presentation in the home to ascertain whether the attendee fully understood it (or questions or rejects the subject

matter) and whether they have decided to make spiritual and lifestyle adjustments integrating the new concepts.

- Make the review brief if the attendee was present to hear the subject. Your objective should be to ensure the understanding and acceptance of the subject, not to re-present the Bible study unless the attendee did not hear it firsthand or just didn't understand. Here you should take nothing for granted.
- Do not assume that the attendee grasped the presentation merely because they quickly and excitedly assented. They may be agreeing because they enjoy your visits, like the meetings, and are comfortable with what's being presented. Or they may have no desire to address any subject that would challenge what they've always believed or require actual changes in their lifestyle. It is important not to settle merely for "Yes," "Sure," "That's all right," "I love Jesus," etc.

Jot down on paper and/or memorize about five subjective questions and the supportive scriptures that you think (or that the evangelist suggests) would confirm the level of understanding, acceptance, and desire to move toward obedience. Each question should lead to a brief discussion that addresses the topic, and perhaps other clarifying questions will spawn from the one asked.

Ms. G was amazed that the Bible actually listed the clean and unclean meats. She knew and recited clearly the unclean seafood, such as shrimp, oysters, and shark, and even turned to the passage in Deuteronomy and began reading to me. There was no need for me to go into any depth on what she already understood. I could have moved on, knowing she was well aware and understood the health message, but I assumed that if she was so readily talking about it, she must find it challenging.

It is my custom to give the big picture first—the principle behind the belief. Therefore, we began by talking about how much God loves us. Scripture assures us that God wants us to prosper and be healthy (3 John 2). Then we moved to the fact that God sees us differently than we see ourselves. When God created us, He brought body and breath together and a human being became a living soul (Gen. 2:7). Ours is not merely a body to God, but a living soul. (Note: I find the best time to begin dispelling the idea of the immortal soul is in the presentation of the health message.) What does that mean? That we depend totally upon God for life and breath. Not only that, He so values our bodies that He considers them holy temples, the dwelling place for the Holy Spirit (1 Cor. 6:19). Our bodies are holy because God created us in His holy image. And not only did He create them, but He sustains them (Acts 17:28). That's why 1 Corinthians 6:20 tells us that we are to glorify God not only in our body, but also our spirit, because both are His. Caring for our bodies and our spirit (our relationship with Him) are what we do to thank God for the gift of life that He has given us not only by creation, but also by redemption. Beginning by eating as He designed is the least we can do, isn't it? If the response is not personal, you can take several approaches:

- We could discuss the original diet and how the addition of meat came about.
- We could talk about the fact that if someone really wants to continue eating meat and/or fish, we have plenty of choices of clean meats and seafoods.
- We could go scientific and deal with the use of hormones and conditions behind the raising and preparation of meat.
- We could go medical and explore the negative health conditions brought about almost strictly from eating meat.
- We could go spiritual and relate the promised blessings of obedience in pursuing a healthy lifestyle and glorifying God in our bodies and spirit that are really His. Also, the promise that God will destroy those who defile their God-given bodies, those holy temples (1 Cor. 3:17 [note: the use of this text came last]).
- Finally, pray together about a willing spirit of obedience for their own spiritual and physical welfare.

In all, we used two questions and five scriptures in the brief health presentation above. But it is merely one approach, however. Depending on where the person is with their understanding and acceptance, the presentation will vary. There is no cookie-cutter approach to presenting a lesson that will work the same for any two attendees. That is why much prayer for the guidance of the Holy Spirit is crucial. The main idea is that the person responds from a converted spirit, and not merely from reason, knowledge, or because they got beaten with Scripture into submission. A resounding principle of God's love for the individual should flow through the Bible study of each doctrine. The love of God and their love for Him must merge in a desire to follow Jesus in obedience on each and every doctrinal belief.

Think ahead. Find ways to prepare the attendee to receive testing truths to come and review those already heard. Each subject presented is interrelated to every other subject. Make those connections in your reviews. For example, the Second Coming has links to Creation, redemption, the Incarnation, the plan of salvation, and our eternal inheritance, and I could go on and on. Your attendee may only have a problem with, for example, the incarnation. That one issue could cause a pullback on every other area. Therefore, it is vital to gain an idea as to where the challenges and misconceptions lie as the evangelist moves forward with each nightly presentation. Listen carefully and interweave into each study some statement or scripture that might trigger a response. In the presentation above, it was Genesis 2:7.

I once gave Bible studies to a woman who accepted the health principles and the law and Sabbath messages. She loved the prophecies of Daniel and Revelation, and so on, but could not accept the fact that the wicked do not go straight to a burning hell to endure eternal torment when they die. She attended the Seventh-day Adventist Church for a while, keeping the Sabbath faithfully, but could not get beyond her belief system to see the love of God in the final death and separation of the sinner from Him who is the sole source of life. As much as the loss saddened me as I left her in the hands of a local Bible instructor upon my departure from the city, it was certainly a learning experience that I shall not soon forget.

Another attendee had grown up believing a similar misconception about the ever-burning hell but was happy and relieved to learn that God was not retributive, but rather emphatic in His seemingly extreme warnings for our benefit, much like a parent. Bill Cosby often warned his television sitcom children that he would "beat them into next week" if they dared to be disobedient. Although one probably cannot interpret such a statement literally, one can certainly explain in simple language what he meant—disobedience could have serious consequences. The biblical statements that relate to sinners burning in the fires of hell were not meant to demonstrate the punitive or retributive side of God, but rather to show His enormous love and concern for our spiritual welfare. He wants us to understand that even dabbling in sin will indeed have eternal results if not repented of. His ideal is for each of us to enjoy life abundantly and eternally. Overwhelmingly relieved to be free from a belief system that had bound him for so many years, my attendee readily gave his heart to the Lord along with his life through baptism. Heaven experiences great joy over even one sinner pulled from the darkness of false doctrine and set free from the chains of scriptural misinterpretation.

Knowing your attendees have unfortunate gaps in their belief system should help in guiding each overview. Learn to find ways to recap past lessons and capture the essence of those yet to come. View people as big ships containing lots of cargo and therefore take much effort and space to turn, rather than small fishing boats that can instantly reverse direction. Start as early as possible turning the ship by carefully and sensitively planting truth in the heart.

If people did not hear the evangelist's presentation on a subject, let them know that you can in no way replace what was missed, but the subject was so important that you would like to at least share the highlights and provide supplementary material on the message. Review your notes with the attendee and ask questions to make sure they understand and accept it. Pick at least one of their questions for the question-and-answer box. Perhaps it will enhance your efforts to gain a commitment to nightly attendance. Reinforce again the value of coming each night and assure them that they cannot afford to miss another meeting.

Besides the review of the lesson, listen carefully for any objections or concerns the attendee may have or challenges they may be facing. Take the time to address them cautiously and sensitively. Only deal with what you as a Bible instructor feel is within your comfort zone. Otherwise, refer them to someone else on the evangelistic team. When you do, you should also take responsibility to arrange the follow-up and make sure it happens.

At the end of the lesson review, use a question that will encourage the attendee to express what they have learned. Then ask for a decision on the subject pointed out in the lesson. Doing the lesson review in this manner will make it easier for them to make decisions later on when they encounter more challenging truths.

Never tear down a person's beliefs, joke about what may be different to you, demean anyone for what they believe, talk over or interrupt, act impatient, share your personal problems or try to solve theirs, or speak out of place about joining the church before the evangelist has indicated it is time to do so. Be professional at all times and represent the Bible instructor vocation well.

> "Every teacher should see to it that his work tends to definite results. Before attempting to teach a subject, he should have a distinct plan in mind, and should know just what he desires to accomplish. He should

not rest satisfied with the presentation of any subject until the student understands the principle involved, perceives its truth, and is able to state clearly what he has learned."[1]

"Your success will not depend so much upon your knowledge and accomplishments, as upon your ability to find your way to the heart."[2]

Chapter Activities

1. Discuss the important responsibilities of the Bible instructor to the attendee during an evangelistic series.
2. Role-play visiting someone who attended the meeting the night before.
3. Role-play visiting someone who missed several meeting nights (first decide on the subjects they missed).

---

[1] E. G. White, *Education*, pp. 233, 234.
[2] E. G. White, *Gospel Workers*, p. 193.

CHAPTER 16

TELLTALE GAPS AND BLACK HOLES

As you review the lessons and presentations with individuals of various faiths, you will find that some biblical concepts will cause deep and sincere conflicts in the hearts of attendees. Usually you can fill such telltale gaps in knowledge or understanding of the Word quite simply by discussing a few applicable scriptures. In addition, you will encounter texts raised by your attendees that have been taught completely out of context. Like the black hole in space that prevents anything, even light, from escaping, such misapplied theories are embedded so deep in their spiritual experience that it seems nothing, not even Scripture, prayer, or personal testimony, will set them free. Such concepts can become the source of strong opposition.

You would be wise not to engage a person in any discussions of scriptures with which they are unfamiliar. It is not unusual to come across those who are convinced about what they believe to the extent that no explanation will change their mind. You could end up either convinced by the attendee's theory or embarrassed about your own. Even worse, a heated argument could result and damage the valued rapport you have spent much time and effort in developing. You never want to jeopardize the relationship over a biblical issue to the extent that the person ends the relationship forever.

It would be far better to encourage a deeper study of the subject. Include a few key scriptures for their consideration and return at another appointed time to go over the findings. You should report the details of the discussion with the pastor/evangelist or the head Bible instructor for additional counsel. Let us here address only a few of the biblical concepts that have created a major divide and even halted Bible studies altogether. They will give you an idea of what some of these "black hole" misconceptions entail.

- **The misconception of the power and authority of laying on of hands and the forgiving of sins:**

"And when he had said this, he breathed on them, and saith unto them, Receive ye the Holy Ghost: Whose soever sins ye remit, they are remitted unto them; and whose soever sins ye retain, they are retained" (John 20:22, 23).

NOTE: It is only by the blood of Jesus Christ and in His name alone that sins are forgiven. Human beings have no power to do so. As Christ's ambassadors we are privileged to be a part of the royal priesthood. As such God has graced His people with the honor of presenting the faults, sins, and challenges of others to Him for His forgiveness, cleansing, and healing. This we can and should do daily (Luke 5:21-24, 2 Cor. 5:18-20, Eph. 4:8-13, 1 Peter 2:9, 1 John 1:9).

- **The misconception that in His coming to our sinful world, living a sinless life, and shedding His blood on the cross, Christ fulfilled the law and thus it is forever after nullified and not applicable to humanity:**

"Think not that I am come to destroy the law, or the prophets: I am not come to destroy, but to fulfill" (Matt. 5:17).

NOTE: We really don't have to go any further than the text itself to see that Jesus did not erase His law. Therefore, "fulfill" must have a broader, or different, connotation, and it does. Jesus Christ came to earth to carry out the ten-commandment law completely, something that human beings could not do for their own salvation. Jesus sacrificed His life to satisfy perfectly the requirements of the law of God, thus making our salvation possible in Him alone and not of ourselves. Sinners saved by grace, we are not to return to sinning, but to live by the power of Christ and His Spirit that dwells in us. Only then can we will and do of His good pleasure, not our own. We actually fulfill the law as well by our response to the love of God for us—loving God with all our mind and strength demonstrated by our obedience to the first four commandments and loving our neighbor as ourselves through obedience to the last six (Matt. 5:17; 22:37-40; 2 Tim. 2:9, 10; Eph. 2:8, 9; Gal. 6:2; Phil. 2:13).

- **The misconception that as long as one prays over the food that one eats, it becomes sanctified (holy) and good for consumption:**

"For every creature of God is good, and nothing to be refused, if it be received with thanksgiving: For it is sanctified by the word of God and prayer" (1 Tim. 4:4, 5).

NOTE: Here again we find the interpretation clearly within the text: "for it is sanctified by the word of God and prayer." Leviticus 11 and Deuteronomy 14 are the Word of God. In these scriptures God has listed what meats were sanctified, or set apart by divine command, for use in our body temples. First Corinthians 6:19, 20 reminds us that our bodies are the holy temples for the indwelling of the Holy Spirit and therefore we should honor our bodies, not because they are ours to do with as we please, but because they belong to God to do with as He pleases.

- **The misconception that speaking in tongues is the one and only sign that one is filled with the Holy Ghost and has received His power:**

"And when the day of Pentecost was fully come, they were all with one accord in one place. And suddenly there came a sound from heaven as of a rushing mighty wind, and it filled all the house where they were sitting. And there appeared unto them cloven tongues like as of fire, and it sat upon each of them. And they were all filled with the Holy Ghost, and began to speak with other tongues, as the Spirit gave them utterance" (Acts 2:1-4).

NOTE: The explanation about what tongues are appears only a few verses later. Pentecost attracted Jews from all over the then known world. They came speaking various languages, but God prepared His disciples to preach the gospel of Jesus Christ to them by endowing them with the gift of tongues, or other languages. That is why in verse 8 the people exclaimed with amazement that they could understand the gospel in their own language. Verses 9-11 actually list the languages.

- **The misconception that God plans to torment the wicked for ever and ever:**

"And the smoke of their torment ascendeth up for ever and ever: and they have no rest day nor night, who worship the beast and his image, and whosoever receiveth the mark of his name" (Rev. 14:11).

NOTE: Although we could take the text at face value as representing the character of God as retributive, further study reveals a God giving the most extreme picture of eternal death as possible as a warning to humanity. It's like a parent exclaiming, "I'll tan your hide if you . . . !" or Bill Cosby's "I'll beat you into next week!" Such statements don't truly represent the extent of the wrath of the parent toward their child, but rather a serious warning. And even though the children know it is not possible for the parent to fulfill their threat, they are certain to get the point that disobedience will have serious consequences. The fires that will rain down from God out of heaven, consuming everything with the taint of sin, is certainly the most serious matter in the Bible and warrants the most dire warning.

God has already said many times that He desires that not one be lost, but rather that all are saved. He combined those statements with the most foreboding language and strongest warnings. Make no mistake about it—hell's fire is prepared for the devil and his angels and all those on earth who choose to follow his lead. It is Satan who would have you believe hell is a divine character issue when it is and has always been a sin issue. God will completely burn up everything containing the taint of sin. However, after that time He will create a new heaven and a new earth where the righteous will dwell in peace for ever and ever. Therefore, the wicked will be no more, not tormented for ever and ever (Mal. 4:1; Matt. 3:12; 1 Tim. 2:4; 2 Peter 2:4-9; Rev. 20:9; 21:1, 5).

- **The misconception that when a person dies they go straight into the presence of God:**

"We are confident, I say, and willing rather to be absent from the body, and to be present with the Lord" (2 Cor. 5:8).

NOTE: Somewhere along the way, Paul's wish got turned into a doctrine. The apostle was not stating a fact but a desire that all who truly love God share—to be present with the Lord. What Christian would not want to experience this? We find no mention of death at all, nor was it intended. The Bible and Paul state clearly that when people die their spirit (or breath) returns to God who gave it and their body decays back to dust. The combination of the two forms the living soul (in our language the human being and/or animal) which, according to the Bible, because it was born in sin, will die. The concept of an immortal soul came from paganism. There will be one and only one resurrection of all the righteous dead at the second coming of Christ (Prov. 8:36; Eccl. 9:5, 6; Jer. 22:10; Eze. 18:4, 20; 1 Cor. 15:51-55; 1 Thess. 4:16, 17).

While the explanations of the above misinterpretations have been quite brief, you must embrace the scriptures through the prism of God's love. Satan would love to have humanity believe that God is a deity of convenience and a vindictive, selfish Being who will one day take out His fury on His rebellious creation. But that is not the God we serve—it is a made-up deity inspired by paganism. Yes, at times God's mercy is conditional, but the principles of Christian belief stand forever. He is love, and again, everything we read in Scripture we must see and interpret filtered through that abiding principle.

Chapter Activities

1. Discuss the advantages and drawbacks in refusing to address a misconception any further when the discussion turns into argument.
2. Discuss each of the misconceptions in detail.
3. Role-play one of the misconceptions with someone who can respond with an argument, thus demonstrating your ability to remain calm and in control.

PART 4

SECURING AND CONFIRMING DECISIONS

CHAPTER 17

BE A SEED PLANTER, NOT A BEAN COUNTER

During the evangelistic series the evangelists lead the way in the successive presentation of each doctrine. Once they have set forth a subject, you must review it in the home as soon as possible because it also leads to the next doctrine. Each home visit must be purposeful and intentional as you drop points of truth in the course of the discussion and confirm the acceptance of elements already presented. If the attendee misses a meeting, you must review in the home the information presented and secure the person's confirmation of it. Take nothing for granted.

As stated many times before, good notes on each night's topic are vital. Study and use them as a guide for summarizing each presentation. The Bible student may even have notes that they have taken on the subject, making them much more comfortable in participating in the lesson review. Most evangelists now provide presentation outlines for the audience. The objective of each lesson review is to determine the attendee's understanding, belief, and acceptance of the doctrine and then whether they intend to personally apply it even if it involves lifestyle changes. What good is it to discuss a doctrine and then not lead the Bible student to begin thinking about how the lifestyle transformation will come about?

It behooves you as a Bible instructor to know thoroughly the subjects covered during the series. But you should not run ahead of the evangelist by answering questions on doctrinal points not yet presented in the nightly meetings. If such questions do arise, encourage the attendee to keep coming nightly, and they will hear an entire sermon on the subject. Also, have them use the question-and-answer box for their Bible inquiries.

Always present reviews and other material in a cordial manner and in a way that they will receive your enthusiasm, or even seriousness, about the subject in the right spirit. It should constantly be your aim as a Bible instructor to make the lesson a win-win experience that leaves everyone blessed by the review, never a win-lose in which the Bible student feels helpless and defenseless, or lose-lose in which no one feels good about the results of the discussion, and definitely not a lose-win experience in which the Bible study student controls the discussion with their erroneous views and interpretations at the expense of your integrity as a knowledgeable Bible authority.

Long before the discussion turns into a debate or appears to be at an impasse, cordially bring the session to a close, give the research assignment, and resume it at another time. This gives both you and the student opportunity to research and pray about the subject under the guidance of the Holy Spirit. Then you can return with a fresh beginning and information. Your research may need to include presenting the challenge to the evangelist, pastor, or a more experienced Bible instructor.

Sandra was determined that immortality was real. It seemed that every time I came to present a Bible study, the subject of the immortal soul would come up. She would fulfill each research assignment I gave her, and she also read my research paper on the subject. After going to her pastor for information, she felt ready to discuss the subject with me, but I declined. We went back over the scriptures she had gathered from her pastor and elsewhere. Then she presented her side of the issue, and I explained my views. But after several sessions with the subject still coming up, we just decided temporarily to agree to disagree. And that's fine, as we know relationships should come first. It's not a matter of winning but of timing. If a person is not ready to receive the principles you are presenting, forcefully pursuing a win could end up a lose-lose. Depending on how far along in the evangelistic series the issues come up, someone more experienced may need to discuss the issue in more detail with the Bible study student.

Chapter Activities

1. Discuss the potential usefulness of taking notes during an evangelistic series.
2. Discuss why it is unprofessional and dangerous to debate Bible doctrines.
3. Discuss how you would go about clearing up a debated subject.

Bible Study Review

If your students have already heard the topic preached at the evangelistic meeting, they do not need a detailed repeat of the sermon in the home. During a series of meetings it is not the objective to give a thorough Bible study to those who have attended them. Rather, you should seek to determine the level of understanding, belief, and acceptance of the subject matter through highlighting significant points of the presentation as a form of review. This is very important. Such a review should bring out any questions on the subject that need further clarification and/or affirmation. Therefore, the Bible instructor's preparation for the review should predetermine what points they will bring out in the home. Such groundwork is crucial.

If the attendee is in full agreement with the sermon and has expressed a desire to apply the new knowledge to personal spiritual growth, you have no need to oversell by continuing to ask questions. The ideal is when attendees eagerly invite you into their home and break into an enthusiastic expression of how much they appreciate what they've heard and how much they agree with the presentation, even though it shatters long-held beliefs. Even more exciting is when they ask you about your church and how they can become a member.

Before one upcoming evangelistic series I had secured the visitors' roster from the church's head greeter. As I went through the names in preparation for contacting those who had come to our local church during the past two years, I came across what turned out to be an elderly woman and her sister who had once visited the church more than a year before with an Adventist niece from out of town. When they informed me that they do not go out at night, I promised them personal Bible studies once the meetings ended. Thrilled to receive the studies, they had been desperately seeking a new church home after the pastor of their small seventh-day Pentecostal church passed away several years prior. They began attending our local Seventh-day Adventist Church. During one session they could not hold it in any longer and were determined to know how they could become members. The two women did not hesitate in accepting Adventist beliefs and even the recommendation of rebaptism. It was almost as though they were trying to prove that they qualified to be members.

It was an exciting day when the two individuals, both in their 80s, went down into the watery grave of baptism. Some people don't need a lot of prodding along the path to Christ. They are already standing at the foot of the cross.

On the other hand, if an attendee does have questions and issues, it is vital that you take time to clear up any confusion or objections. Remember to be very careful that you do not back a person into a corner. That is the wrong approach when meeting objections. Make sure your explanations are scriptural. Take smaller steps with the individual. He or she may have some gaps in understanding somewhere along the way. If the person is sincere, slowing down and filling in those missing pieces could enable them to decide to follow God's will on their own.

Chapter Activities

1. Discuss the preparation that you should make before going to the home to review the evangelist's presentation.
2. What are some signs that the attendee is struggling with some aspects of the evangelist's presentation? Discuss.
3. Discuss why it is important that you stick to Scripture when responding to objections.

Responding to Disagreements

Some people just like to argue their point of view. Others are so certain that their belief is right that they become passionate about it. As a Bible instructor you must keep in mind to respond, rather than react, to the attendee's opinions or statements. You must never get into a debate or argument with an attendee about differences of view on a subject or on Scripture. Although you may be following the example of the Master Teacher by giving scriptural references, if they fall on a resistant heart it may have a negative impact on the relationship. Remember, relationship comes first. It would be much better to give a research assignment and set another time to discuss it. Be very positive about it, ending the discussion but looking forward to the student's presentation of findings. Assure the attendee that at the next meeting you will bring supplementary material that will help to shed additional light on the subject and show why you have taken such a firm position on the subject. In addition, you may share some texts that you or your partner jotted down during the discussion. Always end with prayer for the Holy Spirit to have a welcomed placed in the heart as our divine Teacher.

Ever keep in mind that many pagan views long ago wove themselves into generally accepted Christian beliefs. I find one of the most disturbing to be the idea that God has two sides to His character—His tremendous love for the righteous and His vindictive, retributive hatred of the sinner. Another is the notion of human immortality, which leads to the belief that people live forever whether in heaven or tormented in hell. Unfortunately, the Bible has many phrases that would lead one to see God in such a light. However, when we look through the prism of "God is love," we see the picture of His hatred of sin (not the sinner) and all its destruction of His creation from an entirely different perspective. As we have already noted, the Word of God uses some very extreme language, even threats, to convey the reality of eternal separation from God as the result of continuing in sin. As a parent I have in the past found myself making such remarks to my children to help them understand how serious the matter was. God has done the same in such statements as:

"A fire goeth before him, and burneth up his enemies round about" (Ps. 97:3).

"And the smoke of their torment ascendeth up for ever and ever" (Rev. 14:11).

"And the devil that deceived them was cast into the lake of fire and brimstone, where the beast and the false prophet are, and shall be tormented day and night for ever and ever" (Rev. 20:10).

Such passages are merely a few examples of how the reader of the Bible could misconstrue the character of God as having two sides. It is important to help people to understand them correctly, because it could make the difference between choosing to serve God out of love or becoming legalistic and exacting in service based on fear of a retributive God. God is love. All doctrines and Christian values and beliefs must be interpreted in the light of this fact. It must be the theme of all presentations, the basis of all Bible beliefs, the foundation of all scriptural interpretation, and the overriding reason for coming to Christ and serving Him. That God is love must be the undergirding for every decision call and every reason for confession, repentance, and a new life in Christ.

We have wonderful materials available now on difficult texts. In fact, I would strongly urge every Bible instructor to arm themselves with two outstanding references that could serve as essential companion books, both authored by Mark Finley: *Studying Together* and *Answers to Difficult Bible Texts*. The study of those two small books will help to broaden your own views on some scriptures that continue to be misunderstood yet preached and taught boldly in many Christian churches today.

Chapter Activities

1. Discuss the reasons it is never good to argue about Scripture.

2. List some of the Christian beliefs that have their roots in pagan theology.
3. Is it really possible to see the love of Jesus in some of the most threatening scriptures? Discuss.

How to Handle Resistance

Be a good listener and hear the cry beneath the confusion or objection. It may very well be for an entirely different need. Underneath the surface may lurk family, job, or current church issues that really have very little to do with their specific objection. Their pastor may have recently promoted them to an office with what might be to them an important title, thus they are reluctant to become part of a new, unfamiliar denomination. A family member may have accused them of ignorantly joining a cult, they may still be plagued with an addiction, or a couple may not be legally married.

As a Bible instructor you must listen carefully, cautiously, calmly, and caringly to those under the conviction of the Holy Spirit for what truly underlies their concern. Use the F-F-F technique. Affirm them in their concern (feel), assure them that others have had similar concerns (felt), and then move to get them back on track by lifting up the name of Jesus (found), clarifying His awesome desire for us to inherit the kingdom of heaven that is so much grander than any hindrance they may face. Use words that confirm to them that you understand and genuinely care about them, and then demonstrate that by presenting God's greater love and desire for their life. God already knows what they are facing and will never forsake them.

Now is when faith and trust in the promises of God must come confidently to the forefront. Spend some time reading applicable biblical promises and fervently praying with the challenged ones. Bible instructors are not God and should not try to be Him with all the possible solutions in mind. But rather make God's Word as clear as possible, and then ask them what they feel God is asking of them. Let them spend time with God and hear His voice for themselves. They are adults—treat them as such. Make no demands of people under conviction. Allow them to come to their own decisions. Your role as a Bible instructor is to be prayerful, encouraging, and supportive.

> "And Moses said unto them, Stand still, and I will hear what the Lord will command concerning you" (Num. 9:8).

"Trust in the Lord with all thine heart; and lean not unto thine own understanding. In all thy ways acknowledge him, and he shall direct thy paths" (Prov. 3:5, 6).

"Howbeit when he, the Spirit of truth, is come, he will guide you into all truth" (John 16:13).

All objections must be settled in this loving, respectful way before attendees can move forward with decisions for Christ. Let them talk through it. Here is when listening has great potential. Provide scriptural intervention that makes God's will far more valuable, keeping the explanations simple. Give biblical examples and personal testimonies. Never become argumentative or pushy. Let the Holy Spirit of God bring reasoning and conviction as you uplift Jesus.

"And I, if I be lifted up from the earth, will draw all men unto me" (John 12:32).

"I have sworn by myself, the word is gone out of my mouth in righteousness, and shall not return, That unto me every knee shall bow, every tongue shall swear" (Isa. 45:23).

Be careful not to be so intent on your objective for the home visit that you miss important signs and subliminal messages. Here is also where a partner plays an important role. If one misses the underlying need, perhaps the other will catch it. It's not about you, the Bible instructor, nor even about the lesson to review—it's all about those whom God has placed in your care to love to Jesus. When the Savior taught in the synagogues and one-on-one, He listened from the heart and then approached the individuals from where *they* really were with the Word of God. Remember with whom their battle really rages and understand the true source of their resistance. Through dedicated prayer and even fasting, stand with them, stand for them, and stand still and let the mighty power of God answer their heart's need in ways none could have thought or imagined.

Many of my attendees were plagued with addictions that they had repeatedly tried to break. You should not be surprised to discover that with very few exceptions, your candidates will have some addictions, habits, and/or traditions to overcome. It was not until we brought their challenges to the throne of God together, and they received the support they needed through church intervention programs, that they were healed. What testimonies they have after overcoming under the power of God! What joy they have to be set free. As Bible instructors you must listen and be there to support your attendees through their unique situations as they transition to a life with Christ.

> "Finally, my brethren, be strong in the Lord, and in the power of his might. Put on the whole armour of God, that ye may be able to stand against the wiles of the devil. For we wrestle not against flesh and blood, but against principalities, against powers, against the rulers of the darkness of this world, against spiritual wickedness in high places. Wherefore take unto you the whole armour of God, that ye may be able to withstand in the evil day, and having done all, to stand. Stand therefore, having your loins girt about with truth, and having on the breastplate of righteousness: And your feet shod with the preparation of the gospel of peace; Above all, taking the shield of faith, wherewith ye shall be able to quench all the fiery darts of the wicked. And take the helmet of salvation, and the sword of the Spirit, which is the word of God: Praying always with all prayer and supplication in the Spirit, and watching thereunto with all perseverance and supplication for all saints" (Eph. 6:10-18).

You should expect a decision for Christ to involve spiritual battles and even foes from within the household. Merely the fact that there is a struggle should lead you to feel that the attendee is under the conviction of the Holy Spirit and needs your intense prayer and support. (Note: The confidence in you that has developed in them over time—your sincerity, spirituality, and dependability—should yield positive dividends now during their time of spiritual conflict.) Keep in mind that through the power of suggestion people tend to move in the direction of what others expect of them, so do not give in to objections. So often those that challenge new beliefs the hardest are the very ones who give in to the will of God, while those who are gung ho for everything do not have the depth of understanding to go all the way with Christ.

> "Think not that I am come to send peace on earth: I came not to send peace, but a sword. For I am come to set a man at variance against his father, and the daughter against her mother, and the daughter in law against her mother in law. And a man's foes shall be they of his own household. He that loveth father or mother more than me is not worthy of me: and he that loveth son or daughter more than me is not worthy of me. And he that taketh not his cross, and followeth after me, is not

worthy of me. He that findeth his life shall lose it: and he that loseth his life for my sake shall find it. He that receiveth you receiveth me, and he that receiveth me receiveth him that sent me" (Matt. 10:34-38).

You do not need to be pushy or use force with someone under the conviction of the Holy Spirit. By loving kindness, careful attention to God's Word impressed by the Holy Spirit, and sharing your personal testimonies, the Lord will *give* the one under true conviction into our hands. It's not persuasive discourse but the power of the Holy Spirit that brings conviction to the heart. If anything, pray with the attendee that they will hear and heed the inner voice of conscience and conviction.

"And all this assembly shall know that the Lord saveth not with sword and spear: for the battle is the Lord's, and he will give you into our hands" (1 Sam. 17:47).

"Thus saith the Lord unto you, Be not afraid nor dismayed by reason of this great multitude; for the battle is not yours, but God's" (2 Chron. 20:15).

Before you address the concern of the attendee with scriptures, confirm with them whether the question they brought up is the only thing holding them back. Let them talk and reason through their response. When they finish, repeat their final objection in your own words. Give them time to confirm or correct your conclusion. After the objection (or excuse) is clear, finally ask, "If we could clear this up through the Word of God, could you see yourself accepting God's will for you?" Provide the scripture(s) appropriate to their situation and either let them respond in the affirmative or help them discover the root of their objection, and then ask the question again.

Chapter Activities

1. Role play F-F-F (feel, felt, found).
2. Discuss the implications of the statement "A person convinced against their will is of the same opinion still."
3. What are some body language and subliminal messages an attendee in disagreement may display?

CHAPTER 18

THE BEST OF HEAVEN NOW

"It is a great privilege to be a colaborer with Christ in the salvation of souls."*

Each night of the series of meetings the evangelist will ask the attendees to make some kind of decision for Christ with respect to the subject presented. Some appeals may be more subtle than others. Not all of them will come at the end of the presentation. Several may occur during the sermon. At times they will require a mental rather than an overt response. Some will be more specific than others. The evangelist may ask the audience to mark their card in a certain way, to raise their hand, to stand, or even to come to the front. One thing is for sure—all heaven is astir on these very special occasions and rejoices as each one takes a stand for Christ. Let me remind you of two parables that Jesus told:

"What man of you, having an hundred sheep, if he lose one of them, doth not leave the ninety and nine in the wilderness, and go after that which is lost, until he find it? And when he hath found it, he layeth it on his shoulders, rejoicing. And when he cometh home, he calleth together his friends and neighbours, saying unto them, Rejoice with me; for I have found my sheep which was lost. I say unto you, that likewise joy shall be in heaven over one sinner that repenteth, more than over ninety and nine just persons, which need no repentance" (Luke 15:4-7).

"Either what woman having ten pieces of silver, if she lose one piece, doth not light a candle, and sweep the house, and seek diligently till she find it? And when she hath found it, she calleth her friends and her neighbours together, saying, Rejoice with me; for I have found the piece which I had lost. Likewise, I say unto you, there is joy in the presence of the angels of God over one sinner that repenteth" (verses 8-10).

When the evangelist is about to make the appeal, you as a Bible instructor must be alert, ready with decision cards in hand, along with pencils, for those who might have been missed or were seated late. You must be prepared to meet any need that arises with an attendee during a decision call: card, pencil, clarification, writing assistance, etc. Just as important, you must work closely with the ushers to make sure all decision cards get passed in at the end of the call. Most likely the ushers will use offering buckets to collect the cards.

Ideally, the evangelist will notify the Bible instructor team beforehand of all special occurrences during the meeting, such as handouts, gift-giving, special prayer session, and altar call. However, the Spirit of God might lead the evangelist in an entirely different direction. Do not get upset or confused should that take place. It happens often. Sometimes the evangelist forgets to share important details of what they intend to do during the presentation, or there may be a change of mind at the last minute. It behooves you as a Bible instructor to be alert and prepared for deviations from what may have been planned. Ideally, you should be fully aware of how the decision call will be conducted from night to night. Again, the Holy Spirit might lead the evangelist to make sudden changes. You must expect that and be alert and instantly adjust.

Whenever the evangelist calls for a decision, the Bible instructors, along with the ushers (depending on the size of the crowd), should immediately spread through the auditorium armed with decision cards and pencils to hand out as needed or to listen carefully and follow the directions of the evangelist. Also, when it appears that the ushers are not sure what to do, the Bible instructors should immediately come to their assistance in the most professional manner.

There is nothing more exciting, yet also solemn and sobering, than to see people respond to a call to accept Christ as their Savior. The evangelistic team must be in the flow, not in confusion at this most sacred time. It is the moment when the leadership qualities of the Bible instructor coordinator must rise to the occasion in readily and fully accommodating the evangelist and the attendees. It is also when the prayers in the hearts of God's people must rise in defense of those struggling with a decision for Christ.

The Altar Call

The altar call is always the most sacred and serious time for the audience. It should be reverent in the auditorium. As far as possible, there should be absolutely no movement or distractions unless the evangelist requests it. No one should be in the aisles during the appeal, no walking in or out of the auditorium, no babies crying unattended by an usher or Bible instructor. If people have gone out and now want to return, by all means allow them to do so, but stand inside the door until the appeal concludes. By keeping people out of the auditorium, you may find Satan using you to block someone from giving their heart to Christ. Instead, encourage those outside the auditorium to come in. The evangelist must have the total focus of the entire audience.

All Bible instructors must be alert and follow the directions of the head instructor and/or the evangelist. The Holy Spirit must have the responsive heart and sensitive ear of each and every person in the audience. The appeal to the audience to hear and to obey the call of heaven echoed through the evangelist is always a solemn and serious occasion. You should never treat it as routine, ritualistic, a time stealer, or unnecessary. How many times have individuals left the meeting after making a decision for (or against) Christ and not lived to see the next day? We'll never know how many individuals the Holy Spirit sent to the meeting unbeknownst to them to hear that particular message and respond to that particular appeal. Every meeting has those whom the Holy Spirit has led there for the first time. So many lives have been changed because of that one sermon, that one appeal, that one response. It is the responsibility of the ushers and Bible instructors to ensure that the atmosphere is one in which the Holy Spirit has full, undisturbed expression.

What everyone should do during an altar call is something that should be thoroughly discussed during an observational review meeting. Typically, at the start of audience responses to the appeal (not before the audience actually begins to respond), the Bible instructors should inconspicuously begin to leave their seats and spread out around the auditorium. Timing is everything. If the instructors get up and move around too early, it could become a distraction and, worse yet, people may get the idea that people are leaving the auditorium and they just might want to follow. Any movement by the instructors during an appeal must be at precisely the right time. It is when the evangelist signals for it. He may solicit the audience to stand, or come forward, or mark their cards. When the people in the audience begin to respond is exactly when the Bible instructors start taking their positions. That way the audience may get the impression that their movement results from the appeal, and it might then motivate them to respond likewise. Also, the evangelist directs how they prefer to have the Bible instructor team stationed during the appeal and altar call. Be sure you are aware of what is to take place, where you should be, when to head there, and what materials you should have in hand during the appeal. Some evangelists insist that the Bible instructors remain in place until the respondents begin to leave their seats or start toward the front if the audience is already standing.

Here is a typical scene during an appeal. A couple of Bible instructors will be up front near the evangelist handing out decision cards to individuals as they come forward in response to the altar call. Others should especially be near those on your list (or anyone's list) whom you feel needs special prayer because of potential resistance. With your eyes open, pray in your heart that the voice of the Holy Spirit of God will be heard in their heart, and that the angels of God will minister to those under conviction and battle the enemy of souls. Just as Jesus prayed for Peter that his faith would not fail, pray that your prayer will join the prayer from heaven's sanctuary until each person has made their decision.

As the appeal goes forth, scan the audience and help anyone who absolutely looks like they need assistance to come forward. Remember, the attendee must already be in the aisle before you begin to go to them. Keep in mind that this is a personal decision between them and God. No matter how sincere the Bible instructor may be, they should not try to take God's place by prodding or forcing the person. It must be a choice made in response to the Holy Spirit alone. The Bible instructor must not step into the process in any way. While it is commendable that you as an instructor have a heartfelt desire to see everyone on your list saved and baptized, again you must never be rude, pushy, or in any way feel it is your responsibility to get the person to the altar. It is not. That is totally against Bible teaching. "And the Spirit and the bride say, Come. And let him that heareth say, Come. And let him that is athirst come. And whosoever will, let him take the water of life freely" (Rev. 22:17).

Remember that a decision to respond to an altar call must be a reflection of heart conversion. A forced decision may be exciting to the Bible instructor, but one must ask, did it truly come from a repentant, converted heart? It is the responsibility of instructors to be supportive in whatever ways they can and, most important, spend much time in prayer in behalf of those in attendance. According to John 10:16: "Other sheep I have, which are not of this fold: them also I must bring, and they shall hear my voice; and there shall be one fold, and one shepherd." When they hear the voice of Jesus, He will bring them through the wooing and power of the Holy Spirit, not us. Nonetheless, we have an important part in the spiritual battle: we partner with Christ interceding in the heavenly sanctuary. If we have done our job in the homes, ideally the decision will be made *prior* to the altar call. The appeal should essentially be the result of a decision already made in the home.

What can happen during an appeal always amazes me. I've seen people race to the front or go there in tears. One person will come followed by the whole family, or a spouse or friend. People you never thought would ever respond can surprise you. I had the hardest time catching up with a woman at her home. Fortunately she came out early each night to the meetings, and we were able to talk then. Then I discovered that she came from generations of Catholics and was proud of it. When we finally were able to make arrangements for a home visit, we were treated coolly from the porch and not allowed any further. Night after night I courted her with cordial attention, giving her as much of my time as possible until she felt comfortable with me. At that point we finally got into the home and began learning more about her. She had never before heard about many of the subjects preached and was taken aback at the history of Catholicism. On appeal night—to our amazement—she responded. That was an exciting night. As we continued to review with her each doctrine we saw what an open heart she had. She admitted that only one of her four adult children had remained in the Catholic faith. When she began sharing all that she had learned with each of them, they did not object to her baptism.

You can never predetermine who will be open to more visitation time and who will respond to the appeal. Everyone who attends the meetings must be visited and given the respect due them for their interest in connecting more deeply with God. They should not be alone in their journey to salvation. To allow that is tantamount to leaving them to die by themselves. Some things just should never be. Everyone coming to the meetings deserves the common decency of a home visit, or at the least, a meaningful connection with a Bible instructor to talk through where they are spiritually and what's happening with them as a result of attending the meetings. That is where decisions are spawned and cultivated. The auditorium is where they are confirmed.

Once attendees leave their seats and join the pastor, you should have decision cards and pencils ready to hand out. Candidates should remain up front until the appeal has ended. By then all Bible instructors should have joined them, assisting with either the seating of the candidates in the first few rows of the auditorium, or escorting them to a designated room for counsel and prayer (and to ensure that everyone filled out a decision card). Normally the procedure to follow will get discussed prior to the night's sermon, usually at the observational review meeting.

The Decision Card

Special decision cards are to be ready and distributed during a call. Many evangelists combine the decision card with the nightly quiz card. That way the audience becomes comfortable with not only taking the quiz until it feels nonthreatening but also in the same way registering a decision for Christ in response to an appeal. The possibility of a gift for taking the quiz or for registering attendance heightens the incentive to turn in the card at the end of the meeting. When evangelists combine the decision card with the quiz card, they likely will not collect the card until the conclusion of the meeting so that it can be utilized for both purposes.

Note that some evangelists may decide not to make an altar call first, but rather use a decision card. Others employ the decision card every night of the evangelistic series. When the evangelist indicates and the audience doesn't already have decision cards, the Bible instructors and ushers should distribute them immediately. The audience will follow the directions of the evangelist, who will finally tell them to pass in their card. Again the Bible instructors and ushers will pick up the cards and hand them to the designated person.

Often the evangelist will use the decision cards while the audience is seated, followed by an altar call based on the response options on the decision card. This has the advantage of already having the decision/quiz cards that were turned in, rather than waiting until the altar call to have the candidates fill one out. The method also allows the candidate to return to their seat immediately after the appeal is over. However, evangelists may elect to have the candidates who responded seated in a specific area or escorted to a designated location so they, or an assigned person, can speak and pray with them. While the methods may vary, the Bible instructor should be flexible and adjust to the directions of the evangelists with regard to the handling of candidates during this very delicate time in their life.

The Bible instructor should follow the directions of the evangelist whether to have the candidates seated immediately after the altar call in the front of the auditorium or taken to a particular room. When it is a designated room, be very careful not to lose individuals along the way. This is important, because women may have left their purses on their seats, or other individuals may want to retrieve personal belongings (coats, Bibles, etc.) they left behind. It may be permissible to allow them to secure their belongings and return up front or to the room set aside for them. A Bible instructor may even escort them. Remember, Satan can take advantage of any moment to entice a person to recant their decision. Stay by anyone who has to leave temporarily to get something. Talk to them encouragingly so that the devil can't speak to them, and then get them back to the others receiving counsel.

If the candidates are to be seated immediately, Bible instructors should be available to assist the ushers (if necessary) to remove and reseat people who are occupying the desired seats for the candidates as quickly as possible.

The evangelist or the head Bible instructor will have encouraging words for the candidates and conduct a prayer season. It is your responsibility as a Bible instructor to arrange visits with the candidates, if not before they leave, then as soon as possible. Hopefully the one giving counsel will allow a few minutes for this purpose. If not, the Bible instructors must do all they can before the candidates depart, or at the least, let them know that they will be receiving a call the next day. Contact must be made as soon as possible. Time is a major factor between a decision and the follow-up. The shorter the time between their response and the follow-up, the greater the possibility for better results. Those who have made decisions must have priority and should go to the top of your list for visitation.

Chapter Activities

1. Rehearse the different types of appeals and how you should handle each.
2. Role-play, asking a candidate for an appointment after they have responded to an appeal.
3. Discuss the impact of (positive and/or negative) of any physical movement by Bible instructors during an appeal.

---

* E. G. White, *Gospel Workers*, p. 191.

CHAPTER 19

THE MAGNETISM OF EXPECTATION

Regardless of the situation, as a Bible instructor you must cultivate a positive, and above all, respectful manner when addressing people. Bear in mind 1 Peter 5:8: "Be sober, be vigilant; because your adversary the devil, as a roaring lion, walketh about, seeking whom he may devour." While the evangelist will seek to gain decisions nightly, some will have either missed the meeting and the vital decision-making that took place or for whatever reason did not make the expected decision. It is your privilege as a Bible instructor to partner with the Holy Spirit to take whatever action necessary. Arrange a visit as soon as possible and tactfully determine the reason for the absence or decision break and to review the subject covered in the sermon. Do not jump to conclusions here, assuming that it might be related to a misunderstanding of something the evangelist presented, particularly if the person has been a regular attendee. On the contrary, stay calm and respectful and be prayerfully open to the possibility that it was something other than a boycott that kept them away on an important night.

For the person who hears the spoken Word and receives a detailed review of the presentation, through prayer and careful questioning seek to determine how the individual responded to the appeal. We should view every call for a decision as a moment of truth. This is where the Holy Spirit affirms His transforming work on the heart, and the Bible instructor has the honor of being a partner in the process.

> "Not by might, nor by power, but by my spirit, saith the Lord of hosts" (Zech. 4:6).

Gratitude on the part of the attendee is crucial evidence of a heart being converted. Look for those signs and add to them an attitude of thanksgiving.

The Wiggins model teaches that certain variables influence a person's acting on a decision for Christ. It concludes that there exists a close connection between attitudes (feelings) toward performing an action, expectation (as presented in God's Word), and motivation (WIIFM—what's in it for me), or perceived consequences. It would probably be easy for an attendee to make a decision if they had no consequences to consider. Since children don't always take such things into account as deeply as adults, you will find that under normal circumstances it is much easier for them to make a decision for Christ.

But with adults, consequences often loom in a powerful way, and you must deal with them in a sensitive manner. For example, how will the decision affect basic needs—job; lifestyle; and attitudes of family members, coworkers, and close friends? What will relationships be like in a new church environment? How ready is a person to put aside former or current beliefs held for many years? Satan seems to bombard many candidates with all kinds of perceived conflicts and challenges surrounding a decision for Christ. That is why it is important to learn (and take private notes) as much about a person as necessary as your relationship with them grows. It makes it easier to sense their potential challenges and address them gradually by developing in them love for and faith in God through discussion, prayer, and other means of intervention prior to decision time.

As a Bible instructor you must plan ahead before every visit. You must pray for the Holy Spirit to give you sensitive discernment. It will take that to move attendees from where they are to where they need to be at each point in the evangelistic series. The attendees need to be in agreement with the evangelist each and every night. They should be at a spiritual place where they can hardly wait for the appeal before acting. As a result, they should be mentally and spiritually set to follow the truths and expectations of God's Word as presented. Write down possible questions that will determine the attendee's attitude toward a particular subject that you feel they are struggling with, and then memorize them for later use. Pray over them and claim positive answers from the attendee.

Tina had completed many of the lessons she received from the Bible instructors prior to the start of the evangelistic series. They had already introduced her to the subjects presented by the evangelist. Her questions had been answered, clarifications had been made in the home, and Tina was first of all excited that she understood where the evangelist was coming from on each topic. She felt the presentations were confirmation as to what the Lord was calling her to do. Thus when the appeals came, she eagerly responded. With joy she accepted the new learning and received it with gratitude and was now ready to follow Jesus all the way.

On the other hand, Rachel was struggling with the consequences she must face if she accepted the truths presented. As a result, her pace with the evangelist was way off. She knew that she needed to become a Sabbathkeeper and was willing to do so, but just could not see herself leaving her current church. Loving her pastor, she was very actively involved in the congregation. As a result, she wanted to keep the Sabbath at home on Saturday and attend her own church on Sunday. We sought to assure her that first of all, pastors are quite aware of the Word of God when it comes to the Sabbath but have chosen to remain tied to tradition and to promote it in their congregations to keep from ruffling feathers. They know that while it is not a sin to go to church any day of the week, there is nothing holy about Sunday.

God created the seventh-day Sabbath for one purpose and one only: to be set aside for His holy purpose. It has been so from Creation, and then God later placed it in the Ten Commandments for us to remember that He commands all to keep it holy. Moving from the fact that the Sabbath must be honored, we presented how to do exactly that. We cited Isaiah 58:13, 14 to give a perspective of God's expectations for Sabbath observance. And Ezekiel 20:12, 20 to demonstrate His seriousness about His day as a way to identify His people. Finally, we reinforced that with Revelation 22:14.

For Rachel to observe the Sabbath at home and attend her church on Sunday would put her in the position of following two masters. The Bible tells us that it is impossible to serve two masters (Matt. 6:24). But that passage doesn't stop there. It goes on to say: "Therefore I say unto you, Take no thought for your life, what ye shall eat, or what ye shall drink; nor yet for your body, what ye shall put on. Is not the life more than meat, and the body than raiment" (verse 25)?

Matthew 6 ends with this assurance:

"Therefore take no thought, saying, What shall we eat? or, What shall we drink? or, Wherewithal shall we be clothed? (For after all these things do the Gentiles seek:) for your heavenly Father knoweth that ye have need of all these things. But seek ye first the kingdom of God, and his righteousness; and all these things shall be added unto you" (verses 31-33).

Rachel began to move into step when she realized that she could not serve both God and human beings. It was not a decision that she could avoid, for God was calling her now, and she could not harden her heart against her Savior.

The Bible instructor must wrestle carefully and persistently against the powers of darkness that threaten the soul of each attendee. Stand in the gap between their soul and their Savior before and during each and every visit with them. "For we wrestle not against flesh and blood, but against principalities, against powers, against the rulers of the darkness of this world, against spiritual wickedness in high places" (Eph. 6:12). God has already given you as a Bible instructor the authority to do so. We are ambassadors on behalf of Christ (2 Cor. 5:18-20), and He would have us do as He would in the home.

Carefully ask the right questions, and address every response with encouraging, loving reassurances. Have a predetermined agenda, or theme, that will lead to a desired point of understanding and decision-making on a specific point. At the conclusion of the topical review, show the attendee through the Word of God and personal testimony the great blessings that await them after accepting the concepts taught or reviewed. Point out how valuable those blessings are. It is crucial to establish a favorable attitude (feeling) toward action for the right reason, *not* merely to comply with a doctrine. The love of/for God must be the appropriate incentive.

Christ "spoke directly to every mind and appealed to every heart. He watched the faces of His hearers, marked the lighting up of the countenance, the quick, responsive glance, which told that truth had reached the soul; and there vibrated in His heart the answering chord of sympathetic joy."*

Time is another factor that affects decision and action. The longer the interval between the decision and the behavior desired, the less likely it will happen. You should not wait until the end of the lesson, or encounter, to call for a decision on what has just been taught. Asking for decisions on small points along the way will make it much easier to gain a major commitment on the entire subject and most crucially when encountering testing truths.

Chapter Activities

1. Discuss the dynamics of a person being in step with the evangelist.
2. Discuss what you need to do to ensure the attendee is step with the evangelist.
3. Discuss why timing is so important to a follow-up visit with an attendee after they make a decision in response to an appeal.

---

* E. G. White, *Education*, p. 231.

CHAPTER 20

THREE DEGREES OF SEPARATION

Years ago a theory called "six degrees of separation" gained wide popularly. It proposed that everyone anywhere on earth is in some way or other only six steps or relationships from another person. A decision for Christ is the most important decision a person can make for themselves and the most important stand they can take before friends and relatives. We should not be surprised at all if it comes in stages, or degrees of change, and with great struggle. "As souls are on the point of leaving the enemy's ranks and coming up on the Lord's side, the contest is most severe and close. Satan and his angels are unwilling that any who have served under the banner of darkness should take their position under the bloodstained banner of Prince Immanuel."[1]

Decision-making is a time that Bible instructors should come close to their attendees, empathically feeling the spiritual struggle in which they may be engaged, yet allowing the Holy Spirit to give them strength. "It is through personal contact and association that men are reached by the saving power of the gospel. They are not saved in masses, but as individuals. Personal influence is a power. We must come close to those whom we desire to benefit."[2]

After the sermons and appeals, you must go as a Bible instructor into the homes and clinch decisions for baptism, prepare the candidates, and walk the journey with them to full fellowship in the family of God. "The love of Christ is diffusive and aggressive. If it is dwelling in us, it will flow out to others. We shall come close to them till their hearts are warmed by our unselfish interest and love. The sincere believers diffuse vital energy, which is penetrating and imparts new moral power to the souls for whom they labor. It is not the power of the man himself, but the power of the Holy Spirit that does the transforming work."[3] Therefore, Bible instructors must be just as spiritually prepared for God to use them to lead others to Him as those converts are spiritually desirous to be saved.

Decision-making will take place on many nights as the meetings crescendo toward baptism. It is not unusual for a person who has made a decision for Christ to rethink following through with it. That is why a visit from the Bible instructor as soon as possible following each and every decision night is so vital. Candidates may not have understood the gravity of what they have done. They may experience buyer's remorse when Satan engenders regrets, guilt, unworthiness, a Sabbath work conflict, an addiction, etc., and ultimately they decide against going forward with the choice they have made. Or they may feel inadequate, unprepared, fearful of the future, too sinful, or frightened of change, for starters. Whatever the reason for their hesitancy, you know that the enemy has planted it in their minds.

You must have confidence in their sincerity when they made the decision and work from there with the guidance of the Holy Spirit. Then you can take either a deductive or an inductive approach. Employing the deductive approach, you would start with the big picture and then identify the specific conflicts and address them (with the inductive approach, do just the opposite). Remind them of all that God has opened up to them, and that now He has chosen them to make a decision that will result in blessings beyond what they could ever ask or imagine. Remind them that it is God who has favored them and who is calling them to come out of tradition and join His remnant people worldwide. Next, sensitively probe to determine each of the hindrances the candidate struggles with and meet them with Bible truths. Later we will discuss some of the most frequent objections.

The level of trust and respect that you have developed over time will determine the degree of influence you will have during periods of decision. Pray and fast for your attendees as they move steadily through the degrees of separation to full surrender to Christ, and they should pray for themselves as well. Such moments are what the individual Bible studies and evangelistic presentations were designed to culminate—in a decision for Christ and baptism. Instead of six degrees of separation, we find three levels of readiness.

A-Interest or Ripe Fruit

Nothing could be more exciting than when the attendee asks if they can be baptized. Notice, I said when they *ask* to be baptized. They have been intentional in their search for truth, may have already expressed dissatisfaction with their faith group, and may even have an appreciation for the Seventh-day Adventist Church (it may not be their first encounter with Adventism). Now they want a change in lifestyle and demonstrate a desire to share with others what they have learned. Having accepted major doctrinal concepts all along the way in the home and night after night at the meetings, they have been in sync with the evangelist throughout the evangelistic series. Even though they have responded to the Spirit of God and are firm and excited in their decision to be baptized, you must still remain close to your attendees and affirm them all along the path of preparation.

B-Interest or Developing/Ripening Fruit

With others the struggle will be somewhere between mild to overwhelming. Many will have attended evangelistic meetings just for the knowledge they hope to get. They may know something about Seventh-day Adventists firsthand (attended a Sabbath service, special event, etc.) or had association with them (been a former member or have Adventist friends, family, taken a correspondence course, etc.), but lifestyle and/or relationships, conflicts with doctrines, etc., hinder them from making changes.

Now is the time for you as a Bible instructor to feel that God has sent you to help them address their objections. Once you have discovered their disagreements/or misgivings, succeeding studies and visits should include efforts (1) to reveal the enemy behind the scenes who has been creating their reticence, (2) to discuss clearly the bigger picture of God's power for breakthroughs, and (3) to provide biblical examples and personal testimonies of reassurance. You cannot deal with issues not yet identified. Gain a clear picture of the reason for the objection before bombarding the person with texts. You want to deal only with specific, identified questions. Rolling out texts just to gain a decision may only create more resistance. Keep it calm and simple.

If the struggle is with a Sabbath job, for example, citing texts about the Sabbath completely misses the point. The attendee's heart cry is how to deal with Sabbath employment, and that is what you must address. Since the situation requires counseling, refer the attendee to the pastor. Either invite the pastor to the home or arrange for a meeting in the pastor's office. Sit down with them and determine a course of action. If the person is willing to follow through with the meeting and the suggested action (perhaps a written letter of request for Sabbaths off, other job possibilities, etc.), more than likely they are actually serious in their desire to become part of the family of God.

> "There will be some that will take their position forever under the black banner of the powers of darkness; there are some that will take their position under the blood-stained banner of Prince Immanuel. Our words, our deportment, how we present the truth, may balance minds for or against the truth; and we want in every discourse, whether it is doctrinal or not, we want that Jesus Christ should be presented distinctly, as John declared, 'Behold the Lamb of God, that taketh away the sin of the world.' "[4]

C-Interest or Green Fruit

Some people come to evangelistic meetings simply because it seems to be a nonthreatening opportunity to learn more about the Bible. They have no real interest in leaving their own church or making any changes in their lifestyle. While they may be a recipient of an invitation by way of friend, church member, survey, etc., they have no particular motivation to alter their way of thinking about the doctrines presented from night to night. Such individuals are satisfied with the status quo and enjoy the prestige of the faith group they currently attend.

As a Bible instructor you cannot ignore them. Quite naturally the focus close to the time of baptism is on the A and B category interests, those preparing for that event. What we can do for those in the C category is continue to find avenues to challenge their faith to step up a little higher. God desires to do more for us than we can ask for or imagine, but our faith must be able to see beyond where we are to the possibilities when we trust God with our life for His cause.

- Do all that is possible to address the hesitation of those in category C while encouraging their continued attendance.
- Enroll them in other Bible study courses and, if possible, study with them after the evangelistic series ends.
- Suggest they join a Sabbath school class (preferably a new believer's class).
- Invite them to various events and to join the new believers' follow-up activities.
- Befriend them and introduce them to others willing to befriend them.

- Keep them on your church mailing list.
- Continue to pray for them.

Their casual interest can turn into a greater one, and in the end God will have another member in the kingdom of heaven. Never should we give up on a person until they ask us not to return or indicate that they do not want to continue the Bible studies. Even then they will be on our heart and in our prayers. We must consider our encounter with them as another seed that waits to germinate in their spirits until at some future time they accept the light shown them.

Chapter Activities

1. Review and discuss the attributes of the A, B, and C levels of interest.
2. Role-play pulling for a decision with someone at B-interest level.
3. Discuss how you would handle someone at C-interest level.

---

[1] E. G. White, *Testimonies*, vol.1, p. 646.

[2] Ellen G. White, *Thoughts From the Mount of Blessing* (Mountain View, Calif.: Pacific Press Pub. Assn., 1956), p. 36.

[3] *Ibid.*

[4] E. G. White, *Evangelism*, p. 299.

CHAPTER 21

ABOUT-FACE

A major skill you should have as a Bible instructor is the ease with which you meet objections resulting from the belief system of the attendee. You should remain composed even when you don't feel comfortable addressing the objection. Remember, within the team and materials now available you can always find help to meet any objection Satan might pose. The earlier you address those concerns, the better. Most objections can be handled effectively during the presentation reviews and through the question-and-answer box. That is a major reason it is important to encourage nightly attendance.

When attendees raise objections, it could indicate trust in you on their part, as well as an honest wrestling with the topic. You should welcome such responses and handle them with patience and consideration. They may be a cry for help to sort through the challenges and consequences of making an about-face break from the past. For certain they are an indication of a spiritual battle within, perpetrated by Satan himself.

When someone makes a redemptive about-face decision, it is usually the break that indicates a ready spirit to move forward. You must be very observant, listen carefully, and examine with great sensitivity what you may observe or hear that could be, or become, a roadblock to spiritual progress, a hindrance to that about-face. Be prayerful in your spirit. "For the Holy Ghost shall teach you in the same hour what ye ought to say" (Luke 12:12).

Following are some statements that may surface along with a sample comment and scriptures to address them.

Texts for Hesitating Souls

I am too great a sinner.

Assure them that we are all sinners saved by God's grace. Once we confess our sins to God, He not only truly forgives but cleanses us from all unrighteousness (1 John 1:9).

"Christ Jesus came into the world to save sinners; of whom I am chief" (1 Tim. 1:15)."Wherefore he is able also to save them to the uttermost that come unto God by him, seeing he ever liveth to make intercession for them" (Heb. 7:25).

"Come now, and let us reason together, saith the Lord: though your sins be as scarlet, they shall be as white as snow; though they be red like crimson, they shall be as wool" (Isa. 1:18).

I'm afraid I can't hold on.

Acknowledge their fear and assure them that those who face such fears and turn them into trust will go forward in the strength and presence of God, because they can walk by faith and not by sight (2 Cor. 5:7).

"I can do all things through Christ which strengtheneth me" (Phil. 4:13).

"I have called thee by thy name; thou art mine. When thou passest through the waters, I will be with thee; and through the rivers, they shall not overflow thee: when thou walkest through the fire, thou shalt not be burned; neither shall the flame kindle upon thee" (Isa. 43:1, 2).

"Now unto him that is able to keep you from falling, and to present you faultless before the presence of his glory with exceeding joy" (Jude 24).

I can't live up to the truth.

None of us can in our own strength. "For it is God which worketh in you both to will and to do of his good pleasure" (Phil. 2:13).

"There hath no temptation taken you but such as is common to man: but God is faithful, who will not suffer you to be tempted above that ye are able; but will with the temptation also make a way to escape, that ye may be able to bear it" (1 Cor. 10:13).

"For this thing I besought the Lord thrice, that it might depart from me. And he said unto me, My grace is sufficient for thee: for my strength is made perfect in weakness. Most gladly therefore will I rather glory in my infirmities, that the power of Christ may rest upon me" (2 Cor. 12:8, 9).

"But as many as received him, to them gave he power to become the sons of God, even to them that believe on his name" (John 1:12).

I don't think I can live up to the rules.

Rules are hard to follow when approached from the wrong reason. God really only requires two: to love God with all our strength, and equal to it should be our love for each other (Mark 12:29-31). Then through the Ten Commandments He details what that should involve. Remind them of how much they love God. Also remind them that we don't keep the law to be saved but rather because we are saved. Obeying His law is a natural response to loving Him with all our heart.

"For if there be first a willing mind, it is accepted according to that a man hath, and not according to that he hath not" (2 Cor. 8:12).

"I press toward the mark for the prize of the high calling of God in Christ Jesus" (Phil. 3:14).

"I can do all things through Christ which strengtheneth me" (Phil. 4:13).

I will wait until I get a sign from God.

Waiting for a sign is a wise approach. Let them know that those who have sincerely looked for a sign have found it in God's Word. Direct them to Ezekiel 20:12, 20, in which God made the Sabbath a sign identifying those for whom He is truly their God and the one who sanctifies them.

"Come ye near unto me, hear ye this; I have not spoken in secret from the beginning; from the time that it was, there am I: and now the Lord God, and his Spirit, hath sent me" (Isa. 48:16).

"And hereby we do know that we know him, if we keep his commandments" (1 John 2:3).

One time in the Old Testament God had already given a promise of victory to the people of Israel. Then He challenged Ahaz in Isaiah 7:10-12: "Moreover the Lord spake again unto Ahaz, saying, Ask thee a sign of the Lord thy God; ask it either in the depth, or in the height above. But Ahaz said, I will not ask, neither will I tempt the Lord."

My family will not support me taking this step.

Assure them that it is a common reaction at first, but that God has chosen them out of their family and out of the world (John 15:19). He has a special calling on their life here and for eternity.

"He that loveth father or mother more than me, is not worthy of me: and he that loveth son or daughter more than me, is not worthy of me. And he that taketh not his cross, and followeth after me, is not worthy of me. He that findeth his life shall lose it: and he that loseth his life for my sake, shall find it" (Matt. 10:37-39).

"If ye were of the world, the world would love his own: but because ye are not of the world, but I have chosen you out of the world, therefore the world hateth you" (John 15:19).

"But now they desire a better country, that is, an heavenly: wherefore God is not ashamed to be called their God: for he hath prepared for them a city" (Heb. 11:16).

I can't turn my back on my family and friends.

Explain that they are certainly not turning their back on family and friends but rather leading the way for their eternal salvation. Now they can help others to find the same freedom that God has given them.

"And he said unto them, Verily I say unto you, There is no man that hath left house, or parents, or brethren, or wife, or children, for the kingdom of God's sake, Who shall not receive manifold more in this present time, and in the world to come life everlasting" (Luke 18:29, 30).

"Be not thou therefore ashamed of the testimony of our Lord, nor of me his prisoner: but be thou partaker of the afflictions of the gospel according to the power of God" (2 Tim. 1:8).

I don't believe it is necessary to unite with a church.

Uniting with a church for the wrong reason would not be good, but God does have a purpose for the institution. Direct them to Ephesians 4:11-16, which shows that God uses His true church for the growth of His people. Then go to verses 18-24, which remind us how we have come from ignorance about spiritual things and how the church is there to receive us with open arms and provide the environment for continuing spiritual growth.

"Not forsaking the assembling of ourselves together, as the manner of some is; but exhorting one another: and so much the more, as ye see the day approaching" (Heb. 10:25).

"And he gave some, apostles; and some, prophets; and some, evangelists; and some, pastors and teachers; For the perfecting of the saints, for the work of the ministry, for the edifying of the body of Christ" (Eph. 4:11, 12).

I've been going this way a long time and can't see myself changing.

Assure them of how much a blessing it is to know that God never forgot them and may now be giving them a last opportunity to make their relationship with Him stronger (2 Peter 1:9, 10). As God grows us in Him, we can never give a blind eye to things in His Word that may be new to us. It is His desire that we constantly mature spiritually (Eph. 4:15, 16).

"And the Lord said, My Spirit shall not always strive with man" (Gen. 6:3).

"Trust in the Lord with all thine heart; and lean not unto thine own understanding" (Prov. 3:5).

I will wait until I feel that the Spirit of God has convinced me.

The Holy Spirit has spoken through the clear Word of God. And the Spirit never encourages anyone to wait once they have received truth and have been called to come out of spiritual darkness. Tomorrow may be too late to make a decision. In fact, tomorrow may never arrive.

"We then, as workers together with him, beseech you also that ye receive not the grace of God in vain. (For he saith, I have heard thee in a time accepted, and in the day of salvation have I succoured thee: behold, now is the accepted time; behold, now is the day of salvation.)" (2 Cor. 6:1, 2).

"Then shall the kingdom of heaven be likened unto ten virgins, which took their lamps, and went forth to meet the bridegroom" (Matt. 25:1). Read verses 1-13.

"Howbeit, when he, the Spirit of truth, is come, he will guide you into all truth" (John 16:13).

"Then said Jesus to those Jews which believed on him, If ye continue in my word, then are ye my disciples indeed; And ye shall know the truth, and the truth shall make you free" (John 8:31, 32).

"He that believeth and is baptized, shall be saved; but he that believeth not, shall be damned" (Mark 16:16).

People are already giving me a rough time, and it will only get worse.

You might remind them that those individuals now criticizing them should have done so when the attendees weren't following God all the way, not when they are turning over their life to God who has given them another chance. Rather than discouraging them, such opponents need to consider making the same decision themselves.

"Blessed are ye, when men shall revile you, and persecute you, and shall say all manner of evil against you falsely, for my sake. Rejoice, and be exceeding glad: for great is your reward in heaven: for so persecuted they the prophets which were before you" (Matt. 5:11, 12).

"Yea, and all that will live godly in Christ Jesus shall suffer persecution. But evil men and seducers shall wax worse and worse, deceiving, and being deceived. But continue thou in the things which thou hast learned and hast been assured of, knowing of whom thou hast learned them" (2 Tim. 3:12, 13).

"Fear none of those things which thou shalt suffer: behold, the devil shall cast some of you into prison, that ye may be tried; and ye shall have tribulation ten days: be thou faithful unto death, and I will give thee a crown of life" (Rev. 2:10).

Chapter Activities

1. Discuss your thoughts on why people who say they truly love God object to learning and accepting additional biblical truth.
2. Review and discuss each of the objections addressed above.
3. Role-play handling at least one of the given objections.

Meeting Sabbathkeeping Arguments

Here are some specific Sabbath arguments that often surface. Always be patient, a good listener, and considerate of the person's real—and perceived—challenges. Ideally, they will answer their own questions, given the applicable scriptures, appropriate reasoning, sensitive questioning, and loving support. The material here is provided as examples for the purpose of giving ideas on how to handle such objections along with several Bible references that you can select from, depending on the specific situation. Remember, no more than two or three relevant scriptures discussed in a nonthreatening, noncombative manner should be sufficient.

If the person still seems resistant, either pray together about it and/or go to another subject. Allow the attendee time to contemplate the matter further. Give a research assignment and/or some scriptural references. Set a definite appointment to return and review the assignment. Always ensure that your final words (and your closing prayers) are pleasant and encouraging. Maintaining your good relationship with your attendee is of utmost importance.

The cross did away with the Sabbath. We are now under the new dispensation.

Ask them if it is the only thing holding them back from honoring God on His day. If it could be made clear to them, would they then step out in faith and follow Christ all the way, including honoring His Sabbath? Genesis 2:1-3 tells us that the Sabbath was a part of Creation. It began when God established the seventh day, long before any dispensations. As long as there is a seventh day, it will always be Sabbath, God's holy day. In Ezekiel 20:12, 20 the Lord reiterates the fact that the Sabbath is a sign not only of Creation, but re-creation—redemption. It reminds us forever that just as God set apart the Sabbath for holy use, He does the same thing for those who receive His redemption. The Lord has made the Sabbath a sign that He is our God and we are His completely. That is exactly why the devil has tried through the years to destroy the Sabbath. We must reject him and accept Christ.

"Moreover, also I gave them my sabbaths, to be a sign between me and them, that they might know that I am the Lord that sanctify them." Hallow my sabbaths; and they shall be a sign between me and you, that ye may know that I am the Lord your God" (Eze. 20:12, 20).

"Thus the heavens and the earth were finished, and all the host of them. And on the seventh day God ended his work which he had made; and he rested on the seventh day from all his work which he had made. And God blessed the seventh day, and sanctified it: because that in it he had rested from all his work which God created and made" (Gen. 2:1-3).

"And he said unto them, The sabbath was made for man, and not man for the sabbath: Therefore the Son of man is Lord also of the Sabbath" (Mark 2:27, 28).

"If ye love me, keep my commandments" (John 14:15).

"For if Jesus had given them rest, then would he not afterward have spoken of another day. There remaineth therefore a rest to the people of God. For he that is entered into his rest, he also hath ceased from his own works, as God did from his. Let us labour therefore to enter into that rest, lest any man fall after the same example of unbelief" (Heb. 4:8-11).

I can't make a living in my business if I keep the Sabbath.

Again, ask them if that is the only thing that is holding them back from honoring God on His day. If it can be made clear to them, would they then step out in faith and follow Christ all the way, including honoring His Sabbath? Suggest that if God blessed their business all those years while He waited patiently for them to acknowledge Him and the time He has set aside for rest and communion with Him, would He not bless their business even more once they determined to do His will? Would God not show them even greater favor? Pray with them that the Lord would reveal to them how to transform their business schedule to one that honors Him and His holy day of rest without loss. But before doing that, you should clear up their concern through God's Holy Word.

"Trust in the Lord, and do good; so shalt thou dwell in the land, and verily thou shalt be fed" (Ps. 37:3).

"But he knoweth the way that I take: when he hath tried me, I shall come forth as gold. My foot hath held his steps, his way have I kept, and not declined. Neither have I gone back from the commandment of his lips; I have esteemed the words of his mouth more than my necessary food" (Job 23:10-12).

"Therefore thus saith the Lord God, Behold, my servants shall eat, but ye shall be hungry: behold, my servants shall drink, but ye shall be thirsty: behold, my servants shall rejoice, but ye shall be ashamed: Behold, my servants shall sing for joy of heart, but ye shall cry for sorrow of heart, and shall howl for vexation of spirit" (Isa. 65:13, 14).

"But seek ye first the kingdom of God, and his righteousness; and all these things shall be added unto you" (Matt. 6:33).

"Then said Jesus unto his disciples, If any man will come after me, let him deny himself, and take up his cross, and follow me. For whosoever will save his life, shall lose it: and whosoever will lose his life for my sake shall find it. For what is a man profited, if he shall gain the whole world, and lose his own soul? or what shall a man give in exchange for his soul?" (Matt. 16:24-26).

I risk losing my job.

Explain to the individual that the United States has laws that protect religious freedom and that you can have someone give them more information about their rights. It's possible that something could be negotiated with their supervisor or the owner of the company. If it did come down to them choosing to resign from their job because of Sabbath labor, encourage them to seek the wisdom of God and then have a determined mind to obey and trust Him rather than continuing to trample on the rest time that God declares is holy.

"Fear ye not the reproach of men, neither be ye afraid of their revilings" (Isa. 51:7).

"The law of thy mouth is better unto me than thousands of gold and silver" (Ps. 119:72).

"Thou wilt keep him in perfect peace, whose mind is stayed on thee: because he trusteth in thee. Trust ye in the Lord for ever: for in the Lord Jehovah is everlasting strength" (Isa. 26:3, 4).

"Trust in the Lord with all thine heart; and lean not unto thine own understanding. In all thy ways acknowledge him, and he shall direct thy paths" (Prov. 3:5, 6).

"And also that every man should eat and drink, and enjoy the good of all his labour, it is the gift of God" (Eccl. 3:13).

"But as for you, ye thought evil against me; but God meant it unto good, to bring to pass, as it is this day, to save much people alive" (Gen. 50:20).

I had better save up some money before I do make such a move.

Emphasize that it is always amazing how God steps in once we have committed ourselves to Him. Explain that as they move forward in faith, doors will open that they could never have thought of or imagined.

"The blessing of the Lord, it maketh rich, and he addeth no sorrow with it" (Prov. 10:22).

"A faithful man shall abound with blessings: but he that maketh haste to be rich shall not be innocent" (Prov. 28:20).

"Lay not up for yourselves treasures upon earth, where moth and rust doth corrupt, and where thieves break through and steal: But lay up for yourselves treasures in heaven, where neither moth nor rust doth corrupt, and where thieves do not break through nor steal: For where your treasure is, there will your heart be also" (Matt. 6:19-21).

"But seek ye first the kingdom of God, and his righteousness; and all these things shall be added unto you" (Matt. 6:33).

I have a long history with my church. I am afraid to change now.

Suggest that they should feel highly favored that God has chosen them to receive more knowledge and understanding of His Word. He has entrusted them with the great privilege of more truth, not merely to receive it, but to obey it, even if it means leading the way in following Christ. As a result, they have no idea what awesome ways God will use the testimony of their life as others witness His favor upon them and their determination to deny self and follow Him all the way.

"I made haste, and delayed not to keep thy commandments" (Ps. 119:60).

"If thou turn away thy foot from the sabbath, from doing thy pleasure on my holy day; and call the sabbath a delight, the holy of the Lord, honourable; and shalt honour him, not doing thine own ways, nor finding thine own pleasure, nor speaking thine own words: Then shalt thou delight thyself in the Lord; and I will cause thee to ride upon the high places of the earth, and feed thee with the heritage of Jacob thy father: for the mouth of the Lord hath spoken it" (Isa. 58:13, 14).

"I am the good shepherd, and know my sheep, and am known of mine. As the Father knoweth me, even so know I the Father: and I lay down my life for the sheep. And other sheep I have, which are not of this fold: them also I must bring, and they shall hear my voice; and there shall be one fold, and one shepherd" (John 10:14-16).

"But ye believe not, because ye are not of my sheep, as I said unto you. My sheep hear my voice, and I know them, and they follow me: And I give unto them eternal life; and they shall never perish, neither shall any man pluck them out of my hand" (verses 26-28).

This is so new to me. I don't think it's that important to keep the Sabbath.

Explain that God is Creator and Redeemer. We are not our own, but His creation, bought with the price of the life of His own Son, Jesus Christ. Surely God wants only what aligns itself with His infinite love and His perfect will and purpose. That is what we should seek in order to be in the path of His blessings here and to inherit life eternal.

"And it shall come to pass, if thou shalt hearken diligently unto the voice of the Lord thy God, to observe and to do all his commandments which I command thee this day, that the Lord thy God will set thee on high above all nations of the earth: And all these blessings shall come on thee, and overtake thee, if thou shalt hearken unto the voice of the Lord thy God. . . . And the Lord shall make thee the head, and not the tail; and thou shalt be above only, and thou shalt not be beneath; if that thou hearken unto the commandments of the Lord thy God, which I command thee this day, to observe and to do them: And thou shalt not go aside from any of the words which I command thee this day, to the right hand, or to the left, to go after other gods to serve them. But it shall come to pass, if thou wilt not hearken unto the voice of the Lord thy God, to observe to do all his commandments and his statutes which I command thee this day; that all these curses shall come upon thee, and overtake thee." "If thou wilt not observe to do all the words of this law that are written in this book, that thou mayest fear this glorious and fearful name, The Lord Thy God" (Deut. 28:1-15, 58).

"And Elijah came unto all the people, and said, How long halt ye between two opinions? if the Lord be God, follow him: but if Baal, then follow him. And the people answered him not a word" (1 Kings 18:21).

"Thus saith the Lord, Stand ye in the ways, and see, and ask for the old paths, where is the good way, and walk therein, and ye shall find rest for your souls. But they said, We will not walk therein" (Jer. 6:16).

"Then Peter and the other apostles answered and said, We ought to obey God rather than men" (Acts 5:29).

"Blessed are they that do his commandments, that they may have right to the tree of life, and may enter in through the gates into the city" (Rev. 22:14).

It isn't convenient for me to keep the Sabbath.

Our greatest desire should be to be filled with the Holy Spirit as Jesus was and to walk in His footsteps. Our greatest pleasure should be to love God with all our heart, mind, and strength, and our neighbor as ourselves. And our greatest joy should be in serving God and putting Him first. It is our relationship with God, not a decision based on convenience, that is the basis of how we serve Him and whether we will be determined in our obedience to His will. Tell hesitant individuals that God has chosen them out of the world. Now they will have to decide to answer the call.

"Then said Jesus unto his disciples, If any man will come after me, let him deny himself, and take up his cross, and follow me" (Matt. 16:24).

"And he that taketh not his cross, and followeth after me, is not worthy of me. He that findeth his life shall lose it: and he that loseth his life for my sake shall find it" (Matt. 10:38, 39).

"Jesus said unto him, Thou shalt love the Lord thy God with all thy heart, and with all thy soul, and with all thy mind. This is the first and great commandment. And the second is like unto it, Thou shalt love thy neighbour as thyself. On these two commandments hang all the law and the prophets" (Matt. 22:37-40).

"If ye were of the world, the world would love his own: but because ye are not of the world, but I have chosen you out of the world, therefore the world hateth you. Remember the word that I said unto you, The servant is not greater than his lord. If they have persecuted me, they will also persecute you; if they have kept my saying, they will keep yours also" (John 15:19, 20).

"I have manifested thy name unto the men which thou gavest me out of the world: thine they were, and thou gavest them me; and they have kept thy word" (John 17:6).

"Wherefore also we pray always for you, that our God would count you worthy of this calling, and fulfil all the good pleasure of his goodness, and the work of faith with power: That the name of our Lord Jesus Christ may be glorified in you, and ye in him, according to the grace of our God and the Lord Jesus Christ" (2 Thess. 1:11, 12).

Remember the above texts are samples of some scriptures that you can use to get hesitating individuals back on track. You could employ many other passages, but always keep in mind that using too many texts (more than two or three) to strengthen faith may become an overkill or oversell and therefore have the opposite effect.

Your objective is to question continuously "why" they feel the way they do and to explore the objections using what God has said in His Word as the basis of the discussion, not the attendee's personal issues. The focus should be on the requirement and the blessing pointed out in the scripture, not on criticism of the person's stand. Never use the Bible to beat a person into submission. Remember the adage "A person convinced against their will is of the same opinion still." Rather well-chosen and applicable scriptures should seek to reach the heart with the awesome love of God. Let the attendee accept truth for the right reason, not out of fear of God's wrath.

Assure the attendee that you understand how they *feel.* That they are not alone, as many others in their situation have *felt* the exact same way. "But Mr. Jones, they have *found* . . . [use a scriptural promise]." Again we are employing the simple approach called the F-F-F technique. After you've discussed all their objections and have come done to what appears to be the final snag in their thinking, get a commitment that if the objection could be removed, would they be willing to make a full commitment to following Christ all the way right now? Then restate their objection and answer it with the Word of God. You should be ready to secure the decision at this point.

Remind your attendee:

- Jesus gave His life so that they could inherit eternal life (John 3:16).
- When anyone confesses their sins, God will forgive their sins and cleanse them from all unrighteousness (1 John 1:9).
- They are the apple of God's eye (Deut. 32:10).

- God is bringing them out of darkness into His marvelous light (1 Peter 2:9).
- God has promised always to provide a way of escape from temptation (1 Cor. 10:13).
- God will provide the strength they need to move forward day by day (Phil. 4:13).
- God has thoughts of peace for them and wonderful plans for their life that will only come to fruition when they give their life to Him (Jer. 29:11).
- This world is not their home. They're just passing through. As sons and daughters of God, they have a future, an eternal inheritance (John 17:14).
- They are of great value to God (Matt. 10:30, 31).

Other questions and thoughts you might consider when appropriate are:

- Don't you think the Lord will be pleased to see you baptized on Sabbath morning? Based on what you have told me, don't we agree that you should follow the example of Christ in this matter?
- A decision for baptism is a wise decision. Is it too hard for you? Of course not. And do you know why? Because you love the Lord, and He will give you the courage you need to do the right thing.
- Would you like to go into the water with a friend or by yourself?
- Would you prefer your baptism in the morning or in the evening?
- After you are baptized, you will receive a certificate of baptism, suitable for framing. Write your name on this baptismal card the way you want it spelled on your certificate.
- How many people are you planning to invite to your baptismal ceremony? I know it's going to be big and special. May I help you with the invitations?
- Many people who love the Lord are planning to be baptized on Sabbath. I will be very happy to include your name on that list. Just read and fill out this card. I will be glad to help you if you need assistance.
- Here is a list of things you will need for your baptism. Is there anything that you don't understand?

During your personal study, go over each text given above. Study them carefully. Write out the love of God expressed in each scripture so that when you present them you will be able to explain them in light of the love of God for each one of us. This must be prepared in advance, studied, memorized, and rehearsed. By so doing you give the Holy Spirit fuel to work with in bringing back to your memory at the appropriate time things you have already studied. Then too you will not appear to be cramming scripture down the attendee's throat. Give encouragement and any possible practical assistance. Not only read the text and discuss it, but pray that God will prepare your heart to do His bidding. Calling for a decision for Christ is a very solemn occasion.

Everyone may not accept baptism at the scheduled time, but that does not mean that the Holy Spirit has left them, so neither should you. Patience on your part as a Bible instructor is crucial. Always leave the home with an open door for a welcomed return, whether you gained the decision or not. Remember the Holy Spirit is doing a work of conversion and transformation during your visit and in your absence that no human being can accomplish.

Chapter Activities

1. Review and role-play F-F-F.
2. Discuss some of the objectives for committing to Sabbathkeeping and how you can handle them.
3. Role-play how you would respond to a person who refuses the invitation for baptism.

CHAPTER 22

OLD MAN YESTERDAY, NEW MAN FOREVER

Normally the evangelist publicly prepares the attendee to make a decision for baptism. Every sermon topic seeks to lead a soul to Christ. You, as a Bible instructor, prepare the attendee with each visit, beginning with the very first one, for accepting Christ through baptism. You ask the questions that will lead the individual to reveal their acceptance or rejection of biblical truth. And you will follow up if necessary to address areas in question.

Baptism is one of the most important decisions of a lifetime. When a person chooses to perform this public expression of an inner change, heaven goes into action. God has completely forgiven the candidate's sins, and their names are now written in the Lamb's book of life. They become adopted—even better, grafted—into the family of God so that they become part of the holy nation, royal priesthood, and a distinct people. It qualifies them to sit with Christ on His throne to judge the wicked world and the fallen angels. The old human being is in the past, and God makes all things new. He writes His law in the heart of the new person and baptizes them with the Spirit of God. Satan no longer rules—now it's Christ who lives in them. They become citizens of the kingdom of God, with a right, when Christ returns to claim them, to the tree of life. Rather than a slave to sin, they live a victorious life through Jesus Christ here and throughout eternity, and there is so much more. This indeed is an important step in the life of a new believer, and as a Bible instructor you must guard it with great care.

The Baptismal Bundle

The baptism bundle should be received as a bouquet of roses rather than a loaded gun. It should be handed to the baptismal candidate as a gift with an attached invitation from Jesus Himself, rather than shoved at them with attached threats. The preparation for baptism should be seen as no less special than that for a beautiful wedding. There should be excitement in the air, yet details to cover.

Have the baptism bundle information professionally organized and handy to give to each candidate. You can conveniently place the following items in a large Ziploc bag:

- A small plastic bag in which to place baptism items. You can order special baptism bags, or the small white kitchen trash bags can serve the purpose.
- A baptism bundle card listing the items needed for baptism. Items should be kept simple:
    - shirt and pants to wear in the baptism pool (normally under a provided baptismal robe)
    - pair of socks
    - change of undergarments,
    - bath towel
    - swim or shower cap (optional)

It will be up to the head Bible instructor, or the evangelist, how to handle the baptism bundles. They can deal with them in several ways:

- Give the bundle to the candidate while you wait for them to gather their things.
- Arrange with the candidate how you want to pick it up—whether at their home or brought to you at the meeting auditorium.
- Have the candidate bring their bundle with them when they come to the baptism.
- If it is a very large baptism, you may ask your candidates to wear the clothes they will be baptized in and put in the bundle the other things listed, along with what they plan to wear home.

Always explain to the candidate how the baptism will take place. Sometimes the pastor, or associate pastor, will accompany the Bible instructor to give the baptism bundle to the candidate, but more often it's the responsibility of the Bible instructors to take care of distributing the bundles with the pastors getting involved only if challenges are foreseen. If the baptism numbers are smaller, the pastor may want to meet the candidates beforehand in order to get to know them. Scenarios vary with each pastor.

Go over the items and solicit any questions. Remind the candidate that they should not wear any earrings or jewelry into the baptism pool.

Explain that when they gave their heart to the Lord, He accepted them just as they were, without any pretense or show. They are now coming in a very special way to dedicate their life to God. Jewelry would not be appropriate. (Hopefully a session on such things as jewelry will have already been presented prior to their baptismal date.)

Also glue an ID label onto the bag (if the special baptism bags were not used) for the candidate's name and gender. The information card should be attached (stapled) to the ID label or retained by the Bible instructor, rather than placed inside the bag. Note: No one should ever open or go inside a candidate's baptism bag for any reason. An individual's personal items are in the bag. They have entrusted the Bible instructor with the bag with the understanding that what's in it is confidential.

The information card should list needed information such as:

- full name (the way it is to be written on baptismal certificate)
- full address
- contact information (home and mobile phone numbers, e-mail address)
- age
- complete birth date

Optional items may include:

- names and age range of others living in the home
- favorite song and scripture verse
- what role they would consider serving in the church

Remember, neither the Bible instructor nor anyone else should ever look in or go into a candidate's bag for any reason. If there is something needed out of the bag or something else to be placed in the bag, the candidate must do that. Respect the privacy of the candidate at all times. Place any additional items in another bag and attach it to the original one. Only the candidate should ever put anything in the bag itself.

Review of the Baptism Vows

Follow the instructions of the evangelist or head Bible instructor regarding when and how to review the vows of Christian standards. Normally someone on the pastoral team goes over the vows with the candidates. This is preferable because it gives the candidate and the pastoral team an opportunity to see and interact with each other prior to the baptism.

If the Bible instructors review the vows of the Seventh-day Adventist Church with each candidate for baptism on their list, the candidate should also receive a copy for them to keep. Encourage the candidates to go over all scriptures associated with the vow. They should understand that their baptism is not only a testimony, or witness, of a life committed to Christ, but also a testimony that they have chosen the Seventh-day Adventist Church for their spiritual growth and nurturing. Perhaps on a second visit, or at a general session of baptism candidates, the instructor or evangelist should present a little more about the Seventh-day Adventist Church.

Individual pastors will introduce the new believers to the Seventh-day Adventist Church in different ways, as is often the case with the role and writings of Ellen G. White. Having a little background information about the church's history and structure confirms in the minds of the candidate that indeed they are actually joining the Adventist Church. By giving them some highlights of the history of the denomination's ever-expanding growth and international organizations, the candidate has a little more to take pride in and an enhanced desire to be a part of a worldwide Christian organization. Most people come out of small local congregations (sometimes without even a full-time pastor), while others may have belonged to small family congregations. Thus, joining the Adventist Church will be a major adjustment. They may have few comparisons to the size, diversity, and extensive ministries associated with the Adventist Church.

As a church family Adventists have much to praise God for and to be proud of. Currently one of the fastest-growing religious organizations, we are a world church, well known for its emphasis on education and wholistic health principles. The Adventist Church boasts a membership approaching 20 million people, and if one included the branch Sabbath schools, it would catapult to more than 25 million. Adventists operate churches, schools, and medical facilities in more than 200 countries and territories, and operate numerous publishing houses and media centers that broadcast its three major private networks and numerous programs. Adventist universities and colleges rank among the best in many nations. It is easy to purchase information for the candidates or direct them to the official Web site of the General Conference: www.adventist.org.

We should provide such information, because the notion that the Seventh-day Adventist Church is a cult that follows Ellen White remains strong everywhere I go. Hopefully some actual facts will help dispel the fallacy if candidates find themselves barraged by well-intentioned friends and family. Normally the evangelist will provide the audience with a presentation on prophecy and the introduction of Ellen G. White to the

Millerite movement that led to the establishment of the church in the 1860s.

Normally a litany of concerns will emerge as the candidates struggle with their decision to be baptized into the family of God. Some questions may seem insurmountable to the new candidate. Should they let their pastor know about their change of denomination? Because their parents will not support their decision, what should they do? They cannot understand why they should give up their jewelry. Perhaps they work on Saturdays. Take each of their concerns very seriously. If you don't feel equipped to handle the situation that arises, let the candidates know that someone more capable of giving them appropriate guidance will answer their questions. However, as a Bible instructor, it is your responsibility to be prepared for such issues. Discuss possible questions in Bible instructor observational reviews and do your research by speaking to the pastors and/or head Bible instructor. You will find much good material available now addressing such challenging questions.

You should teach attendees in such a way that the individuals will feel the urgency not only to accept what is being taught but also to put it into practice. It is the work of the Holy Spirit to take the candidate from where they are and move them to their high calling in Christ Jesus. Thus changes in the life and lifestyle indicate the work of the Holy Spirit on the heart. For God is interested in not merely spiritual growth but also our moral awareness, our physical conscientiousness, our financial and material blessings and opportunities, and our social life.

> "Beloved, I wish above all things that thou mayest prosper and be in health, even as thy soul prospereth" (3 John 2).

It is the responsibility of the Bible instructor to take note of any addictions, behaviors, or lifestyle challenges that will conflict with the baptism vows that we are asking the candidates to accept. If they are not already in harmony with the baptismal vows (such areas as living together outside of marriage, working on the Sabbath or in a field frowned upon by the church, addicted to harmful and/or illegal substances, eating unclean meats, and wearing excessive jewelry), make the pastor/evangelist and head Bible instructor aware of it as soon as possible and address the issues utilizing the highest standards of professionalism. Preferably deal with such conflicts prior to baptism. While it is much easier to resolve conflicts early on as they are presented by the evangelist during the evangelism series, it is never too late to confront them in the spirit of Christ and find workable remedies. Countless times, individuals have testified of how God healed and delivered determined and committed ones from addictions to tobacco and illegal drugs, for example. The Lord is on the side of those who truly desire to be set free. And that is the place to which the Bible instructor must guide the candidate.

Leading them to a determined commitment to be freed from the world and all its vices and conflicts with a life in Christ is another most important charge for all Bible instructors, and something that cannot be overstated. It is your responsibility as a Bible instructor to be observant and to ask careful questions as a subject comes up during the evangelistic series and/or in the Bible study guides and then to deal with it at that point. Help the candidates to embrace the view that their bodies are holy temples being prepared to be dedicated to God for His higher calling.

Paul described our bodies are the temple for the indwelling of the Holy Spirit. "What? know ye not that your body is the temple of the Holy Ghost which is in you, which ye have of God, and ye are not your own? For ye are bought with a price: therefore glorify God in your body, and in your spirit, which are God's" (1 Cor. 6:19, 20).

As a Bible instructor you have the awesome privilege of helping free others from the bondage of addictions, habits, lifestyles, and belief systems that have kept them from fully realizing a fruitful relationship with God. Be there for them. Urge them. Work with them. Fast and pray for and with them until God delivers them from the shackles that bind them.

Work with the pastor, if necessary, to find support groups and specific programs dealing with the candidates' problems. If permitted, bring others into their lives who have overcome in the areas in which they are struggling.

For more years than she'd want to count, Jacqueline hadn't left the house without her heavy makeup, rings on every finger, and all kinds of other jewelry. She couldn't imagine removing her jewelry to begin her new life with Christ. That was more difficult than disposing of the shrimp and pork in her refrigerator and completely changing her diet, more challenging than walking away from her longtime dedication to her church, or even stopping her house cleaning on Sabbath. This one thing halted any forward movement toward baptism. One of our new Bible instructors had had a similar challenge. We asked her to come with us to share her experience with Jacqueline. It was such a beautiful testimony of struggle and triumph that it brought Jacqueline to tears. The conviction reached her heart that evening, and we witnessed her complete deliverance.

Joe had chewed tobacco since childhood. Not one day (other than the days he unsuccessfully tried to quit the habit) could he recall not having a plug in his mouth. He had attempted to overcome the habit several times and failed. We asked a pastor who likewise had struggled with the habit to meet with Joe. Again, a personal testimony of deliverance was compelling. The pastor did not stop with just his story, but took Joe through the steps for breaking the addiction and offered to be his prayer buddy. Joe agreed to try again. With his wife's help, he collected all the tobacco hidden throughout the house and car and bagged it for the pastor. Nervous, but determined, Joe knelt with us for prayer—and has never looked back.

Personal testimonies combined with fervent prayer and support can bring someone to complete surrender like nothing else. You must do all you can to help potential baptismal candidates achieve victory over their addictions. However, there will be cases in which deliverance does not come completely before baptism. Such incidences can become a challenging call simply because no one can judge the heart. People have been known to lie about and hide their addictions from the Bible instructor because of their enormous challenge to overcome on the one hand, and their enormous desire to be baptized on the other. Your responsibility as a Bible instructor is not to decide how near to "perfect" the candidate is according to Seventh-day Adventist rules, but rather to determine how close the candidate is to seeing God and experiencing His love. While we might have to walk a mile in the shoes of a person challenged with an addiction even to begin to understand their plight, we can approach such a situation in the assurance of three scriptures:

> "So shall my word be that goeth forth out of my mouth: it shall not return unto me void, but it shall accomplish that which I please, and it shall prosper in the thing whereto I sent it. For ye shall go out with joy, and be led forth with peace: the mountains and the hills shall break forth before you into singing, and all the trees of the field shall clap their hands" (Isa 55:11, 12).
>
> "If we confess our sins, he is faithful and just to forgive us our sins, and to cleanse us from all unrighteousness" (1 John 1:9).
>
> "For whatsoever is born of God overcometh the world: and this is the victory that overcometh the world, even our faith" (1 John 5:4).

Depending on where the candidate is in their relationship to the baptismal vows, the pastor should have the last word based upon the recommendation of the Bible instructor. The goal is not to discourage anyone, and circumstances do vary widely, but it is usually better to set a goal of a future baptism for those still struggling with problems than to baptize them under false pretenses.

Make every effort to help candidates grow in faith and in experiential knowledge of Jesus Christ so that they can stand before the congregation with integrity as they recite their baptismal vows. The focus should be on winning spiritual battles by the power of God. Individuals with addictions of any kind should be able to come to the people of God and be led to victory not only from the addiction but in knowing Him in a way never before experienced. They should not leave the way they came, and will not if the church combines its faith and prayer power to make them whole.

God wants to set sinners free, so as a church we must ask ourselves, have we succumbed to an environment like many of the towns and cities Jesus went to but could not work any miracles because of their unbelief? Addiction battles are no time to lower our guard, shrink from, or shirk our responsibility. On the contrary, it is time to bring in the heavy artillery of fasting and prayer, drawing the candidate closer to the throne of God and crying out like Jacob in Genesis 32:26: "I will not let you go, Lord, until you bless me with the victory." Encourage the candidate to pray (and fast) and meditate on scriptures such as:

"I will not let thee go, except thou bless me" (Gen. 32:26).

"And said with tears, Lord, I believe; help thou mine unbelief" (Mark 9:24).

"I can do all things through Christ which strengtheneth me" (Phil. 4:13).

"But thanks be to God, which giveth us [me] the victory through our Lord Jesus Christ (1 Cor. 15:57).

Schedule times during the day to check on the candidates and pray with them. Quote the scriptures with them to strengthen their resolve and reignite their faith in and love for God. Teach the candidate to stand on the Word of God. Remain by their side until they have gained victories. When God gifts them with the breakthrough in answer to all the prayers, stop and celebrate with praises to God. They shall never forget the part you played in God's setting them free from the bonds of addiction. And they will always be grateful to Him for the release.

Here are some scriptures that you can add to Bible instructor arsenal:

"Even God, who quickeneth the dead, and calleth those things which be not as though they were" (Rom. 4:17).

"Be still, and know that I am God: I will be exalted among the heathen, I will be exalted in the earth" (Ps. 46:10).

"Declaring the end from the beginning, and from ancient times the things that are not yet done, saying, My counsel shall stand, and I will do all my pleasure" (Isa. 46:10).

"Wherefore take unto you the whole armour of God, that ye may be able to withstand in the evil day, and having done all, to stand" (Eph. 6:13).

Carol had mentioned her drug addiction to someone at work whom she thought was a Christian and would pray with her. Big mistake! Now it seemed everyone knew. How embarrassing! She had started dabbling in college and became hooked. No one knew of her addiction. Now that she was active in her career and in spiritual things, she longed to be set free. I had only known Carol a short time when, at the recommendation of her pastor, she decided to discontinue her Bible studies.

Early one morning I received a phone call. Tearfully Carol told me what she was experiencing. Of all the people she knew, she felt that I was the only one whom she could trust. What a surprise! (One never knows the impact of the moments God gives you with others. That's why every minute with a person should be of utmost seriousness—nothing taken for granted.) She was desperate. We talked for a long time about what she was going through. I sought to give her hope and assurance, and gave her the four scriptures above to meditate on throughout the day. Then we arranged to pray together each morning for one week.

Unbeknownst to her, in addition, I fasted from all television and sweets that week and focused as much of my time and attention on claiming the promise of victory for her as I could. Needless to say, Carol began feeling stronger and better by the very next day, and by the end of the week (actually before week's end) she felt her deliverance had come—her cravings had vanished! It is the Word of God and prayer that draw individuals close to God:

"And I, if I be lifted up from the earth, will draw all men unto me" (John 12:32).

It is the Word of God and prayer that strengthen faith and resolve:

"So then faith cometh by hearing, and hearing by the word of God" (Rom. 10:17).

Through the Word of God and prayer come overcoming power and victory:

"Nay, in all these things we are more than conquerors through him that loved us" (Rom. 8:37).

Not only will individuals achieve victory in the given situation, but the faith and fortitude they gain from the experience will take their relationship with God to new heights that will come into play in future spiritual battles. Now the victorious one also has a compelling testimony to share and a faith to lend to others in similar circumstances.

In addition to baptism by water representing the cleansing blood of our Lord, the candidate also has the covenant promise of the baptism of the Holy Spirit. Through it they receive power to walk a Christ-centered life daily. They can read about the experience of Nicodemus in John 3:1-16. Their new church family is there to support them in many ways. Even though the evangelist no doubt will present the benefits of joining an organized church family (the Seventh-day Adventist Church in particular), you should also share information about the organizational structure, departments, and auxiliaries of the church. It's always nice to have information prepared to hand to the candidate and review with them. There are very helpful pamphlets and booklets that you can purchase for the purpose of discipling new members.

Let's review some of the biblical standards that could be major lifestyle changes the candidate for baptism should be made aware of and make major efforts to address beforehand.

The Right Age

Many times questions arise about the age of readiness for children desiring baptism. My greater concern, however, is with parents who discourage their children from being baptized. That should never be. Once children hear it from the pastor and their parents and conclude in mind and spirit that they are not "ready" to be baptized, it seems to resonate forever. While intentionally seeking to ensure that the young ones are mature enough to understand what they are committing to, such adults unintentionally guarantee that the child never feels ready. It especially and unfortunately happens with too many of our own children who were born and raised in the Seventh-day Adventist Church.

After being told that they are not old enough, children will often have enormous difficulty switching gears to feel that they are finally ready, and therefore put it off again and again and too often never get baptized. Unfortunately, many eventually leave the church altogether as a result of never feeling they know or are mature enough. Children hearing such things month after month and year after year become the most difficult to convince that God accepted them into His special family of heaven when they first gave their heart to Him, no matter how young they were.

> "Then were there brought unto him little children, that he should put his hands on them, and pray: and the disciples rebuked them" (Matt. 19:13).

We should first of all congratulate children on their desire to make Jesus Lord of their life. Commend them for accepting God's calling, for He has chosen them to be special for Him. Praise and pray with them again and again (daily at worship time is not too often) as they look forward to that wonderful experience. Encourage their love of God and teach them to thank Him daily for choosing them. Ask God to help them to continue to be obedient to His will for their lives. When they bring up baptism, read to them and/or remind them of the story of Samuel in 1 Samuel 3. Teach them the prayer of Samuel and encourage them to continue to be faithful like him as they look forward to the day of their baptism. Assure them that the process to prepare them for baptism will begin immediately. Never use such expressions as "not the right age," "not enough knowledge," "don't know enough," "don't know what they're doing," or "not old enough."

Young children can understand looking forward to baptism even though they may not grasp the concept of time. With a little creativity, you can distract them or redirect their attention to other meaningful associations and preparatory activities. Why not take them to the pastor for special anointing and prayer as they immediately embark upon their special Bible studies. Perhaps you could give them a birthday age with which to associate the right time (never stating that they are not old enough), and always with the assurance that it is something all are looking forward to. During church baptisms why not explain to the young children its symbolism. We can handle all this in many different ways while keeping them excitedly looking forward to baptism in a year or two. Most of all, do not forget that Jesus is displeased when we forbid children from coming to Him. He does not turn them away, and neither should anyone in the church.

> "But when Jesus saw it, he was much displeased, and said unto them, Suffer the little children to come unto me, and forbid them not: for of such is the kingdom of God" (Mark 10:14).

Encourage children of all ages to take Bible studies and work very hard to understand God's love for them and His plan and purpose for their life. The lessons should be more than finding texts and filling in the blanks. Lead the child to see the love of God for them in each study guide and feel an ever growing desire to be in His presence and to emulate His character. Parents should reinforce and/or affirm the lessons through daily, consistent family worship. We could say much about the necessity and benefits of the family worship hour. Also give the children opportunities to participate in outreach activities sharing the love of Jesus, along with church involvement through the children's ministry department and other auxiliaries.

Such activities will produce visible evidences of readiness. Neither rush nor delay the process. It will happen at a younger age for some than for others. The permissible age usually ranges from 8 to 12—some earlier, some later. While some churches and/or pastors have loose regulations they abide by, no one wants to be accused of quenching the spirit of a little one who is determined not to take no for an answer.

Inspire parents to take an active part in preparing their children for baptism. Many shy away from giving their children Bible studies, feeling inadequate to provide the quality of learning they desire for them. If they feel that way, why not turn that sense of inadequacy into a personal spiritual growth project. Also encourage them to study the lessons in advance and present them to their children in creative ways, or to go through them along with their child and you. You can provide any needed assistance and, if necessary, oversee the lesson series as presented by the parents. Doing so will undoubtedly bless the parents as much as the child. Parents and child can grow together in understanding the principles of God's Word. At times as a result of the parents' growth in the values of Christian beliefs, the parents request rebaptism and are baptized along with their child.

It is my strong feeling that even though you may take the lead in providing the studies, the parents should feel it the greatest honor of parenting to have a part in leading their child to Christ and to be as active in supporting the process as possible. As they do so, it provides a perfect time for discussions about God's true church and its responsibility for spreading the gospel. Along with that, one can teach children how to pray, and begin praying daily that God will lead them into the knowledge and understanding of His purpose and will for their life. Seek to interest them in spiritual growth reading and journaling. As a Bible instructor you have a responsibility to work with families in the church in such activities.

Chapter Activities

1. Discuss the pros and cons of baptizing children.
2. Discuss the danger of turning a child off from being baptized based solely on their age.
3. Role-play how a parent could handle a child's desire for baptism at the age of 5.

Modesty in Dress and Jewelry

Today's media has set the standard for what society classifies as beauty. It is not a new phenomenon, however. The world has always defined beauty by the amount of makeup, the style of fashion, and the amount of money one possesses or can attract. Obviously no one in the world of cosmetics and fashion has looked into the Bible to see what our Creator had to say regarding how we should represent ourselves and God in physical appearance. Yet, it is there.

- First Timothy 2:9 simply encourages modest apparel, being humble and reserved, and discourages the wearing of jewelry, braided hair, or costly apparel. Adorning should be both convenient and necessary. Paul notes that outward excesses could lead to pride, vanity, immodesty, and indecency.
- First Peter 3:3, 4 determines that adornment should reflect the content of the heart, i.e., internal graces that lend to natural beauty and adorn the character with the fruit of the spirit, not external extravagances.
- Ephesians 4:22-24, through the symbolism of a change of clothes, discusses the need to put off the old corrupt lifestyle and don one created by a renewing of the mind. (The King James Version of the Bible uses "conversation," an old English word meaning "lifestyle.")
- Romans 13:14 reminds us that when we accept Christ, we are indeed putting on the Lord Jesus Christ and rejecting the desires of our sinful nature.
- Exodus 35:22 tells us how the Israelites responded to Moses' instructions to bring their jewelry that they had brought from Egypt as material for the building of the tabernacle. God had no intention for the children of Israel to keep the jewelry given by the Egyptians for their personal adornment.
- Isaiah 3:16 describes the Lord's disgust with the daughters of Zion (children of God) for what they had allowed themselves to become

as a result of following the cultures around them, particularly in their dress. He Himself would take away the jewelry and unacceptable apparel and replace it with a plague, or curse.

- Isaiah 3:16-24 explains that it is a prideful heart that lies behind the display of jewelry. Often those obsessed with adornment would not leave home without it even if it's merely for a casual occasion. God never wanted anything to control us to this extent.

Certainly God created precious stones to display more of His unlimited appreciation of beauty. Scripture uses precious stones to symbolize the heavenly city (Rev. 21:19-21). The Lord had the Ten Commandments written on stones (Ex. 34:1, 4). God employed them as memorials and even communicated with His people Israel through such jewels (Ex. 39). The Garden of Eden had every precious stone (Eze. 28:13). One day we shall be as the stones of a crown, highly valued and honored in the kingdom of God forever. "And the Lord their God shall save them in that day as the flock of his people: for they shall be as the stones of a crown, lifted up as an ensign upon his land" (Zech. 9:16). The precious stones were to have a useful, meaningful purpose. God never meant for their beauty to shift from enhancing our appreciation of our Creator to exalting the pride of the created. Thus whenever God sought to bring His people back to a renewed, restored relationship, He emphatically commanded them to remove the prideful jewelry (see scriptures above). Let's take it off and focus on adorning the heart with the fruit of the Spirit (Gal. 5:22, 23).

Chapter Activities

Discuss the following questions:

1. Is it still relevant to require the taking off of jewelry as part of becoming a member of the Seventh-day Adventist Church?
2. What do you tell someone who has removed all their jewelry and then sees others in the church wearing it?
3. What is the church's stand on the wedding band?

Drinking Alcoholic Beverages, Smoking, and Using Other Addictive Substances

The same God who created us and redeemed us is the same Deity who has a right to claim us as His own. In all that we do we should demonstrate before the world a heart of gratitude to Him for His abundant goodness to us and show that we answer to a higher power and a higher calling. Our lives and lifestyles are a witness for or against the gospel of Jesus Christ, as well as whether the power of the Holy Spirit, or lack thereof, influences our decisions.

- First Corinthians 6:19, 20 reminds us that our bodies are the temple of the Holy Spirit. It makes emphatically clear that we are not our own to do with our bodies whatever we please. Bought with the price of a crucified Savior, we therefore have a responsibility to respond to God's favor by glorifying Him in our body and in our spirit—both of which belong to God.
- First Corinthians 10:31 reiterates the high standard of glorifying God in all that we do, including eating and drinking.
- Leviticus 10:9 gives a picture of how seriously God wanted the priestly family of Levites to take His admonition against alcohol. If they went into the tabernacle after drinking wine or strong drink, they would immediately die.
- First Peter 2:9 describes God's last-day saints as a part of the royal priesthood (cf. Ex. 19:5, 6).
- Proverbs 20:1 expresses the wisdom of Solomon regarding strong drink. Those who drink are not wise.

Your candidate may have an addiction that requires more than merely a desire to overcome. The pastoral and/or evangelism team should be prepared to assist individuals seeking to free themselves from any addiction. The healing of the demoniac and the sick, the deaf, and the blind, and even bringing the dead back to life again offer proof positive that God specializes in cases deemed impossible. There exist programs for dealing with addictions and those who would be glad to be support buddies, etc. Make them available as resources. God wants to shatter the shackles that bind people to addictive behaviors and substances. If the Lord has set them free, let us in ministry ensure that they are free indeed.

Chapter Activities

1. Research and gather materials from three different Christian addiction support groups.
2. Research and gather materials about Adventist addiction support groups.
3. Discuss how you would handle a case in which a person wanted to escape alcohol or tobacco.

The Eating of Clean Meats

God didn't originally create animals for human consumption. The original diet detailed in Genesis 1:29, 30 consisted of fruit, nuts, grains, and vegetables. However, after the Flood, God permitted clean meats. Leviticus 11 and Deuteronomy 14 detail those meats now allowed.

We addressed this issue in great detail in an example in Chapter 15: Hack Good Divots. The Seventh-day Adventist Church is known for its promotion of health principles. The people of God should be a source of help in dietary matters. Adventists should conduct ongoing cooking, exercise, and health classes that promote natural remedies in all of our churches. New believers, young in the faith and eager to meet God's approval in every area of their life, especially need them. Our stand on the principles of health strengthens the resolve of new believers to do what is right and pleasing to God and grounds them in the faith. As a Bible instructor you should encourage and promote health principles as much as you would any other doctrinal beliefs.

I shall never forget the largest cooking class I ever attended. It was a community event sponsored by the local Seventh-day Adventist church. Beautiful flyers had blanketed the community, and the RSVP calls started flowing in daily. Even though it charged a small fee, more than 200 people from all over the community attended the four evening sessions, and they were not disappointed. The interest was amazing, and so were the food samples. During four special nights the attendees learned much about health and natural remedies, and many lives and homes would never be the same. It was one of the projects to create interest in the upcoming evangelistic series.

These have been merely a few of the lifestyle changes that may challenge a new believer. But we should not go into so much depth in the preparation for baptism that the candidate becomes discouraged. Because the candidates have committed their life to Christ and are willing to follow Him all the way, that should be sufficient for a sound base from which they can grow over time. An attempt to cover "everything" has a grave danger that much of such discussion will turn into personal opinion rather than sound biblical counsel. Keeping requirements as few and simple as possible is the key to maintaining the focus on a saving relationship with Christ. It is wise to review those things that are made clear by the Word of God.

The story of the Ethiopian eunuch in Acts 8:35-39 offers an example of the simplicity of the qualifications for baptism. The more we complicate the qualifiers to govern behavior, the more we move away from the saving grace of Jesus Christ. Your responsibility as a Bible instructor is to bring people to the Savior and let Him work out all the ills and errors. Our check lists of do's and don'ts will never make saints out of sinners, but being saved by grace will.

It would behoove you not to make issues more challenging than they already are. Instead, encourage the new believers to pray that the Holy Spirit will lead them in all that they do, to seek God's guidance, and to follow the concepts taught and revealed in God's Word. Stick with the principles and allow the Holy Spirit to guide in the individual application. You need to give much more focus to developing candidates who have come to know God, who are drawn to the Word of God, and who are filled with the Holy Spirit.

Chapter Activities

1. Discuss what we should consider as the essentials in preparing a person for baptism. What should candidates know and demonstrate in their lives?
2. Discuss what things human beings might regard as essentials for the baptismal candidate that God might not necessarily consider as of first importance.
3. Review and role-play standing by the side of someone struggling to overcome an addiction.

Visitation for Baptism

As a Bible instructor you must be aware of four major areas of visitation that serve as turning points for gaining decisions:

1. The visit to solicit a decision to accept Bible studies.
2. The visits for conducting Bible studies and securing decisions with each one.
3. The visit for presenting and gaining a decision to attend the nightly evangelistic series.
4. The visit to gain a decision for Christ and baptism.

The day of baptism is one that all look forward to. You should do everything possible to see that it meets every expectation of order and excitement. The candidates should be well prepared and enthusiastic about their time of new beginnings with God. You should be so filled with joy that it is contagious. Still, take nothing for granted. Consider each candidate as a fragile babe in Christ that must receive special individual care and support. Some will be as visibly excited as you, while others will still be struggling with decisions they need to make. Review the example of a presentation on baptism in chapter 11, Example Bible Study Presentation: Baptism.

Once in the home, explicitly follow the instructions given by the evangelist or head Bible instructor. They will likely advise you to be cheerful and excited for the candidate who has made a decision for baptism. Again take nothing for granted, however, keeping in mind that human nature tends to move in the direction of what others expect of them. So talk with the spirit of expectation and use the power of suggestion. Remind them of the date for the baptism and a little about what will happen then. Encourage them to invite friends and family, and urge them to stay for the big dinner afterward (or some other event following the baptism). Let them know that along with all the heavenly host, you are rejoicing with them, "because your names are written in heaven" (Luke 10:20).

> "And when she hath found it, she calleth her friends and her neighbours together, saying, Rejoice with me; for I have found the piece which I had lost. Likewise, I say unto you, there is joy in the presence of the angels of God over one sinner that repenteth" (Luke 15:9, 10).

It is usually a much easier decision for those who already have family and/or friends who belong to the Seventh-day Adventist Church. Such individuals have probably been aware of the Adventist faith for as long as their family member or friend has been a member. The Adventist family member or acquaintance could ideally be a wonderful asset in supporting the new believer's assimilation into the culture of Adventism as well as clarifying doctrinal beliefs. Lifestyle changes are usually the most challenging. So a conversation about the Adventists the candidates already know might even add to their encouragement about the new life they are about to embark upon.

At this point the candidate may have already attended the local Seventh-day Adventist church. If possible, bring some information about the congregation they will be attending to give to the candidate. If they assumed that they would be attending another church, or keeping the Sabbath at home, that could be discussed also. Of course, answer any questions the candidate may have. And deal with the baptism bundle in one of the ways presented in the previous subsection. Finally, have prayer and leave. The visit should only be as long as it takes to answer questions and provide some information, and, of course, deal with the baptism bag.

On the other hand, some will need their decision massaged, or as some Bible instructors would say, *pulled* from them. In their minds they have been wrestling with perceived difficulties, hindrances, and challenges. Such perceptions are their reality whether actual or not. As a Bible instructor you are there to help them sort out their objections. Listen attentively and sincerely to their objections. Don't move too fast, or too slow, but in the Spirit of God outline an approach to address each one calmly and humbly. Deal with each objection in a way that leaves Satan no crack to wedge his way in. Without being too pushy, ask leading questions and wait in silence for their answer no matter how long it takes. Follow the counsel presented in chapter 11 on testing truths and in chapter 17 on responding to resistance. If you know that the individual has embraced the values and beliefs as presented—and most of all, accepted Christ in their life—then you also should realize that they now need our help to combat satanic forces.

Your job is not to baptize at all cost. When a person is not prepared in mind or spirit, they especially need your help. It doesn't necessarily take a long time to bring a person to a point of being ready, but it does take a lot of patience, and it should be a prerequisite to a decision for baptism.

Chapter Activities

1. Discuss the reasons you should be excited in the home of the one anticipating baptism.
2. How would you handle yourself differently in the home of one who is of B-interest as compared to one who is A-interest in preparing for baptism?
3. Discuss what counsel you should give to family members of a baptismal candidate.

The Day of Baptism

While the deaconesses and deacons are responsible for preparing the baptismal robes and pool, in addition to organizing everything for the baptism itself, the Bible instructors should remain visible and available to the candidates and those actively involved in the ceremony. If for no other reason, it is good to show excitement and support and, of course, to join in the prayer with/for the candidates before the baptism begins. Some evangelists may request the instructors to wear uniform dress for such a major event.

The baptism should provide privacy and security for both genders. Should robes be used, be sure that they are cleaned, ironed, and separated for males, females, and children. If bundles were brought in advance, arrange them so that the name labels are clearly shown and they are separated by gender. The pastor/evangelist will determine at what point in the service the baptism will take place, where the candidates will assemble, and when the candidates should file into the auditorium (or sanctuary) and take their seats. All Bible instructors should sit with or near the candidates, for it is the instructors' celebration day as well.

The head Bible instructor and/or the instructor responsible for the candidate will announce the name of the person to be baptized. It is nice when the name is also flashed on the church's monitor screen with a few factoids (favorite song, talents for ministry, etc.). Check and make certain that one deacon/deaconess always remains inside and one outside the room where the candidates have left their personal belongings before, during, and after the baptism until all have dressed and reclaimed their possessions. Don't let a missing item mar an otherwise beautiful baptismal service.

You should be on the alert for a final appeal that the evangelist will very likely make. Have your decision cards, pencils, and baptismal vows ready. There may be a call for another baptism that very day. Whatever the case, the Bible instructors (and church deacons and deaconesses) should be ready under the direction of the evangelist either to prepare additional candidates for baptism immediately or to counsel with those filling out decision cards and preparing them for an upcoming baptism. Baptism numbers have been know to double and even triple as a result of appeals made on baptism day.

Often Adventist churches present the candidates to the congregation by extending the "right hand of fellowship" after the baptism and allowing time for the members to greet the new believers either during or at the end of the worship service. Most will put off the welcome to another Sabbath and combine the welcoming ceremony with the handing out of baptismal certificates. Many churches hold fellowship dinners on baptism day, encouraging the entire membership to stay a while to meet the new additions to the church family.

PART 5

FOLLOW-UP STRATEGIES

HFTH-8

CHAPTER 23

KEEP THEM COMING

Once the evangelistic series has ended, it by no means indicates that evangelism itself has concluded. Nurturing the spiritual growth of new members is of equal importance to leading them to a new life in Christ Jesus. Therefore, the teaching reviews, training seminars, and building of a network of church support has only just begun.

A flurry of excitement always takes place the day new members join the congregation. It's as though the congregation receives a shot in the arm of evangelistic fervor and renewed spiritual energy and desires to be at its best. If plans of action and strategies for successfully integrating new members are appropriately in place, the local church could experience explosive growth as excited new members reach out to loved ones and friends.

Every department of the church should include not only an evangelistic focus and flavor but also a follow-up ministry in which to integrate the new members. In fact, it should be part of the process of laying plans for the evangelistic series itself and not an afterthought. Months ahead of time the church should develop methods of integrating the new members into the Seventh-day Adventist Church and nurturing them for at least two years. Such plans should not forget the preparation also necessary (in fact, an imperative) for current members to be welcoming and part of the process. It can be the most daunting part of the process and thus must begin early.

Visitation and Prayer

Most new members face overwhelming challenges during the assimilation process the first year or two, some for much longer. Change can be very difficult, and the Seventh-day Adventist Church can present many of them—changes involving friendships, health principles, Sabbath observance, worship service style, and Sabbath school classes, as well as possible job shifts and new ways of relating to family and friends. For this reason, and many others, praying for and visitation of the new converts should continue on a regular basis. And it should begin immediately to help them grow spiritually from the outset of their Christian walk as Seventh-day Adventists. Personal contact by the pastor, elders, Bible instructors, and/or assigned guardians will do as much to mature and keep new converts in the faith as anything else. When they are left alone, traces of the familiar, old lifestyle quickly creep in and eventually become all-consuming, and Satan takes charge from there.

As a Bible instructor you should be freed up to pursue new interests while the entire church specializes in the follow-up, but unfortunately that is not the norm. Instructors in the local church will need at least to check on the new believer or with their guardian from time to time. So often even guardianship gets placed on the shoulders of the Bible instructor. This should be avoided.

Guardian Sponsor

Every church should develop a guardian sponsorship ministry. They are church members who have at the least gone through a detailed orientation and have been trained on how to minister to new members on a personal level. Church leadership can immediately assign a sponsor for each new convert. Ideally, when the sponsors are introduced during a visitation prior to baptism, the rapport will begin then, and the new members will feel a welcomed part of their new church family.

The official welcome given new members and introduction to their sponsors often formally takes place during the worship service. Guardian sponsors should be active church members who truly love evangelism and care about the nurturing of new members. Good role models with knowledge of the Adventist message and system, they should prepare to give much time to the care of the new believer.

The guardian sponsor plays a crucial role in supporting the new believers along their journey toward assimilation. Here are 10 responsibilities the guardian sponsor should consider:

1. Provide information on additional study resources, opportunities for Bible studies, prayer groups, etc., and be willing to conduct weekly Bible studies with them and/or others in the household.
2. Ensure attendance to Sabbath school, church, prayer meetings, and other special events such as church business sessions and Week of Prayer.

3. Introduce and assist in the application of Christian beliefs, values, and the health message. For the latter, invite them to dinner occasionally, help them in learning to prepare healthy foods, encourage natural remedies, emphasize the eight laws of health, and set an example of a healthy lifestyle.
4. Give guidance in daily Christian living (e.g., devotional time, Sabbath observance, social activities, daily Sabbath school lesson study, and outreach witnessing to loved ones and the community).
5. Provide careful, caring guidance with regard to clothing. Many people never dress up (and some churches don't make a point of it), while others may need encouragement not to fall back into wearing jewelry during the week, etc. Do not force a dress style, or redress new members with well-used clothes. Rather, accept them as they are, and allow them to develop their own style over time.
6. Ensure introductions to and relationship building with other church members as the new converts integrate into the social network of the church (refrain from gossip and judging). Keep them abreast of church-related events and help them assimilate.
7. Refer to appropriate help and support to solve problems they are having difficulty handling. Involve the pastor when necessary, cautiously provide counsel, refer to church and community specialists, etc.
8. Encourage the use of their talents through participation in various programs and the ministries of the church, such as choir and ushering.
9. Assist with special needs (e.g., transportation, Sabbath school lessons, and directing to resources for housing, food, new job, financial assistance, or overcoming addictions).
10. Be personally devoted to the new believer (e.g., phone and check on them from time to time and pray together, invite them to personal events, and be there for them when they call on you).

New Believers Orientation and/or Sabbath School Class

Most Seventh-day Adventist churches have a new believers' Sabbath school class or new believers' orientation that meets every Sabbath morning during the regular Sabbath school time. (Sometimes they are separate classes—one taught by the pastoral team, the other conducted by the Bible instructor.) The teacher is normally a member of the pastoral team. The lessons review certain Bible doctrines and provide a bigger view of the Seventh-day Adventist denomination, its history, and how it operates. The new believers' class also affords a wonderful opportunity for new members to become acquainted with each other. It establishes them in the faith with sound doctrinal understanding and affirms them as Seventh-day Adventist Christians.

New Believer's Bible Study Guides

Because the new converts have learned so much in such a short period of time, to ensure their becoming grounded in the fundamental beliefs and doctrines of the Seventh-day Adventist Church it is advisable for the Bible instructors or one of the church elders to enroll them in another Bible study course and then study the series with them in their home. It can become a good opportunity for a new Bible instructor fresh out of training. You will now find available a selection of Bible study guides for integrating new believers. Materials also exist to teach them about the Seventh-day Adventist system and operational structure. Another advantage of such follow-up studies is the opportunity to encourage others in the home to take part in the studies and to attend church with the new believers. The courses also provide an opportunity for family and friends to have their questions about the new faith of their loved one answered.

Reaching Out to Family

Family members and friends may have attended some of the evangelistic meetings and/or the church with the new members. They thus become prime candidates to invite for Bible studies. Find appropriate ways to become more visible and friendly to others in the household. Encourage the new believer to invite them not only to church but to all social events and special meeting series.

Baptism Class

It is not uncommon for others to request baptism, especially after major baptisms, who were only considering it previously. Invite them to join a baptismal class. While usually taught by Bible instructors, the pastor or an elder can conduct it. In most churches it is an ongoing, open entry class. Sometimes new members interested in revisiting the basic doctrines and structure of the Seventh-day Adventist Church will also attend. In addition, it can also serve as an introductory class for visitors interested in Bible studies or who want to learn more about basic Christian beliefs as taught by Seventh-day Adventists.

The baptismal class offers many opportunities as a ministry. Encourage its members to invite friends and family to join them and to learn together. The class is personal enough for attendees to build relationships and begin teaming up for witnessing, social activities, and building a strong support network for special prayer, spiritual encouragement, clarifying Bible concepts, and other types of interaction.

Accepting New Members as They Are

The new believers may not have formal church dress and may still struggle with inappropriate habits or practices. Caution current members on how they interact with new believers on such issues. Allow recent converts plenty of space and love during their period of transition. Some may need more than others. Give them time to grow in the area of dress, for example, rather than lavishing them with used clothes that may not be of their taste yet. Providing such garments could be more embarrassing to them than helpful. It may send a statement that babes in Christ are not acceptable as they are, not good enough, etc. Sometimes the new believer will feel their self-worth has been lowered by church members trying to "make" them fit in and look like everyone else. Even though it may be well intentioned, such efforts could be socially and spiritually damaging.

New believers will not remain long if they do not feel part of the church family. Doris was one. Her job necessitated her to wear casual pants, so she really didn't have many dresses suitable for church. We gathered some in her size from various members, made sure they were cleaned and pressed, and proudly delivered them to her. Stunned, she didn't quite know how to respond. As she looked over the clothes and made comments, I could immediately tell they were not necessarily her style, but she graciously accepted them. She attended church a few times never wearing anything we gave her and then stopped coming altogether. She again began working (as a beautician) on Sabbaths. I often wonder what statement we made to her when we brought her the secondhand clothes without her asking for help in that area. Perhaps other factors played into her falling away, but I never forgot her reaction to the clothes. We must be careful how we transition individuals into the Adventist culture. It is far better to allow God to do that while we do the loving and caring for them.

When Donna and her two sons first started attending church, they looked as though they could use help, but we decided on an open arms approach, making them feel very welcomed regardless. Today, after three years, they have shown continual progress and now look so much different. Given time, people tend to move toward the bar of expectation. We do not need to run ahead of the process. God puts up with each of us with exceedingly great patience and love and merely asks us to follow His example as we relate to others.

> "And beside this, giving all diligence, add to your faith virtue; and to virtue knowledge; and to knowledge temperance; and to temperance patience; and to patience godliness; and to godliness brotherly kindness; and to brotherly kindness charity" (2 Peter 1:5-7).
>
> "That in the ages to come he might shew the exceeding riches of his grace in his kindness toward us through Christ Jesus" (Eph. 2:7).
>
> "Put on therefore, as the elect of God, holy and beloved, bowels of mercies, kindness, humbleness of mind, meekness, longsuffering; Forbearing one another, and forgiving one another, if any man have a quarrel against any: even as Christ forgave you, so also do ye. And above all these things put on charity, which is the bond of perfectness" (Col. 3:12-14).
>
> "O praise the Lord, all ye nations: praise him, all ye people. For his merciful kindness is great toward us" (Ps. 117:1).

More than anything, new believers need our love and acceptance, friendship, prayers, and encouragement as God grows them from where they are to what He intends for them. Let's not try to be God or to do the work of the Holy Spirit, but rather let's continue to hold their hands as they take one step at a time. Again as an example, we do not have to change the dress of the new member right away. Instead, let them develop their own Sabbath dress while showing them love and acceptance.

Discovering Gifts of Talent

Every new believer has talents that the church should utilize for building up the kingdom of God. It is the responsibility of each congregation to discover a place for them. The Bible instructor, the sponsor, and the church officers should ensure that the new members become active in the church's ministries as soon as possible. They may start in the choir or ushering; assist with the Adventist Youth team; or join the prayer ministry, men's/

women's ministry, personal outreach ministries, or community service. There is a place for everyone to minister to others.

Sabbath Activity

For the next several weeks, until new members become better acclimated, dinner with other church members is preferable to letting them spend the Sabbath alone. It offers opportunities to review lessons and gain new associations, and it lessens the possibility that old friends and even family members will call on them to do things not in keeping with Sabbath principles. The new member guardian could take the lead in ensuring that converts spend Sabbath afternoons productively. By the way, after a major baptism is always a good time to start a series of cooking classes.

New Member Witnessing

We should encourage new believers to share their newfound faith. With the Bible instructor, guardian sponsor, and pastoral team available to support them, the new members will have all the guidance, direction, materials, and help they need to lead others to the faith they now hold dear.

The personal ministries leader should develop a clear path for the full integration of the new member into various types of witnessing. Encourage the departments, ministries, and auxiliaries of the church to make a concerted effort to befriend and incorporate new believers.

Social Activities

It is good to have on the calendar a series of social events following a major baptism. An informal social event, such as a monthly potluck dinner or an old-fashioned Saturday night social, is a great way to initiate relationships. Bible instructors can be an asset here also, introducing old members to new ones and ensuring the latter have a memorable time.

Keep the new members abreast of upcoming events. Make sure they have needed transportation and complimentary tickets where appropriate. Get other departmental leaders involved in taking responsibility for making sure new members know what is happening.

CHAPTER 24

RATTLING THE HEDGES

Let's review your role as a Bible instructor following the evangelistic series. Again, it will vary from being the sole guardian (hopefully avoided) to merely being an observer of the progress of new members and being ready to step in when needed or asked. There are always, however, those on the brink of being baptized at the end of every major series. Here's where *rattling the hedges* becomes your major focus. New members can certainly take part in encouraging friends and family to follow their example in Bible studies. However, we should not leave them to battle with family and friends about biblical issues alone. Your responsibility at this point is to look for every opportunity to interest the circle of family and friends of new members in having their Bible questions answered and helping them understand more about Seventh-day Adventists. The phase of seeking new Bible study students begins again immediately as the evangelistic series moves toward its final baptism.

In addition, you may get asked to teach the new believers' Sabbath school class or provide a series of new believers' orientation classes at a time other than Sabbath morning. However, since a Bible instructor normally teaches the baptismal class, someone on the pastoral team would typically cover the new believers' Sabbath school class. When that is the case, you would work with the pastoral team to ensure that the new believers consistently attend the class.

You may assist the pastoral team in deciding the subjects to cover and during what period of time. In addition, you may find it necessary to take responsibility for follow-up by reviewing the studies in the homes of the new believers. Very often new believers are grateful for the opportunity, because the clarification grounds them in the Word of God. Thus they look forward to the weekly support of prayer and encouragement.

New members often face special challenges, such as breaking addictive habits (including the use of profanity) and behaviors, spousal and family conflicts, Sabbath employment and/or academic classes, health and dietary changes, music and social life issues, and careers in certain fields (entertainment, liquor/tobacco, etc.), to name a few. Rattling the hedges includes discovering those challenges early on and working with the pastoral team to provide programs and referrals to support the new members' efforts to gain victory over anything detrimental to their Christian walk. The local church should have in place a referral list for such community programs as Alcoholics Anonymous (AA) and other addiction support groups, family counselors, etc. Also make available Adventist support programs, such as Five-Day Plan to Stop Smoking, cooking classes, health and fitness activities, and legal consultants for the church. My advice to you is to be slow to give counsel and quick to refer. Having said all this, your priority is the frontal attack of fasting and prayer and the Word of God covered in chapter 22: Old Man Yesterday, New Man Forever.

If you are a wise Bible instructor, you will also listen for any disturbing member interaction with the new converts and provide immediate intervention. As a church we must continually train our members to have a wide-open-arm approach with new believers. Too often more concerned about our appearance to onlookers, we allow genuine love and acceptance to disappear once someone becomes a member, which therefore leads to the disappearance of the new believers. Another task for you as a Bible instructor is to encourage current members to allow the new ones space to grow at their own pace. Demonstrating a genuinely caring spirit toward them will go a much longer way in keeping them in the fold and nurturing their growth than nitpicking every perceived imperfection. Whatever concerns the older members have, they should bring them directly to the pastor, the Bible instructor, and/or an elder, and then leave them in the hands of those leaders.

The older members have not been working with the new believers and should not feel that now that such individuals are on their "turf," they have every right to "whip" them into submission to the church's culture. It is not true, and leadership must correct this kind of spirit whenever it raises its ugly head. I will never forget how excited Avian was finally to have a church home. She lived not far from the local Seventh-day Adventist church but never really noticed it until the evangelistic series began. Following up on a door-to-door survey, Avian began Bible studies, and when the meetings started, she willingly attended with her two sons, made wonderful progress, and was determined to be in the first baptism. Her sincerity was like the kind of person a Bible instructor would love to clone about a thousand times. On her very first Sabbath attending the Adventist church following baptism, someone scolded her about her very pale lipstick, and before she could enter the church, another approached her about the fact that she wasn't wearing stockings. Leaving the church, she went home in tears.

One could only imagine how much talking and prayer and supporting and loving and begging and determination it required to get her back. I even took one of the church women with me to the house to apologize and hug Avian and then asked her to give the prayer in the home. I hope and believe that the experience changed her heart toward new members. Fortunately, Avian came back to stay, but so many others never return and refuse to have anything more to do with Adventists. While you must intervene and protect the new members from the "unintentional dragons" that prey on them, you must also rattle the hedges to shake out and train the pew members to be like Jesus would be toward the babes in Christ.

Chapter Activities

1. Discuss how lavishing new members with used clothes could have more of a negative than positive impact.
2. Discuss the need to train current members on how to relate to spiritual babes.
3. Discuss special challenges new members may experience and how to address them.

CHAPTER 25

KEEP ON KEEPING ON

This training guide has covered many aspects of your role as a Bible instructor. But greater depths will emerge as you move from the classroom to the field. While it may seem overwhelming at first, it doesn't take many experiences in major evangelism to find footing in the ebb and flow of witnessing and soul winning if one is truly called and dedicated. From there, merely staying active and led by the Spirit of God, along with mentoring others, will continuously increase your skill and capabilities. Just keep on keeping on, and God will expand your borders of ministry as a Bible instructor.

Such dedicated, hardworking individuals are in great demand as the right arm of evangelism. When evangelists find such truly committed people, they have discovered something extremely valuable. Many claim to be Bible instructors but actually lack the self-sacrificial commitment to soul winning. They may be lazy, be easily discouraged, have ulterior motives (including temporary employment), have self-grandiose issues, etc. Although they may have wonderful testimonies and prayers, they too often demonstrate opinionated positions and fail to perform professionally in meetings and in the field. Some may even have a track record of leading people to baptism, but, like Jonah, their motive is far from Christ-centered. On the other hand, when the Bible instructor is consistent, hardworking, and an inspiration to be around, they will be welcomed by any evangelist. They will be true prayer warriors that demonstrate a command of the Bible in the home and carry themselves with Holy Spirit professionalism in the meetings and in the field.

Fortunately their numbers are growing. Bible instructors increasingly view themselves as part of the whole, rather than holding an elite exclusivity. Therefore, they are much more willing to share their ministry and build up Bible instruction at the local level. The days of the solo instructor are finally behind us. Teams are the growing norm. It is not uncommon to hear of churches that have developed five to 25 or more full- and part-time active Bible instructors.

If you are willing and able to make a three- to six-month commitment to an evangelistic series, the travel prospects are exciting. Professional instructors today have opportunities to work in evangelistic campaigns across the nation and worldwide. They enjoy the awesome privilege to work with and develop relationships with Seventh-day Adventist members in local communities in various cities and with other Bible instructors from all over the country. It has enhanced the possibilities of camaraderie among instructors everywhere as well as becoming a way of identifying outstanding ones.

Pastors and evangelists are also the recipients of the benefits of a growing force of willing and capable Bible instructors. As pastors take more responsibility to ensure that such training is an essential part of local church evangelism, more career individuals will become available. If each year only two or three instructors received training and experience in major evangelism, what a difference that would make in the support of personal ministries and other outreach endeavors of the local church and major evangelistic campaigns around the world.

The first and foremost objective of the gospel of Jesus Christ is to seek and to save the lost. Second Corinthians 5:19-21 explains clearly that the church has the awesome and God-appointed ministry of reconciliation—the ministry of bringing harmony between heaven and earth, peace between God and sinner. With that in mind, the goal that we must continually strive for should be for every able Seventh-day Adventist Christian to become a capable and active Bible instructor. Let us keep on pursuing the God-ordained charge of releasing men and women from the grip of Satan and placing them in the arms of Christ forever.

"'Unto every one of us is given grace according to the measure of the gift of Christ. . . . When he ascended up on high, he led captivity captive, and gave gifts unto men. . . . He gave some, apostles; and some, prophets; and some, evangelists; and some, pastors and teachers; For the perfecting of the saints, for the work of the ministry, for the edifying of the body of Christ: Till we all come in the unity of the faith, and of the knowledge of the Son of God, unto a perfect man, unto the measure of the stature of the fulness of Christ" (Eph. 4:7-13). Here the members of the church of God are shown acting their different parts, all under the supervision of the great

Master Worker, who knows just what each one in His service should do to meet the necessities that arise."[1]

"This time demands that advance moves be made, that resolute, persevering faith be exercised, that a patient, self-denying, long-suffering spirit be manifested by every member of our churches, and that each one who professes to follow Christ shall become a worker in his moral vineyard. The God-fearing members of the church can do more good by devoted, personal effort than our ministers can accomplish when they feel no burden to labor from house to house. Our ordained ministers must do what they can, but it must not be expected that one man can do the work of all. The Master has appointed unto every man his work. There are visits to be made, there is praying to be done, there is sympathy to be imparted; and the piety—the heart and hand—of the whole church is to be employed, if the work is to be accomplished."[2]

As ambassadors for our Lord, we are all on the same team. Let's keep on keeping on as anointed workers sent forth under the banner and charge of the Master. I invite your comments for the continuous improvement of the art and science of Bible work.

Gloria J. Bell
Globell3@yahoo.com

---

[1] Ellen G. White, "Strength and Power in Unity," *Bible Training School,* April 1903.

[2] Ellen G. White, *Pastoral Ministry* (Silver Spring, Md.: Ministerial Association, General Conference of Seventh-day Adventists, 1995), p. 147.